LATIN POETRY · THE NEW POETS AND THE AUGUSTANS

LATIN POETRY ◯

THE NEW POETS &

THE AUGUSTANS

◯ CLARENCE W. MENDELL

YALE UNIVERSITY PRESS, NEW HAVEN & LONDON

PREFACE

hile I sincerely hope that the specialist in Latin literature may find points of interest in my treatment of the development of Latin poetry, this book is intended primarily for readers whose Latin has largely deserted them but who may have a vague and perhaps nostalgic memory of Catullus and Vergil and Horace. Where I have diverged from traditional interpretation I have tried to give sound evidence for my own position. I am of course deeply in debt to editors, old and new, of all the classic poets and also to such modern critics as Fraenkel, Prescott, Rand, Duckworth, Commager, and many others, but I did not think it wise to burden the book with constant references to their scholarly contributions. My greatest debt is to George Lincoln Hendrickson, with whom for more than fifty years I enjoyed the companionship of the Latin poets.

I have avoided the application to classical authors of the methods used in contemporary criticism of English poetry because it is my conviction that the point of view of the poet's own day is a better guide to an understanding of his work and that the modern terminology (often ill-defined) is too frequently baffling rather than illuminating. The translations are my own: I have used verse as my medium in the hope of giving a better idea of the tone and impact of each poem.

Classical scholars will hardly desire any sort of bibliography in a book which deals with eight of the most relentlessly dissected poets of Rome. But that legendary being, the general reader, should he find himself curious to know something more of these authors and their poetry, ought surely to be encouraged. The following suggestions are offered for his guidance.

For further reading of the poetry itself, the Loeb Classical Library, published by the Harvard University Press, provides both Latin text and English translation of all the important Greek and Roman authors. The texts are conservative and dependable, the translations more than competent, and both are by highly qualified scholars. For a discussion of the literary history of the period not yet outdated and free from any bias of contemporary poetic theories, the two volumes of W. Y. Sellar, *The Roman Poets of the Augustan Age* (4th ed. Oxford, 1924), are incomparable for the period they cover. For a brief appreciation of all Roman writers of the classical age J. W. Mackail's small volume, *Latin Literature* (New York, 1923), is the most sympathetic and readable. H. G. Rose, *A Handbook of Latin Literature* (New York, 1936), is a useful work of reference.

Should the general reader be intrigued by some particular poet and wish to know more about his qualities and methods, he will find ample material listed in M. Platnauer, *Fifty Years of Classical Scholarship* (Oxford, 1955). The following suggestions may also be helpful.

LUCILIUS. With only fragments of his work surviving, Lucilius will probably appeal most to the specialist. Others will find all that they need and doubtless much more in G. C. Fiske, *Lucilius and Horace* (Madison, 1920), a learned and somewhat heavy source of solid information.

LUCRETIUS. J. Masson, *Lucretius, Epicurean and Poet* (New York, 1907), and E. E. Sikes, *Lucretius, Poet and Philosopher* (Cambridge, 1936), will give the general reader ample background. He should, however, be on his guard against letting the philosophic questions which they raise interfere with his pleasure in reading the poet himself, and may judiciously want to skip the more prosaic problems which are perhaps no darker to him than they were to Lucretius.

CATULLUS. Fundamental to the mass of material on Catullus which has appeared during the last quarter of a century are two outstanding books: A. L. Wheeler, *Catullus and the*

Tradition of Ancient Poetry (Berkeley, 1934), and E. A. Havelock, *The Lyric Genius of Catullus* (Oxford, 1939), the former more conventional, less pioneering, the latter more saturated with enthusiasm and more intriguing. It was largely Havelock's book which motivated the spate of articles which are to be found recorded in Platnauer's bibliography.

VERGIL. T. Frank, *Vergil* (New York, 1922), deals primarily with Vergil the man, the background and facts of his life. E. K. Rand, *The Magical Art of Virgil* (Cambridge, Mass., 1931), on the other hand, is concerned more with poetic qualities, which he analyses and develops sympathetically and brilliantly. More matter of fact is H. W. Prescott, *The Development of Virgil's Art* (Chicago, 1927), which is, to a large extent, a presentation in English of the essential elements of R. Heinze's *Virgil's epische Technik* (Leipzig and Berlin, 1902). The literature of the last quarter-century on Vergil and his works is equaled in extent only by that on Catullus and Horace and will for the most part not appeal to the general reader.

HORACE. One epoch-making book has recently appeared which very nearly supersedes all that has gone before so far as strictly literary criticism is concerned: Edouard Fraenkel, *Horace* (Oxford, 1957). It is least satisfactory in its treatment of the most personal of the poems and it lacks the human warmth of Mackail. It is immensely learned and not as appealing to the general reader as is a book like S. Commager, *The Odes of Horace* (New Haven, 1963), which applies up-to-the-minute methods of poetic criticism and illumines many of the odes. N. E. Collinge, *The Structure of Horace's Odes* (London, 1961), adds something to our understanding of the poet's workmanship. Much, however, of the best in Horatian criticism is to be found in the periodical literature listed by Platnauer. This is particularly true of the numerous definitive articles by G. L. Hendrickson on satire, and on Horace's *Satires* in particular.

ELEGIAC POETS. Much has been written about Tibullus,

Propertius, and Ovid in recent years but, for the most part, in somewhat technical articles. The general reader will find all that he needs in Sellar and Rose.

C. W. M.

Bethany, Connecticut
June 1964

CONTENTS

I · THE NEW POETS

hen Tacitus was young enough to be interested in school arguments about style, he created, in the *Dialogus,* a charming character named Aper, the enthusiastic partisan of the younger generation against the suffocating prestige of the old school. He speaks one immortal line: "What is different is not necessarily worse." It speaks for the pioneers of every generation as they struggle toward freedom from the dead hand of the past. Always the "new" poets, the "new" artists meet with the shocked ridicule of the conservatives. Often they are impelled by the opposition into excesses which go far to justify their critics. But, as time passes, the excesses are left behind and, by virtue of the air and light which the young enthusiasts have had the courage to admit, the older traditions are revitalized and perhaps given a new direction, until presently the revolutionaries themselves become the defenders of tradition against a new generation of innovators. We ourselves have seen the radical Romantics become the old-fashioned Victorians, the ridiculed Impressionists almost conservatives.

It must have been much the same at Rome in the days of Cicero and Catullus. A group of young poets was shocking the world of letters by producing the first expression in Latin of intimate personal emotion. These young men were in rebellion against the whole conception of traditional poetry, not merely its outward form and manner. Their self-revelations seemed to the older conservatives un-Roman if not indecent. Cicero's disgust with their lack of respect for the old master, Ennius, was the result of shock such as that which conservative opinion of the 1920s suffered from the outspoken realism of the younger prose writers. But Cicero did not comprehend the sweep of the new movement, and the skirmish which Horace later fought against the professional, schoolteacher poets of his day was not the major action of the war. That had already been won by the New Poets.

The break with the past which the New Poets made was a complete one. They would have no more to do with the time-worn, impersonal poetry, with its national impulse and its tone of Stoic morality; no longer would they turn solely to the past. They would live and write in the present, as individuals, not as a part of the state. They would express their own emotions, their own loves and hates, and they would write not for the glory of Rome but for their own satisfaction and fame.

If we are going to understand their dissatisfaction and the enthusiasm of their assault we must recall a few facts of Roman history and tradition. The beginnings of Latin literature are significant. Poetry came to Rome through a schoolteacher, a captive slave, set free in 275 B.C. to instruct the children of his Roman conquerors. Livius Andronicus, a cultivated Greek from Tarentum, translated the *Odyssey* of Homer into Latin verse to be a textbook for teaching his young charges. But Homer was only a beginning textbook. The poets with whom Livius was best acquainted were of a much later period.

Greek civilization, in this third century before Christ, had long since passed beyond the glories of the Age of Pericles. Dominant throughout the eastern Mediterranean, with Alexandria as its focal point, Greek literature had adapted itself to its cosmopolitan market. It was just coming to the attention of the rude power rising in the west. Rome had conquered Italy and so come face to face with the culture of Greece in one direction and the might of Carthage in the other. Her own civilization was centuries behind the Greek. Such poetry as she had consisted of nursery rhymes, folk songs, rituals, and possibly ballads. Her verses followed the tramp of marching feet rather than the music of the lyre.

But the Romans were practical people, quick to learn, and they knew how to get others to do for them what they could not do themselves. Livius Andronicus was followed by other clever Greeks and, when he had added to his schoolteaching the writing of a victory ode for his masters, he and his colleagues were given a room in a temple on the Aventine to be the headquarters of their new guild of poets and grammarians. There is significance in this assignment. The guild, like all the other guilds, was an association of workmen. They were in no position to build a club for themselves nor had they homes in which they could meet as a group. Socially they were far below the salt. The Aventine was by tradition the district of the foreigner and the unprivileged.

It was under such auspices that poetry came to Rome. It was more a trade than an inspired art. As time went on it developed two functions aside from that of providing school texts. First, the furnishing of plays, mostly adaptations from the later Greek comedy of manners, to be performed at the many Roman festivals which were not wholly unlike our county fairs. These plays were sold to the aediles who ran the games. In the second place, poetry could be useful to the aristocrats to preserve and enhance the glory of Rome's history and the traditions or myths of her leading families. The first function was jealously guarded by the guild, for from it came the livelihood of its members. The second involved no profit and was regularly left to individuals patronized by their social betters for their own advantage or by the occasional man of patriotic nature for the glory of Rome. In no case do we find citizens of standing engaged in poetic composition. Life was far too serious and full of action for them during the long period of Rome's defensive conquest of the peninsula and her struggles with Carthage for the control of the western Mediterranean. The citizen of standing found his life filled with essential duties: tilling the Roman soil, administering the Roman state, fighting Rome's battles, and raising a Roman family. But when Carthage had succumbed and then Macedon, involving the Greek federations in its fall, there came a period of comparative relaxation. The battle of Pydna (168 B.C.) may be taken as a landmark. Peace brought with it an enormous access of wealth, including hordes of captive slaves, which changed completely the economy of Rome.

Hostages also came from Greece, and it was thus that Rome's first great Hellenist became intimate with Polybius, the Greek historian. Scipio, son of the victorious commander at Pydna and heir to the library of King Perseus, used the period of comparative leisure for the next twenty-five years to satisfy his delight in things Greek. Around him was gathered the so-called Scipionic Circle, including Romans of the aristocratic class interested in literature and their humbler but often abler protégés. Polybius was the oracle of the group, which, as a result, was primarily interested in prose literature. But not wholly: one of Scipio's earliest discoveries was Terence, a writer of comedies. Spared the need of earning a living, Terence incurred the envy and hostility of the guild. Furthermore, in the hands of the Circle, he applied himself not to satisfying popular demand but to producing works of art in the purest Latin. The contrast is obvious between the spontaneous, boisterous, colloquial Plautus and Terence, with his polished imitations of realism, his close adherence to Greek plots and techniques, and his pure Latinity.

What the influence of the Circle was is clear at once. Here was the first self-conscious study and imitation at Rome of Greek literature not for the practical purposes of school instruction and public amusement but as an ornament of culture. To be sure, culture was sought in the name of patriotism. The members of the Circle were leaders in the state who sought the glory of Rome not only through arms but also and more essentially through letters. This national emphasis became more marked when, in 146 B.C., an outbreak in Greece persuaded Rome to exterminate Corinth. Along with the wealth of that great commercial city there came to Rome the Stoic philosopher Panaetius. He gravitated naturally to the Scipionic Circle, where his modified Stoicism (he had adopted Aristotle's theory of the mean) served well the needs of the Roman leaders. The old state religion, which had long served to keep the mass of the people in ignorant subservience to the elect, was losing its hold as contacts with other peoples became more general. People were even beginning to think for themselves. Hitherto philosophers had been banished along with other subversive aliens but with less than complete success. Here was a philosophy which could be merged with the basic Roman morality of virtue and obedience and reinforce the sanctions of religion. Its adoption did open a door to other less amenable philosophies, but this fact was not considered for the moment: Stoicism became an essential part of orthodox Roman belief and therefore a part of orthodox Roman literature. Under the patronage of the Scipionic Circle, letters assumed not only an aura of Greek culture but also a strong national trend, revealed in its patriotic color and its pursuit of pure Latinity and in semiofficial sponsorship of the Stoic code of behavior. History and oratory were the chief beneficiaries of the concern shown by Scipio's group, and both of these fields were developed by men of the aristocratic class and not by the members of the guild. Poetry was not really included in the literary activity of the group. They did, in their early days, patronize Terence, and in their later period they received Lucilius into their number.

Lucilius was not really a poet nor was he a wholly orthodox member of the group. His output, which was later to be called satire, had a tremendous influence on Roman literature, but this was due largely to the content: popular Stoic ethics, elementary literary criticism, and a general critical survey of the contemporary scene, all expressed with caustic wit and blunt personal criticism. Stylistically he never conformed with the principles of strict Latinity, and his verse fell below any real standard of poetry. Greek words were freely interspersed among the Latin, and little attention was given to artistic form. All these characteristics were of importance in later literary developments and in the arguments which accompanied them, but they do not give him any claim to being a poetic representative of the Scipionic Circle. His importance lay rather in his independence of any school. Well before the death of Lucilius (103 B.C.) the luxury and short-sightedness of the aristocracy had given birth to the social revolution which dominated approximately a century, from the first activity of Tiberius Gracchus to the battle of Actium (31 B.C.). The introduction of Greek culture, accompanied by an unparalleled influx of wealth resulting from the conquest of the eastern Mediterranean world, had produced an era of extravagant luxury on the part of the newly rich and at the same time an era of restless revolt on the part of the rapidly increasing and overwhelming majority of the unprivileged proletariat. Of the one per cent of the population that still ruled Rome, more than half were members of the aristocracy solely by grace of the money that gave them their power. The class that dominated Rome was scarcely one to create great poetry. Their first and only literary concern was to learn the laws of rhetoric, which could give them the power of speech to control the courts, the assemblies, and the mob. The older aristocrats might occupy themselves with the history of their more glorious past or with the comforts of philosophy. Such poetry as the period produced had to come from the professional guild, which continued to turn out plays for the entertainment of the holiday crowds.

However, as the revolution began to take on the character of civil war in the early part of the first century, a different situation arose with regard to literary output. Whether senators or knights, the aristocracy was divided in allegiance between the various leaders who sought the supreme power by force, supported by professional soldiers and partisan mobs. For those involved, the contests were all-absorbing, but there were many who could find no reason to support one side or another as the struggle became personal. More and more, a considerable number of the intellectuals were

thrown back on their own resources, and some of them turned
to literature instead of politics. The high tension in Rome
for long periods and the excitement of constant change they
could hardly avoid. The whole situation was ripe for a new
sort of poetical expression, more highly charged with personal emotion, less conventional, and more original. The
old accepted types of epic and drama could not satisfy a
younger generation of men-about-town excited by the tension
of civil strife but not directly involved in its violence.

These young poets did not form a literary circle. The impression that they did comes from the fact that their aims
and style of writing have so much in common and that they
came very soon to be grouped together by their critics as the
"new poets." The earliest of their number were, as a matter
of fact, actually associated to a certain extent by their common devotion to the outstanding teacher of the day. Valerius
Cato was a grammaticus, somewhat above the average of his
class, who lectured on poets and poetry and who himself
wrote at least one poem about which we know, an epyllion
called "Lydia." He had a high standing as a critic, with the
reputation of being able to make or break a young poet. His
standards and his models were Alexandrian. He stressed the
artistic value of form, even intricate form, of metrical re-
finements and dexterity hitherto confined to the Greek, and
of a minute study and intimate analysis of personal emotion.
In brief, he rejected the broad lines of plot and character-
drawing familiar in tragedy and epic in favor of the narrower
and more detailed study of more personal incidents. His
appeal was strong and he won a quick response from the
disturbed and already rebellious young poets of the seventies
and sixties. Aside from Catullus, we know of Calvus who
wrote an "Io," epigrams, a lament, and a marriage hymn; of
Cinna who wrote a "Smyrna" and a propempticon; of one
Cassius with elegies and epigrams, of Caecilius with a "Cybele"; of Ticidas, author of erotic poetry; and of many others
who are little more than forgotten names. Catullus, with
greater genius than the rest, was probably the least subser-

vient to the Alexandrian models. In general it was the miniature epic, the epyllion, which attracted them, with its possibilities for exhibiting intricate form and academic learning. It would seem that the lesser grammatici were in complete sympathy with the ideals of Valerius Cato. At any rate, by the time of Horace it was natural for him to look upon them as an entrenched group of critics with lamentable Alexandrian taste, antagonistic to what he considered the sounder poetry based on the earlier and more classic Greek models but nevertheless wholly Roman. Their followers he condemned and themselves he consigned to the limbo of their classrooms.

Lucretius, contemporary with Catullus, was as much a rebel as any of the new poets. It was, however, the Stoic element in orthodox poetry and in Roman life against which he rebelled. In essence he was as much a new poet as Catullus, but his mighty creation was bound to have few if any rivals or followers, for sustained effort was not in harmony with the spirit of the times. It was not that the other new poets were idlers or triflers. The amount of work which Catullus put into his "Peleus and Thetis" or Cinna into his "Smyrna" was prodigious. The energies which others put into politics these brilliant young men devoted with remarkable enthusiasm and success to intricate and highly polished poetry. But what principally shocked Cicero and Horace was the fact that their products were no longer motivated by national pride or any moral concern but by the desire for personal satisfaction and, if possible, personal glory. The separation of the poet's function from the service of the state and the creation of a body of personal poetry, more realistic than the standard models, more contemporary and more emotionally satisfying, was the accomplishment of these young rebels. The proof of their success is the release of their most severe critic, Horace, from the bonds of tradition, and the achievements of the Augustan poets, impossible but for the innovations of the new poets, innovations which

Horace condemned and Vergil welcomed and by which both profited immeasurably.

During the thirty years between the publishing of Catullus' book heralding the new point of view in poetry and Horace's first publication of a rival type of lyric, the world of Roman politics underwent a dramatic change. The prize for which the dictators fought had fallen into the hands of an advocate of peace. After the battle of Actium (31 B.C.) Octavian had begun to reconcile the warring factions and was fast winning the foremost of his opponents with his policy of restoration and peace. He was ably supported by Maecenas, an unwarlike patron of literature, who rapidly gathered together a new semiofficial circle of poets devoted to the new regime and to a Rome which was largely a figment of the imagination. For Octavian's restoration of the republic was in reality a very practical compromise, glorifying the past which it claimed to perpetuate while quietly but resolutely assuring to a new aristocracy a power more nearly absolute than that of the old. With the doors of Janus closed for the first time in generations and strong emphasis placed on the cultural life, such sufferers from the civil wars as Horace and Vergil could wholeheartedly accept the new regime without scrutinizing too closely the texture of its organization. There was no insincerity in their eulogies of the man who had brought about the changes which to them seemed to be ushering in a new age of gold. Once more the "orthodox" poetry assumes the nationalistic tone of enthusiastic patriotism. It differs somewhat from the nationalism of Scipio's group in that it is more Italian than narrowly Roman and that, perhaps in reaction against Antony's Alexandrian venturings, it is less tolerant of Greek influence. It was at least partly because of these divergences that Vergil's poetry idealized the Italian countryside and that Horace's criticism of the new poets centered on their Graecisms. He could hardly criticize them for striking out into new fields when it was his own proud boast that he was first in several fields of poetic creation. He certainly could not criticize their expression of personal opinion or their passion for variety. But what he considered their subservience to Greek technique came close in his opinion to being unpatriotic.

One thing more should be added for an appreciation of Horace's position. His reconciliation with the regime of Octavian was due in part to his pride in being accepted by the elite of Rome. As the son of a freedman holding a humble job in the quaestor's office he had been a member of the scribe's guild. After reading the satires it is impossible to question the touch of snobbishness which appears in his pride as a member of the circle of Maecenas. The guild members may well have reacted to this with the Roman equivalent of Browning's

> Just for a handful of silver he left us,
> Just for a riband to stick in his coat.

Such are the outlines of the story of the new poets, their origin and the first reactions to their work. What, if anything, was there in Latin literature before Catullus on which they could build? First, the unconscious influence of native Italic verse cannot be overlooked, little as we know about it. In the simpler age of early Rome, when master and slave worked together on the farm, the rustic festivals with their lusty Italian gaiety, had some sort of songs and dances. We hear of highly personal give and take of a boisterous sort in rude verse. The religious rituals had a loose metrical form. All this disappeared, at least from the surface, when the highly complex Greek literature overwhelmed the native beginnings, but some trace may well have survived of a direct and personal expression.

Second, in the borrowed Greek literature, the contemporary comedy furnished a first step toward the use of everyday subject matter and commonplace realism. It dealt with familiar people of middle class status, with slaves and freemen, with fishermen and pastry cooks. To be sure, it was not the vehicle for an egocentric and sentimental poet, but it too furnished a suggestion that poetry could be used for something less austere than the epic and the drama.

Third, a real break with orthodoxy had undoubtedly been made by Lucilius. He was scarcely a poet, but it is more than a probability that his free expression of personal opinions was the first step in the new poets' revolt from tradition.

Friend of Scipio and Laelius, Lucilius was in sympathy with the national spirit and modified Stoicism of the Circle, but he developed the hexameter satire as a vehicle for his own criticisms of contemporary life. The very use of the hexameter for the definitely colloquial style of satire was in itself a revolutionary step. Ennius, the pioneer in the Latin epic meter, never consciously lowered its dignity throughout the *Annals,* which for a century and a half held its proud position as *the* Roman epic.

On the formality and monotony of the patriotic narrative style, on all the openly recognized poetry of his day, Lucilius squarely turned his back. This is not the place to discuss the sources, technique, and history of satire, not even its precise definition. There is sufficient agreement between qualified scholars to serve our purpose. Satires are short hexameter essays commenting in the author's own person and from his own point of view on any phase of contemporary life which may interest him. They started with a strong tendency toward *moral* comment, with a clear bias in favor of the modified Stoicism of Panaetius. They always retained this bias, though they dwelt with more relish on the exposure of vices than on the eulogizing of virtue. But if the moral slant is usually discernible it is not overemphasized. Humor is almost always in evidence; homely illustration is frequent. Lucilius, who seems to have been a knight of highly independent character, indulged in much personal vituperation of a violently abusive sort. Variety, however, is the soul of satire, with Lucilius as with his successors, and justifies the name, *satura,* which indicates a miscellany or even a hodgepodge and was first attached in derision to Horace's book of satires nearly a hundred years later. Lucilius very modestly spoke of his own works as *ludus,* trifling, or *sermones,* conversations, or even *schedia,* skits. He wrote about a fanciful council of the gods over a contemporary named Lupus, head of the senate; he wrote an attack on luxury and the vices of the rich, the diary of a trip to Capua, grammatical discussions, reviews of contemporary politics and morals.

We have little enough material in the 1,300 fragments which survived to judge the work of Lucilius fairly. On the whole, however, it confirms the verdict of the Roman critics. Learned and witty, says Cicero; Horace: clever, keen on the scent, courteous and witty; liberally endowed, says Quintilian, with learning, outspokenness, bitterness, and plenty of salt sting. On the other hand, Horace says that Lucilius was garrulous and too lazy to write with nice care, that much of what he wrote might well be jettisoned. Varro puts him in the stylistic class whose hallmark was *gracilitas,* plainness or even baldness, but the term was also used of the plain style affected by the Scipionic group. Horace has another illuminating remark, that the whole life of Lucilius lies exposed for us in his verse. As there is no indication of biographical material, we must take this as meaning that the poet exposed thoroughly his own personality, his ideas, his character, his likes and dislikes. And therein lay his importance for the future of Latin poetry. He opened the door to personal expression. His colloquial style showed that, even though he himself was not really a poet, the way was open for poets to express themselves and to use the contemporary scene for subject matter.

It was many years before a great poet followed the lead of Lucilius, but this need cause little surprise. The years of his literary activity saw the failure of the old republican aristocracy, weakened in character by the imperial successes of Rome and by the flood of wealth channeled into its coffers without benefit to the great bulk of the populace. They saw too the stirring of that populace under the leadership of such men as the Gracchi. It was not a period to inspire great poetry, but Lucilius was not forgotten. We know from

Suetonius that he was read and lectured on by a succession of grammatici culminating in Valerius Cato, who also seems to have produced an edition of his works. As we have seen, it was he who influenced fundamentally the group of young men who were to become the new poets, and Cato may well have been the motivating medium who used the pioneering work of Lucilius to encourage his enthusiastic students into still more ambitious ventures.

II · LUCRETIUS

ucretius has not been generally considered one of the New Poets although he was a contemporary of Calvus and Catullus and wrote a poem as unusual for the time as anything which they produced. One reason for this is that the general conception of what the new poetry was has been too narrowly confined to certain types of Hellenistic verse. If Lucretius had been considered thoroughly orthodox it is hard to understand why he is never mentioned by Horace in spite of the familiarity which both he and Vergil show with Lucretius' poem. The didactic poem was a favorite type with the Alexandrians and appears first in Latin with Lucretius, and the most cursory study of the *De rerum natura* shows how strongly the writer was influenced by the new spirit which came from Alexandria.

Compare with Homer's appeal to the Muse in the opening lines of both the *Iliad* and *Odyssey* the invocation of Venus with which Lucretius begins his "epic" of life.

Thou mother of Aeneas' race, beloved
Of gods and men, Venus all-nourishing,
Who, 'neath the constellations gliding through
High heaven above, dost with thy presence fill
The sail-set ocean and fruit-bearing earth,
Since 'tis by thee that every living thing
Is first conceived and rising sees the sun:
Before thee, goddess, flee the winds, the clouds
Of heaven, before thy coming; dappled earth
For thee puts forth sweet flowers, for thee
The waves of ocean laugh and heaven appeased
Shines with an all-pervading radiance.
For when the spring reveals its first glad day

When breathes again the fertile west wind's breeze
The birds of heaven herald thy glad return
And hail thee, goddess, filled with thy magic power,
The herds inspired dance o'er the fertile fields,
Swim through the rushing streams and, willing slaves,
Each follows eager where thy summons leads.   (I.1–16)

It is not the Muse whom Lucretius invokes. It is the goddess of love, the force that peoples the world of living nature, and she is not asked to sing for him but to be his ally as he tells (in self-conscious verse) the tale of nature. Nor is she addressed curtly in a single word: she is appealed to with all the attributes of her rich endowment. Here is romance, color, suggestive symbolism, far removed from the *Works and Days* or the *Wrath of Achilles*. There follows a dedication to Memmius, another Hellenistic and Roman touch, and a further appeal to Venus to still the din of war that the gentler tones of poetry may be heard. This appeal involves a vivid word picture of Venus in the arms of Mars, relaxing his grim battle lust in her soft charm of love. Again the poet returns to the immediate and prosaic to state his subject. So, after sixty-one lines of preparation, he launches forth.

When mortal life lay desperately exposed
Upon the earth to superstition grim
That showed itself from out the realms of heaven
With horrid mien threatening our human race,
A man of Greece first lifting mortal eye
Dared challenge Superstition's mastery.
Him neither storied gods nor lightning bolt
Nor heaven with awe-inspiring voice could quell
But all the more he spurred his restless brain
To burst the bolts of Nature's fast-closed gates.
His piercing mind prevailed and soared beyond
The flaming bastions of the universe,
Explored the mighty void and brought us back
Victorious the truth of what *can* be,
What *cannot,* and the limits set for each,

The reasons why, the predetermined bounds.
And Superstition groveled in turn beneath
The heel of Reason till his victory
Has made us equals of the powers of heaven.   (I.62–79)

This is still introductory matter, but at line 150 begins at last the more prosaic pursuit of Lucretius' subject: nothing can come from nothing by act of creation. The universe consists of atoms (matter) and void (space) and nothing else. The atoms, streaming through the void in parallel lines, swerve slightly from time to time for no apparent reason and so produce collisions and combinations which we behold as material objects. The rest of the six books discuss the implications of the fundamental proposition that nothing can come from nothing, nothing can be reduced to nothing. It is a theory of materialism produced by reason out of imagination unsupported by experimental proof. Analogy there is, but not scientific proof, yet with magnificent courage and superb vision the poet presents the materialistic theory of body, soul, and mind, the theory of sense perception and the material basis of sexual passion, the evolution of civilization, and finally (in a sort of unfinished appendix) the explanation of what appear to be contradictory phenomena.

Such, in briefest outline, is the didactic poem of Lucretius on Epicurean philosophy and its materialism. It is of small consequence that we know practically nothing of the poet's life. The late notices of madness and suicide as the result of a love potion are conjectures of incompetent critics drawn from their own reactions to the poem, of value only as they inspired Tennyson to create a moving but wholly mythical Lucretius. The poem itself is sufficient to place the man. He is a rebel against the traditional bonds of orthodox religion and the Stoic philosophy that was officially accepted in its support. These were what inspired the fear of death and impaired the power of individual man to live to the full a free life. While contemporary poets were more concerned with the forms and spirit of poetry, Lucretius was primarily interested in his subject, so much so that he becomes at times the impassioned evangelist of a doctrine of freedom. He does not speak as a patriotic nationalist but as a fervent individualist. He was, however, a poet and, like his contemporary poets, he wished ardently to create something new in poetry. Catullus might hint, by speaking of his *new* book, that he was pioneering in new territory, but Lucretius stated boldly: "I am traversing / The pathless region of the Pierides / Untrodden else by any foot of man" (I.925–27). Experimentation was in the air and, with a more sustained effort and with greater success than most of his contemporaries, Lucretius was a New Poet though never a Singer of Euphorion.

Such an assertion must be further substantiated, for Lucretius is usually thought of as a follower of Ennius rather than as a secessionist. He did choose the hexameter as the meter best suited to a long poem and so falls superficially into the epic category. He revered the pioneer genius of Ennius and pays him generous tribute as the Roman Homer. He made use of many archaic expressions and was a master of alliteration, one of the few artistic devices of earlier Latin verse. He made free use of single five-syllable words to fill the last two feet of the line and he frequently ended the line with a monosyllable. All these were practices frowned on by later taste. He was more sparing than his contemporaries in the use of spondaic lines. At this point his poetic kinship with Ennius ends.

For Lucretius wrote a didactic poem, a familiar practice in Alexandria but not at Rome. Furthermore, his was the Hellenistic type of didactic poem, far removed from the classic work of Hesiod. Hesiod wrote to give practical instruction. He wrote in verse because prose as a literary vehicle was unheard of in his day. He knew whereof he was writing and his *Works and Days* was intended for the dirt farmer. When, in their search for variety, the Alexandrians revived the form, they no longer wrote as experts in the field of their subject but as poets adorning borrowed material for the delectation of a sophisticated reader and for the glory of their own names. Poetical adornment, in Hesiod a rare and accidental matter, was to them primary. The content of their didactic poems might be and usually was inexact, partial, and, from a practical point of view, disorderly in organization. Now Lucretius in his eagerness to end forever the tyranny of superstition maintained a logical sequence of argument. But he was quite ready to accept his philosophy secondhand, was at times inaccurate, and always strove to make his sermonizing palatable by his poetic art. He appears in the first person constantly throughout the poem, not merely as speaker but in self-explanation, in appeals to his patron Memmius, in eulogies of Epicurus. His aim was twofold: to emancipate the individual from the constraining fear established by traditional superstition and to win glory for himself as a pioneering poet.

Lucretius lived from 94 to 54 B.C. The reference to his work in Cicero's correspondence confirms this chronology and gives evidence that he was not unknown at the time. We may be sure that he was not active in the troubled political life of his day, for, if he had been, there would surely have been some further reference to him, however casual, in the surviving literature; and it is difficult to believe that an active politician could have written the six books of the *De rerum natura* before he was forty years old, packed as they are with evidence of wide reading, deep thought, careful workmanship, and intense feeling. Nor can we believe that Memmius was an admiring patron who made possible for Lucretius a literary life free from financial worries. Such a belief is inconsistent with Memmius' utterly unsympathetic attitude toward the Epicureans and their shrine, the home of the master. We must assume, I think, that Lucretius was an independent writer who gave his life to the production of a great poem on a single subject dear to his heart.

It is often emphasized that Lucretius is much closer to Ennius in poetic style than are Catullus and Vergil or even Cicero. The truth is that Ennius was the fountainhead of all

Latin hexameter verse, which even in Lucretius' day had not become a truly congenial medium but was still in the process of naturalization, slowly freeing itself from those elements of the Greek prototype which were not compatible with the peculiarities of Latin versification. Catullus made considerable advance in the process of adaptation, but Catullus' hexameters are often monotonous and there is a softness in his rhythm which would have been wholly inappropriate to the harder quality of Lucretius' subject matter. Lucretius, too, made a great advance toward the mastery of the hexameter but along different lines from those of Catullus. He was less interested in the musical flow of the lines than in their inherent dignity and impressive power. His concentration on the content of his argument often led him to disregard poetic qualities and drive home his argument in prosaic lines lacking in poetic imagination. But surely he as well as Catullus contributed to the development of the Latin hexameter, which awaited the touch of Vergil for its final perfection.

There seems to be little doubt that the manuscript of Lucretius' poem was edited or at least published by Cicero. While this was in hand he speaks of the work in a letter to his brother Quintus as having both inspiration (*ingenium*) and artistic merit (*ars*). Natural genius and artificial skill were an easy and popular contrast still serving the critics in Augustus' day. Cicero, from an early flirtation with Alexandrian poetry, had come to have a special reverence for the *ingenium* of Ennius, a quality which he fails to find in the Singers of Euphorion, as he calls the New Poets. It must be remembered, however, that this disparaging phrase occurs in the *Tusculan Disputations* which were written in 45 or 44, ten years after the publication of the *De rerum natura*. The scorn which it pours on the neoterics is directed not at all Alexandrian poetry in Latin but at the lesser and (to him) trifling output, verse which had art but not, he believed, genius.

It is the art which we must look for if we are to establish Lucretius among the New Poets. We have already glanced at the invocation to Venus with which the poem begins. In it appeared the elaboration, the vivid depiction of nature and her beauties, the use of myth, the intrusion of the author and the dedication to a patron, all devices associated with the school of Alexandria. As the argument for materialism advances we may forget at times that Lucretius was first of all a poet and, as though he realized this danger, he more than once reminds the reader that he *is* a poet and that he yearns for recognition as such. Toward the end of the first book he tells us: "mighty hope of praise has struck my heart with the sharp thyrsus" (I.922–23). The symbolic use of the thyrsus, the mythical weapon of the followers of Dionysus, gives the key to his slightly cryptic line and he proceeds to make his meaning doubly clear.

> Into my heart is thrust the entrancing love
> Of the fair Muses wherewithal inspired,
> With mind alerted I am traversing
> The pathless region of the Pierides
> Untrodden else by any foot of man.
> I would approach and quaff unsullied springs
> And cull new flowers that so the Muses might
> Crown me as yet no man has e'er been crowned.
>
> (I.923–30)

Again in the last book the poet summons the Muse to help him finish his course with glory:

> So guide me now, thou wise Calliope,
> Comfort of man, delight of all the gods,
> As in my course I near the whitened line
> Marking the goal, that with thee as my guide
> Mine be the prize captured with signal praise.
>
> (VI.92–95)

At the beginning of Book IV Lucretius repeated the lines from the end of Book I already quoted. Whether, in the final revision, he would have placed them here or not is today a

matter of conjecture, but there can be no doubt of his original
impulse to assert his poetic ambition at this point.

One of the best-known flights of poetic fancy is the opening of the second book:

> Sweet is it, safe upon the solid land,
> When mighty winds across the open sea
> Heave high the waves, to watch the dreadful toil
> Of others. Not that another's pain gives joy
> But seeing unscathed evils that touch us not.
> Sweet is it too to watch the strife of war
> Waged o'er the plains in which we have no part.
> But nought is sweeter than to hold the heights
> Of calm philosophy and so look down
> Upon the wandering world of men below
> Seeking a pathway in a life of doubt,
> Striving to match their wits, rivals for fame,
> By day and night with unremitting toil
> Battling to make the goal of wealth and power.
>
> (II.1–13)

The imagery and the realism are both Alexandrian and both
are equally typical of Lucretius. It is in this second book,
with its especially close argumentation, that we find the most
persistent attempt to illuminate the prosaic with the figures
of poetry. Directly following the opening lines quoted above,
two contrasted pictures are drawn, one of the rich palace and
one of the simple countryside, which later on will be presented in full for another purpose. It is enough, here, to indicate the care bestowed upon the pictures and on the choice
of words. The sculptured lamps, the coffered ceilings are
quite enough to conjure up the rich palace; the coursing
brook, the grassy bank, and the green meadows flecked with
bright wildflowers do the same for the countryside. But in
addition Lucretius has chosen words which add vivid life
to both panels. The house glows (*fulget*) with silver and
glitters (*renidet*) with gold. The weather smiles (*adridet*)
on the picnickers and the seasons sprinkle (*conspergunt*) the

gay flowers over the fields. Catullus, Vergil, and Horace all pilfered this small masterpiece without shame. Forty lines further on the succession of the generations is "like racing runners who hand on the torch of life." Meteors are the "mighty torches of heaven, leaving behind them in their flight long trails of flame." Again, "the woolly flocks creep off to where the alluring grass invites them, jeweled with fresh dew." Crowded with pathos is the picture of the mother cow whose calf has been sacrificed at the altar. This bit of sentimentality, too long drawn out perhaps, but wrought with sympathetic care, is worth quoting.

> Mother bereft, she wanders through the glades
> Following the footprints of his cloven hoof,
> Searching each spot if she may only have
> A glimpse of her lost offspring, while she fills
> The grove with loud complaint, ever returns
> Back to the farmyard, longing for her young.
> Nor can the tender willows nor the grass
> Fresh with the morning dew distract her heart
> Or 'suage her woe. The brooks that swell their banks
> Avail her not nor can the other calves
> Grazing the fruitful fields comfort her mind.
> So well she knows her own and longs for him.
>
> (II:355–66)

Very different is the simile with which the poet illustrates the hopeless confusion which would result if the false theory of our ignorant belief were true, that the number of atoms of any given shape were finite. They could never meet together to form their proper object.

> But as, in mighty shipwrecks, the wide sea
> Tosses about benches and hollow spars,
> Prows, masts, and floating oars, scatters them wide
> Along the beach, that men may see and know
> The treacherous falsehood of the almighty sea
> Nor ever trust it, though with deceitful guile

It smiles an invitation, so if you set
A finite limit . . .   (II.552–60)

It is in these extended similes that Lucretius shows the ability
to match meter to subject and to satisfy the most exacting re-
quirements of the Alexandrians. For our taste, he somewhat
overdoes this in his description of the followers of the Great
Mother, but that is a matter of judgment, and Catullus found
the passage worthy of imitation. The effect can be appre-
ciated only in the Latin; translation loses the intricate sound
effect.

Tympana tenta tonant palmis et cymbala circum
Concava raucisonoque minantur cornua cantu.
                                   (II.618–19)

(All taut, the tambourines resound beneath the hands and
the hollow cymbals, and the trumpets threaten with hoarse
blare.)

These are by no means all of the passages in the second
book which mark Lucretius as a romantic poet capable of
lyric expression, and the second book is not radically different in this regard from the rest. Like Books I and III, it
may have been given more final revision and polish than the
others, but throughout the whole poem the flowers of poetry
are conspicuous, and they are not casual but deliberate. Even
as he nears the end, Lucretius says: much still remains to
be adorned with polished verse. He had already exposed
clearly his method of procedure, not only in his formal introduction but again more vividly in the beginning of Book
IV.

For just as doctors, when their healing art
Bids them give children bitter medicine,
Will smear the cup's lip with a coat of honey
That so deceived they'll drink the bitter draught
And thus be cured, so I, knowing how grim
May seem to some my stern philosophy,
Have sought to clothe in sweet Pierian song,

The honey of the Muse, my argument,
If thus I might beguile your mind with song
Till it should fathom fully Nature's plan.   (IV.11–25)

The simile here presented at once calls to mind the similar figure in Horace's defense of his own method of relieving his serious preaching by the introduction of humor just as, he says, teachers give cookies to boys to make them try to learn their ABC's. The analogy extends beneath the surface. Philosophy for the Roman was practical, a search for that rule of behavior which should lead to the happy life (*vita beata*). Satire had originally been to a considerable degree the popular presentation of the Stoic doctrine of ethics, the approach to contentment by way of the path of duty. Lucilius, the pioneer in the field of satire, had presented virtue as the aim of an ethical life, for Stoicism was the accepted code of behavior for the Roman. Now Lucretius rose in rebellion against the whole Stoic position. Because his own philosophy, Epicureanism, *was* revolutionary and in fact shocking to the average cultured Roman, he felt bound to set forth at length and in convincing detail the whole body of belief which lay behind Epicurean ethics. This meant nothing less than the removal of the gods and with them the fear of death. The practical end was still the teaching of a way of life, and to this end Lucretius used the same method as the satirist, the approach by means of homely illustration and easily understood maxims, stated if possible in striking, epigrammatic form. The Stoic Lucilius, with his bold individualism, had indeed opened the way for his even more independent rival, Lucretius. It is remarkable how closely the conclusions of the two philosophies agree when it comes to the code of behavior recommended as leading to the happy life. Either Lucilius or Horace could have endorsed the doctrine put forward by Lucretius in this passage from Book II referred to earlier.

Oh wretched mind of man, oh blinded heart,
In what dark murk, amid what threatening ills

Our little life, whate'er it be, is spent,
That we see not how Nature asks but this,
That, with the body free from pain, the mind
May savor pleasure without care or fear.
So we perceive that for our body's nature
Few things at all are needful, only such
As may prevent all pain. And though at times
They may supply in pleasant fashion much
Delight, still Nature feels no detriment
If in our homes there be no golden statues
Of youths with fiery torches in their hands
To light rich evening banquets, if the house
Shine not with gold and silver nor the lyre
Resound from coffered ceilings cased in gold,
If, nonetheless, beside a coursing stream
We lie together on the cushioned bank
Beneath the branches of a lofty tree
And without luxury refresh ourselves
When most the weather smiles and spring bestows
Her wild flowers sprinkled through the verdant grass.

(II.14–33)

It would be futile to illustrate extensively the words,
phrases, and figures which give evidence of the relation of
Lucretius to the satiric line of descent from Lucilius to
Horace. It is another phase of Lucretius' pioneering spirit
and of the contribution of one new poet to the tradition of
Latin poetry. The familiar punishments of hell are made
symbols of living experience (III.978); nature converses directly with the man who fears death (III.931); there is a
vivid picture of the restless man who cannot escape himself (III.1053); with small excuse the labors of Hercules are
elaborated (V.20); Heraclitus is attacked directly and with
great vigor, one of the more striking phrases being *clarus ob
obscuram linguam* (illustrious for his obscure tongue, I.629).
All of this has the familiar ring of satire and not a little of

it reappears in Horace. Such epigrammatic phrases as *mortalem vitam mors cum immortalis ademit* (when immortal death has filched our mortal life, III.869), are not notably common in Lucretius, but the pungent phraseology of the satirist is fairly frequent. When man is wretched, he tells us, his true self is revealed: *persona eripitur, manet res,* (the mask is torn away, the truth remains, III.55), and this truth reveals avarice and greed for office as leading men to crime and misery. Day and night men strive with utmost toil to rise to topmost wealth, and presently they cruelly rejoice at a brother's death while they hate and fear the tables of their kin. Horace and Juvenal could imitate the satiric in Lucretius but not greatly improve on it.

This phase of practical philosophy verging on satire is, I think, one element of the new poetry. The old traditional forms are abandoned, variety is passionately cultivated, realism is affected but at the same time poetic symbolism and erudite allusion. Eventually new forms will be developed. Those which are too consistently artificial will meet with sharp criticism and perhaps disappear; the rest will find their proper place in an honorable tradition. In Lucretius' poem the various elements are all discernible but made subservient to the overmastering purpose of which the poet never loses sight. When he finds himself able to claim achievement the grandeur of his goal is fairly matched by the dignity of his poetry.

> Death then is nothing nor concerns us aught
> Since these our souls are mortal matter too.
> And as the clashing arms of long ago
> Cause us no pain nor all the vast distress
> When Carthage to the conflict hurled her might
> And with the din of war the universe
> Resounded while the rule of earth and sea
> Hung in the balance, so when we are no more,
> When soul and body by whose unity

We now exist are sundered into space
It shall be naught to us who shall be naught
Though chaos claim earth, sea, and heaven above.

(III.830–42)

III · CATULLUS

atullus came to Rome from Verona while still a young man, some time in the sixties B.C. His father must have been a man of considerable means and importance, for it was he who entertained Julius Caesar when the general was passing through Cisalpine Gaul. The son did not see eye to eye with his father in politics, but the older man must have kept him well supplied with funds, for he played enthusiastically the part of a young man-about-town in extravagant Rome, owned a yacht, and had a villa at Sirmio on the Lago di Garda. He had a brother who died and was buried in the Troad, under what circumstances we do not know. Catullus himself, so far as our information goes, made a single trip out of Italy. He went to Bithynia with Memmius when this rather dubious politician was governer of that province. His position on the gubernatorial staff would seem to have been a purely ornamental one, and he returned independently of his colleagues on the yacht which he had had built for himself in Bithynia. He never held political office himself, but all of the people whom he mentions in his poems with either fondness or dislike were people of consequence, and most of them were actively engaged in the bitter political warfare of the day.

Politics, as we have already seen, was a cutthroat business in the sixties and fifties. Party lines were drawn not in relation to principles but to personalities. The civil war between Pompey and Caesar was shaping up, and it was already obvious that the division of the legions would be more decisive than the ballot box. The old sense of responsibility for public service was fast disappearing. The senate was becoming a sounding board for factional leaders, and the courts

[28]

were largely used to prosecute personal enemies in the tense struggle for individual power. The shameless political deal that is pompously called in our schoolbooks the First Triumvirate had dealt the death blow to democratic government. The times were perilous and exciting. There must have been many a young man who, like Catullus, preferred to follow his own inclination and enjoy life while it lasted rather than burden himself with a public career that could not fail to involve him deeply in the partisan struggle.

If we were to judge Catullus' short life (he died, according to Jerome, at thirty) by the content of his poetry, we might casually conclude that he devoted it solely to pleasure, and that of a not too admirable quality. Undoubtedly he knew well and from personal experience the gaudy and shabby life of love and intrigue that characterized the society in which he moved. But when we study more carefully the small volume of poetry which he left to posterity, we can only marvel at the amount of thought and study and sustained effort that this apparent flaneur devoted to his art during some ten crowded years. Even his trifles turn out on inspection to be constructed with meticulous care, and at least two of his longer creations are masterpieces of poetic technique possible only to a workman of integrity, who was willing and able to discipline his own unquestioned genius.

In Catullus' social set the writing of poetry was fashionable. The name of the orator Calvus is always bracketed by later writers with that of Catullus, and these two may well have been the leaders of what came to be known as the New Poets. Though we read of many others whose poems have been lost, the new school in its first generation must be judged almost solely by the one small volume of Catullus. How startlingly new it was can be realized only with an understanding of what Latin poetry had been up to this time.

It was now two hundred years since Livius Andronicus had produced his translation of the *Odyssey*. That and the epic of Naevius on the First Punic War, which shortly followed it, were in native Saturnian verse, an accentual meter doomed to give way before the quantitative and more musical Greek hexameter. Mastery of the new metrical mode of expression came slowly to the Romans, and the long drudgery involved in writing an epic poem in an unsympathetic medium accounts for the few attempts made. Also, Ennius' *Annals,* crude as many of the surviving fragments sound to us, attained by virtue of its high dignity and fervid patriotism such an entrenched position of honor as the great Roman epic as to discourage further efforts in the same line. It set a standard, however, and made epic poetry one of the three recognized branches of the art. The other two were tragedy and comedy. These were written in profusion and practically to the exclusion of any other type of poetry. Lucilius, as we have seen, made something of a break with tradition, but he was not really a poet and the new poets were actually breaking new ground. It is not to be wondered at that their verse made a resounding sensation.

The new expression of individualism also confronted a long tradition of almost puritanical prejudice in the realm of morals. The simplicity and strict integrity of both public and private life had, it is true, suffered a serious decline, but the old standards were still the official standards and were solemnly preached if not meticulously observed by the old guard of patrician families. Meanwhile the flood of immigration with its importation of foreign wealth and new ideas was beating against the dikes of conservative tradition. The new poets expressed the reaction of the younger generation to what seemed to them a welcome emancipation. That is why literary criticism has often been wrong in stressing too much the learning and artificiality of the new poets, what has been called their Alexandrianism. The erudition which they undoubtedly do show at times, and which often mars their work, was but one element of the new breadth and variety to which they so eagerly applied their excited efforts. Realism was as legitimate a goal for them as artificiality; learning was no more to be scorned than simplicity. The unforgivable sins were conformity and monotony.

The small volume which Catullus published is most immediately striking because of the variety of its contents. It would not be comparably surprising today, but it came at a time when a poet published an epic or a tragedy, not a book of "collected poems." Catullus did not even know what to call his collection but speaks of his "little book" and the "trifles" it contains. The verses in which he speaks of it in this vein comprise the dedicatory poem to Cornelius Nepos, in hendecasyllables. This definitely informal meter, best known for its use in vituperative verse, is the most frequent medium of expression in the first third of the book. Catullus, however, extends its use to all kinds of short poems: bursts of high emotion, both love and hate, trifling jokes, small anecdotes, political potshots. And the hendecasyllabic skits are mingled with short poems in straight iambics, choliambics, two even in Sapphic stanzas. This is but the beginning of his variety, for the second third of the volume consists of longer poems, two wedding hymns in wholly different metrical dress, an epyllion in hexameters, two ventures into the field of erotic elegy, and a magnificent picture of religious frenzy in exotic galliambics. Finally, the third section of the book consists of what might be loosely called epigrams in conventional elegiac couplets. But, though the elegiac couplets are conventional, their contents are not.

It seems, then, not at all improbable that when Catullus speaks of this volume as "new" he implies something more than its technical spit and polish. The word has something of the nature of a manifesto from the new poets and as such is suitably addressed to the conservative author of history, Cornelius Nepos.

> To whom shall I present this little book,
> Dainty and new, polished with the pumice stone?
> To you, Cornelius, for you used to think
> My trifles had some value, none too great,
> While you alone of all the Italian race
> Were venturing heroically to expound

The history of the world in volumes three,
Learned, ye gods, and how laborious!
So take it, whatsoe'er my little book
May have and, oh my patron Muse, I pray,
Grant it to live at least beyond my day.　　(1)

In the first place, the new poet uses a deceptively deprecatory tone. His poems are mere trifles, his book is small, and
all that he praises in it is its physical elegance. He pays
respect to the more serious work of Nepos, his conventional
history. But beneath the surface tone of self-depreciation,
Catullus is boldly entering the field of published poetry with
a personal address and a discussion, slight as it is, of his own
product. He is not calling on the Muse to sing—*he* will do
that: no shirking of the responsibility for what he writes.
These may be trifles but he presumes to hope that, published now, they may live and be read. Furthermore, there
is a slight tone of raillery in the reference to Nepos' mighty
tomes. The affectation of simplicity in the choice of meter
conceals a careful construction, his own book holding the
stage in the first few lines and again in the last three, while
Nepos and his history furnish a contrasting picture in the
central core of the poem. The smooth transition from the
first part to the second, in sharp contrast with the abrupt
transition from the second to the third part, is well calcu-
lated to catch not only Nepos' attention but the reader's also.
As already noted, the conspicuous "new" seems to be a
covert suggestion of the novelty of the contents.

The continual emphasis, from Cicero's day to the present,
on the new poets as the exponents of Alexandrian artificiality
makes it easy to overlook one of their first contributions—
the introduction of realism. The short poems of Catullus
deal regularly with familiar personal incidents in realistic language and from a realistic personal point of view. Almost
always the poet speaks directly in his own person and usually
to some individual. Lucilius had prepared the way with his
personal satire and he also undoubtedly suggested to Catul-

lus some of his subjects, at least their concern with current
gossip. A considerable group of poems deals with Catullus'
own love affairs, especially with the one which most influenced his life, his infatuation with the notorious Clodia
or, as he calls her, Lesbia. Into these and a few others there
enters a sincere passion that puts them in a class by themselves. It is the more casual verses which should be considered first, for these illustrate the clearest break with the past,
the abrupt departure from the elevated poetry of tradition.

In their simplest form these may recount some amusing or
at least interesting incident, Asinius going home from dinner with one of Catullus' favorite napkins under his tunic,
Calvus orating furiously, Rufus' failure to take sufficient
baths, Arrius' affected accent, Quintia's attempt to rival Lesbia, the gossip about Clodius and his sister or about Gellius'
improprieties. Among these, attacks on well-known political
characters are prominent. Caesar's friends are conspicuous
among the victims of Catullus' pen, and it is with attacks
rather than praise that this genius is busy. Caesar himself
is the object of a blunt epigrammatic rebuff:

> Caesar, I care not if your love I lack
> Nor fret myself if you be white or black. (93)

But Caesar is also, along with his son-in-law, Pompey, the
victim of a more elaborate and malicious attack in which,
to be sure, the names do not appear, though no one could
miss the obvious allusions.

> Lives there a man can bear this horrid sight
> Except some shameless, greedy profligate?
> Mamurra now possesses what was once
> The long haired Gauls', what Britain once controlled.
> You bastard Romulus, can you look and live?
> Shall he so proud in stolen opulence
> Frequent the chambers of our palaces
> Like some pet dove, Adonis' counterpart?
> You bastard Romulus, can you look and live?

Then you're the shameless greedy profligate.
Was it for this, oh matchless general,
You sought the farthest island of the west
That that foul, jaded Mentula of yours
Might so devour its uncomputed wealth?
Was it too little that he swallowed up
His patrimony, next, unsatisfied,
The Punic plunder, then, in a third debauch,
Iberia's wealth washed down by Tagus' stream?
So now must Gaul and Britain fear his maw?
Why do you spare him? What can he achieve
Save to devour the wealth of all the world?
Was it for this you wrecked our universe,
Father-in-law in league with son-in-law?   (29)

This, it is true, goes beyond the limit of trifles, but the
new poet will not be confined to categories. It is extended
and elaborated, but it has the qualities of the short hendecasyllables: realism, including a colloquial plainness of speech
descending to vulgarity, personal directness of approach,
and wholly contemporaneous appeal. Such wit as it exhibits
lies in the apt choice of words, in the exaggerated picture of
the political grafter and in the skilled use of repeated lines.

In four poems Catullus employs this last device effectively
by repeating the first line in the last to give a certain framework and to bind the whole into a closer unity. Three of
the four are vindictive poems of outspoken indecency and
will not be translated here. The fourth (56) is a trifling exhibition of preciosity.

Foul *Annals* of Volusius,
Pay ye the vow my Beauteous
To Venus made and Cupid too,
Swearing, if I once more were true
And ceased to hurl the Iambic shaft,
She'ld offer up the choicest draught
Of earth's worst poet to be destroyed
In fire the clubfoot god employed.

'Twas so my sweetheart thought her wit
Condemned my verses to the pit.
But, Goddess born of ocean's foam,
That ever honors as thy home
Amathus and Idalium,
Golgi and Dyrrachium,
Urii, Ancona too,
Cnidus' reedy shore so blue—
Give me receipt for vow well paid
While these, in rustic filth arrayed,
Expire in flames, not fabulous,
Foul *Annals* of Volusius. (36)

Of better quality is the ironical blast at the great Cicero, so urbane as to be taken literally by many critics as humble praise.

Most learned of the sons of Romulus
That have been ever, Marcus Tullius,
Or are or shall be in the years to come,
His greatest thanks Catullus sends to you,
Catullus, worst of all the poetic tribe—
As much the worst of all the poetic tribe
As you are best of all the orators. (49)

One is almost tempted to believe that our date for Catullus' death is really wrong and that he lived to hear Cicero's sneer at the new poets as "Singers of Euphorion." Occasionally the short poem has the real characteristics of the epigram. So the 53d.

I had a laugh the other day:
    Listening to little Calvus squander
His mighty organ tones to flay
    Vatinius, I heard some bounder
Raising his arms to heaven, say:
    Ye gods! a learned salamander! (53)

The true epigrams, with something of the Greek sense of

restraint, expressing sadness without sentimentality, yet never far removed from self-pity, are reserved for the third part of Catullus' volume and are written in the traditional elegiac couplets. Such is the 70th poem:

> My sweetheart says she would not choose to wed
>> Any but me—not if great Jupiter
> Should sue. But woman's words of love
>> Are writ in running water or in wind.   (70)

This epigram suggests a more important group of poems than the incidental trifles which we have been looking at. These are the poems of sentiment and passion which have endeared Catullus to the world. Here again the variety is amazing. One of the best-known may be taken as representing the poems of happy and requited love.

> Come Lesbia mine, let us but live and love
> And all the tattling tales of gossiping age
> Count not a pennyworth. For *suns* may set
> And rise again, but *we,* our brief life gone,
> Must sleep one long and never ending night.
> Give me a thousand kisses, then a hundred,
> A second thousand and a hundred more,
> A thousand then, another hundred. So,
> When we have kissed so *many* thousand times
> We'll lose all count, that no malicious soul
> Shall know we kissed *so* many thousand times.   (5)

Another phase of the lovers' happier experiences appears in a poem which is generally taken to picture the poet's despair when he has lost his love forever. With some diffidence, I would find a different interpretation. The Greek "limping meter," the choliambic, in which the poem is written, offers a slight warning against taking too seriously what it has to say. Catullus' tendency to end a piece with a surprise line, a striking characteristic of the later Roman epigram deriving from Catullus, confirms the suspicion that this poem may represent a not unhappy state of mind, that it may be the purposely exaggerated expression of a transient lovers' quarrel, a bid for the expected return of mutual happiness.

> My poor Catullus, play no more the fool,
> And what you see is gone reckon as lost.
> The suns shone bright for you in those glad days
> When you but followed where your sweetheart led,
> That sweetheart loved by you as none shall be.
> Those were the days of happy frolickings
> That you loved and your sweetheart loved as well.
> Now she will have no more. You too give over
> Nor follow where she flees. No longer live
> In misery but, with stern heart, endure.
> Farewell, my love, Catullus now is firm.
> But you will grieve when no one pleads with you.
> Ah, wretched girl, what life will now be yours!
> Who will pursue you? Who will think you fair?
> Whom will you love? Who now will call you his?
> Whom will you kiss? Whose lips in passion bite?
> But, come—tut, tut, Catullus, you be firm.   (8)

There is a vast difference between the half mocking tone of these verses and the final bitterness when all is really over between Catullus and Lesbia, and he indites in Sapphic stanzas his brutal final word. There is an added sting to this last message, for it is written in the meter which he used only one other time and that when, a callow youth, he first saw Lesbia, who was to be the blessing and curse of his short life. But that first address to his love was a translation from Sappho before experience had made him a poet in his own right. His last words to her are not borrowed ones.

> Aurelius and Furius, comrades sworn
> To follow where Catullus calls—beyond
> The farthest Indies or that shadowy shore
>   Lashed by the eastern sea,
>
> Or if his goal be the Hyrcanians,

The soft Arabians, or the Parthian hordes,
Or those who live where seven-mouthed Nile dyes
     The Inland Ocean's blue,

Or should he march across the mighty Alps
To view the monuments of Caesar's pride,
The Gallic Rhine, the northern ocean dread
     And Britain's farthest tribes;

Prepared to meet all these and whatsoe'er
Heaven may decree beside—I ask you this:
Only to carry to my sweetheart's ear
     Words few nor comforting.

Let her live on with her lewd following
Of lovers numberless whom now she holds
Fast in her toils, loving none faithfully,
     Destroying all alike.

Nor let her hope to win my love again
Which by her faithlessness lies withering
Like some frail flower on the meadow's edge
     Touched by the passing plow. (11)

The artificiality of the first two-thirds of the poem, with the rather ponderous listing of distant places, is clearly intended as a contrasting background for the short, simple, and bitter message which he commits to his two friends for delivery (within a few squares in Rome) to his faithless sweetheart. A second deliberate contrast is effected by the brutal coarseness of stanza five and the exquisite simplicity and pathos of six. To himself he addressed a final poem in the Lesbia cycle of his less literary and perhaps more sincere expression of personal emotion.

If in the memory of kindness done
Man may take pleasure, thinking of his own
Unbroken loyalty, his faith maintained,
That he has never sworn to other's hurt,
Then you, Catullus, may expect much joy

In years to come from this ungrateful love.
For all that man in kindness does or says
This have you said and done—and all is lost,
Bequeathed by you to a disloyal heart.
Why torture then yourself? Nay, steel your soul
And end your agony when gods oppose.
'Tis hard to lay aside an accustomed love,
'Tis hard but, God knows how, it must be done.
Here is your one salvation, this you must win,
This you must do whether you can or no.
Ye gods, if ye know pity, if any man
Even at death's door your pity may have saved,
Look on my woe and if my life be pure
Deliver me from this destroying plague.
Alas, a numbness, creeping o'er my frame,
Has stolen from my heart all sense of joy.
I ask no more that she return my love
Nor yet, what cannot be, that she be chaste:
I pray but to be healed, to lose this curse.
Grant this, ye gods, for my long faithfulness.   (76)

Three poems, representing three phases of his trip to Bithynia in the train of Memmius, furnish expressions of three different emotions. His feelings about his commanding officer were expressed frankly and coarsely in short, stinging hendecasyllables. For his fellow travelers he may have had warmer sentiments, but his departure for home ahead of them in his own boat, built for the purpose, combined with the arrival of spring, produced only an outburst of joy.

At last the spring comes with its melting warmth,
At last the rage of equinoctial skies
Is silenced by the gentle zephyr's breath.
Up, up, Catullus, brave the Phrygian plain
And hot Nicaea's farmlands lush with crops:
Fly to the famous towns of Asia's coast.
The eager heart pants for the open road,

The very feet rejoice in new-found strength.
Comrades of happy memory, farewell.
Far, far from home together came we here:
Each by a different way shall we return.   (46)

On the return voyage to Rome Catullus stopped in the Troad to visit the tomb of his brother and has left us the unforgettable record of his emotion evoked by the occasion.

Through many peoples and o'er many seas
I come, my brother, to this piteous rite,
To proffer you in death the last sad gift,
Speak to your ashes one last word—in vain.
Since Fate untimely snatched you from my sight,
Ah, brother, stolen from me ruthlessly,
Now, what I can, I bring, by custom blessed,
These meager offerings to thy spirit gone.
Receive them, watered with a brother's tears
And to eternity, hail and farewell.   (101)

The direct simplicity and sincerity of these lines did not deserve the maltreatment which they received at the hand of Tennyson's sentimentality.

When the trip was safely over, Catullus sentimentally took his little boat to the Lago di Garda, below his villa at Sirmio, where it was evidently hauled up to be a constant reminder of his experience. The poem he writes about it is fraught with no deep emotion. It may be slightly nostalgic but is really only the mature development of a short incidental poem, given body and importance by the mild warmth of affection expressed with a formality just sufficient to be effective. For the picture of the retired craft in the opening and closing lines frames gracefully the twofold sketch of the trip, picturing the succession of scenes first in reverse order, from Sirmio to Bithynia, then in swift summary home again. The slightly exotic names are not learned: they are real reminiscences and familiar at least to the friends to whom the poem is addressed.

That little boat you see before you, friends,
Claims to have been the swiftest of all craft;
Nothing that floats, she says, could distance her
Whether with oars they sped or under sail.
Never, she vows, will Adria's threatening shore
Deny her boast nor yet the Cyclades
Nor Rhodes of noble fame nor horrid Thrace,
Propontus or the treacherous Pontic gulf
Where she who's now a boat was long ago
A leafy tree. For on Cytorus' ridge
She used to whisper with her rustling green.
Pontic Amastris and Cytorus' woods,
You know and still remember, says my boat,
For on your hill she once was born and grew
And in your waters first baptized her oars.
Thence through the raging seas she bore her lord
Whether from left or right the breezes blew
Or, full astern, Zeus favored neither sheet.
No vows she paid to settle with the gods
As proudly home she came and snugly made
Her final harbor in this placid lake.
All this was long ago: now she grows old,
Safe in sequestered peace, and dedicates
Herself to Castor and to Castor's twin.   (4)

Enough has been said to illustrate the variety of the
shorter poems. Mention should be made, however, of the
gay hymn to Diana in glyconics to be sung by boys and girls.
It alone has no personal reference, no stark realism, no incidental appropriateness. It is the challenge of the new poet
to the writers of the conventional hymn, letting in a shaft
of light and banishing all penitential grimness.

In all of the collection there is almost nothing of the
academic aura generally ascribed to the new poets, which
would suggest that the critics have neglected the shorter
poems for the more easily dissected long ones. There is,
however, one short poem which must be faced before we

can say that there is *no* burdensome learning. It is the highly controversial seventh.

> You ask how many kisses, Lesbia,
> Would satisfy, and more, Catullus' love.
> As many as the sands of Libya
> That blow about Cyrene rich in herbs
> Between the oracle of torrid Jove
> And ancient Battus' sacred sepulcher;
> As many as the stars, when night is still,
> That spy upon the furtive loves of men.
> To give to you so many kisses might
> Content, and more, Catullus' maddening love,
> So many kisses which the curious
> Could never count, to curse with envious tongue.   (7)

The rendering does not completely expose the exaggerated touch of learning, for the literally translated epithet of Cyrene would not be the bald "rich in herbs" but the pedantically accurate "asaphoetida-bearing." The oracle of Zeus in the African oasis consulted by Alexander is not too remote a reference but the tomb of Battus smacks of the schoolroom. Before we condemn the poet too finally, it is well to look at the poem as a whole. Here once again is the familiar framework with the first and last three lines embracing a central core. And, as happens in other poems, the central core is divided into two contrasted panels. Only here the contrast is between an artificial and a natural comparison. The sands of the desert and the stars of heaven are not new figures of speech: what is new is the ornate dressing up of one and the incomparable simplicity of the other. *Cum tacet nox,* when night is silent, is perfect and the following line falls not far short of it. The slightly offensive learning, then, has a definite purpose, and is not the mere display of an exhibitionist. Whether we like it or not, the poem is typical of the way Catullus combined realism and personal emotion with something of that artistic form which was to be so characteristic of his longer productions.

There can hardly be a question of where Catullus turned for a model when he undertook these more formal and pretentious creations. He would hardly have translated with devoted care into Latin elegiacs a ninety-four-line poem of Callimachus if he had not thought well of the work. As a matter of fact, the Alexandrian poet was himself a rebel well-known for his revolt against the lengthy epic. "A big book is a big evil" was said to have been his expression of protest. He represents to us the group of scholar-poets who, in Greek poetry, were the prototypes of the New Poets at Rome. They too wrote short epigrams and vituperative verse but their most characteristic production was probably the short epic, the epyllion. It was not so called in antiquity. It was simply the epic reduced to a size suitable for a single sitting, roughly some four or five hundred lines. The poem which Catullus chose for translation from among the products of the master, "Berenice's Lock," can hardly have been wholly characteristic of the type. It is just under a hundred lines in length, and the tale, such as it is, comes to us from a lock of hair cut from the head of Queen Berenice and transformed into a bright constellation in the heavens. The story is slight and is made to carry a heavy burden of accessory information, including some more than commonplace astronomy. But the technical qualities are of the greatest interest. The lock identifies itself in the opening lines as the constellation discovered by the royal astronomer Conon and explains concisely that Berenice had vowed its consecration if the gods would save her warring consort. The last lines of the poem return to the queen and the lock begs for her remembrance, to be expressed with suitable offerings, the while it still protests its desire to return to its mistress' head. Within this framework is enclosed, not a second or supplementary story, but allusive reminders of the young girl who, by daring act, became queen, of the devoted bride who made the vow, and the brave consort who conquered Asia, all in warm contrast with the cold astronomy which presents the resulting life of the devoted lock. There is also something

of an inner frame, for the transition from the opening lines
to the scene of Berenice's vow is made by means of a question raised by the lock:

> Do young brides then hate love or is the truth
> That mothers mock its joy with feigned lament,
> Shedding profuse tears midst the wedding joys?
> Yea (may God help me) all their groans are false.
> The proof, my queen's complaints as in the arms
> Of her new bridegroom I beheld her joy.
> Or did you not in very truth bemoan
> Your couch deserted and the bridegroom gone?
>
> (66.15–22)

And the return to Queen Berenice at the close of the poem
is made by way of an appeal to all brides to remember the
lock on their wedding night.

> And thou too, oh my Queen, lifting thine eyes
> Up to the stars of heaven, when thou shalt pray
> To Venus, leave me not forgotten; crown
> My loyalty with thy munificence.
> For I could wish the starry heavens might fall
> And I become again a royal lock.   (66.89–93)

Apart from the structural symmetry, the content of the
poem shows a confusing mixture of sensuous warmth in the
realistic touches of first love and curiously academic learning in its development. The lock expresses its impotence before the steel which severed it but confirms this by recalling
how steel cut the canal for the Medes and by praying that all
the race of Chalybes (the mythical steelmakers) may perish.
And, after the fairly simple ending, as given above, there
comes as a shock one final line:

> So leave Orion beside Hydrochous.

The illusion is shattered, but the astronomy is quite correct.
   "Berenice's Lock" was Catullus' apprentice work. From
it he learned much in the way of technique but he never

imitated the particular poem in his own creations. We know that Callimachus wrote a more conventional epyllion called "Hekale" about Heracles and the bull of Marathon. On his way to the adventure the hero visits Hekale in her humble home to which he returns after his triumph only to find that his old hostess has died. What Catullus may have drawn from Callimachus will be evident in a study of the "Peleus and Thetis," his contribution to the epyllion tradition, the poem which, of all that he wrote, had the greatest influence on subsequent writers (see Appendix).

Into it he put an amount of care that it is hard to exaggerate. In one of his "trifles" he speaks of the nine years devoted by his friend Cinna to *his* epyllion called "Smyrna." The new poets were not grudging of effort. If an epic was to be reduced to a mere four hundred lines, those lines must meet successfully the scrutiny of meticulous critics. The details assume major importance: a miniature is different in kind from a mural. The poem begins with the sweep of a romantic epic:

Once on a time the pines on Pelion's height
Took form, they say, and swam through Neptune's wave
To Phasis' strand and King Aeetes' realm
When chosen youth, the flower of Argive strength,
From Colchis set to bring the golden fleece,
Dared in swift ship to scour the salty sea.   (64.1–6)

In swift and picturesque narrative we have the story of the Argonauts, building the ship, sailing out of harbor, and being met by the wondering Nereids who emerge from the depths to behold the strange sight of the first ship. Swiftly follows the love at first sight between Peleus and the sea nymph, Thetis. Zeus resigns his claim to Thetis and all consent to the perfect match of man and goddess. In twenty-one lines, a long and exciting story has been suggested and now the great adventure which followed, the recovery of the golden fleece, is wholly passed over and the tale leaps to the wedding day of Thetis and Peleus.

So when the long-awaited day had dawned
All Thessaly came thronging joyously
To crowd the portals of the royal home.   (64.31–33)

The countryside is deserted as the guests crowd into the palace and behold its splendor. The contrast is heavily stressed.

None tills the fields, the bullocks' necks grow soft,
The vine no more is trimmed, with downturned share,
The steer no longer cuts the stubborn glebe
Nor pruning hook the shadowy foliage,
And squalid rust consumes the idle plow.
But Peleus' palace with its vistaed halls
Shines with a blaze of silver and of gold.
Bright gleam the ivory couch, the goblets rare:
The house laughs with its royal treasure trove.
And in the central hall, the wedding couch
Awaits the goddess, its white ivory
Bedizened with a crimson coverlet.   (64.38–49)

It is soon clear that the poet has been leading up to the story embroidered on the coverlet as his objective.

With subtle art the tapestry portrays
The famous deeds of heroes long ago.
For, from the sounding waves of Dia's shore
Swiftly the ship of Theseus sails away
And Ariadne, fury in her heart,
Straining her eyes, believes not what she sees
Nor that at last, aroused from treacherous sleep,
She stands deserted on that lonely strand.   (64.50–57)

Fifty lines have brought the story to the tapestry and its picture of abandoned Ariadne. Two hundred lines follow, telling the tragic tale of Theseus and Ariadne, weaving back and forth in time and place from the scene on the island of Dia, the central element being the lament of Ariadne. Then the human guests depart and the gods come to the wedding.

For them the Parcae sing the prophecy of Thetis' son Achilles. Instead of picturing the departure of the gods, Catullus concludes the epyllion with twenty-five lines explaining the final departure of the divinities from earth, why men and gods no longer mingle. This final member completes the framework of the poem as a whole, balancing the lines at the beginning, which presented the meeting of man and goddess, but it is at the same time the concluding member of the framework of the symmetrically constructed story of the wedding.

The structure of the poem will be clear from the diagram which follows, but so great is the art of the poet that, in reading the poem, the mechanism, with its transitions, is never felt. Also it should be noted that corresponding elements are never of exactly the same length. Catullus had the sense and feeling of the Gothic architect in the infinite variety within his symmetrical whole.

I. Introduction, 1–30
    1. The Argonauts, 1–11
      2. Meeting of Peleus and Thetis, 12–21
    3. The Argonauts, 22–30

II. The Wedding, 31–408
  A. 1. Human Guests Arrive, 31–49
     2. The Coverlet, 50–51
       3. Ariadne, 52–131
        4. The Lament, 132–201
       5. Theseus, 202–64
      6. The Coverlet, 265–66
    7. Human Guests Depart, 267–77
  B. Divine Guests Arrive, 278–302
    1. The Parcae, 301–22
      2. Song of the Parcae, 323–81
    3. The Parcae, 382–83

III. Conclusion
    Why Divine Guests Are No More, 384–408.

From one point of view, we have a second story, antecedent to the major tale, inserted by means of the tapestry device and constituting a little more than half of the poem. From another point of view, the overall framework presents the relationship of gods and men, happy at first, tragic in the end, enclosing two contrasting panels. One deals with human character, the other with divine. One represents a love affair originating in strife and terror, unsanctioned and unfulfilled. The other presents a love which is blessed of heaven and fulfilled within the auspices of traditional religion. The central feature of one is a human lament over human cruelty, of the other a divine blessing on sacred love. The theme throughout is love, one-sided in the first panel, mutual in the second.

Within the first and longer panel is evident the same device of concentric frames, the same combination of correspondence and contrast to form a symmetrical pattern.

1. The Coverlet, 50–51
2. Ariadne on the Shore, Theseus Departing, 52–75
3. Arrival of Theseus in Crete, 76–115
4. Theseus and Ariadne to Dia, 116–23
5. Ariadne Alone on the Shore, 124–31
ARIADNE'S LAMENT, 132–201
6. Ariadne Alone on the Shore, 202–06
7. Theseus without Ariadne to Athens, 207–11
8. Departure of Theseus from Athens, 212–48
9. Ariadne on the Shore, Dionysus Arriving, 249–64
10. The Coverlet, 265–66

Such is the formal construction of the poem, the scaffolding concealed by the poet's genius. How different from the drive and action of the *Iliad*. How different from the unity of the *Odyssey,* achieved by the sustained interest in a single hero or that obtained, less successfully, by Ennius through the chronological sequence of history. Striking as this complex unity of structure is, there are more fundamental novelties of poetic quality which just as surely characterize the poem.

Undoubtedly the most pervasive element which sharply differentiates this epyllion from the traditional epic is the overall tone. Hitherto the great narrative poems had concentrated on the tale they told, a heroic tale of stirring action and sustained motion. There were, to be sure, incidents of a softer and more romantic quality: the parting of Hector and Andromache, Nausicaa and her playmates, probably Dido and Aeneas in the lost epic of Naevius. But in the "Peleus and Thetis" we have something quite different. It is the action which is incidental. It is vivid and compelling, but it is only the link between the emotional scenes for which the poem exists. One illustration will be sufficient. Theseus has arrived at the court of Minos ready to meet the Minotaur in the labyrinth to settle forever the quarrel between Crete and Athens. The princess Ariadne, at her father's side, is overwhelmed with love at first sight.

With what great waves of passion Venus swept
The maid as she beheld, with heart on fire,
This stranger, golden haired, and deeply sighing
Turned pale with fear that clutched her fainting heart.
For Theseus, firm to meet the ravenous beast,
Was seeking instant death or glorious fame.
And still, with promises that reached their goal,
She kindled on her lips a silent prayer.
For as some oak with branches far outflung
On Taurus' peak or pine with pitchy bark,
The storm wind with indomitable blast
Tears from the ground—it crashes headlong down
Uprooted, spreading havoc far and wide—
So Theseus laid the mighty monster low
Tossing in vain to heaven its spreading horns,
Then safe with glory he retraced his way,
Guiding his footsteps by her slender thread

> Lest in those labyrinthine wanderings
> By treacherous error he might forfeit all.   (64.97–115)

To Homer the battle with the Minotaur would have been an heroic episode, drawn out for the relish of both poet and hearer. For Catullus, the importance of the incident lies in the emotional response of Ariadne and the result of her act in saving Theseus. Between these two elements the great physical struggle is covered in a seven-line simile; knowledge of the facts is assumed.

And so, throughout the poem, the action moves from one emotional scene to another; the meeting of Peleus and Thetis, the wedding day, the pitiable state of abandoned Ariadne, the scene at Cnossos discussed above, lamenting Ariadne, old Aegeus bereft and plunging from the cliff, the arrival of Dionysus and his Bacchic rout, the departure of the human guests and the arrival of the gods, the Parcae and their prophecy. Where action is necessary it is handled swiftly and effectively but it is subsidiary. Following directly on the lines just quoted, the return to the shore of Dia, where Ariadne has been forlornly waiting, is accomplished by the most summary action.

> But why stray from my song to tell the tale
> How Ariadne turned from her father's face,
> Her sister's last embrace, her mother's too
> Who still rejoiced even in her daughter's loss,
> And chose instead to follow Theseus' love,
> Or how she sailed to Dia's foaming shore
> Or how, her eyes still closed in peaceful sleep,
> Her lover left her with forgetful heart.   (64.116–23)

A whole book of thrilling narrative is thrust aside to maintain the poet's chosen method.

There are two particularly striking facts about this succession of emotional scenes. First, the chronological order is broken not once, as in the *Odyssey* (when Odysseus relates his experiences at the court of Alcinous) but repeatedly, constantly weaving backward and forward. This must have been a deliberate revolt from epic monotony. Second, the method is notably visual. It is not merely that the Ariadne story stems from the picture on the tapestry. Each scene is visualized and made vivid by realistic detail and particularly by color and color contrast: the white foam tossed up by Argo's oars against the dark blue of the Aegean Sea, the crimson coverlet on the ivory couch, the white hair of the Parcae held by crimson fillets. If color is not the chosen element it is often the realistic detail which creates a visual picture. The scene of the Thessalians thronging to the wedding of Peleus and Thetis is made vivid by the complementary picture of the deserted countryside with the idle cattle, the discarded pruning hooks, and the plowshare left to rust in the abandoned furrow. Ariadne's pathetic situation is enhanced by the picture of the waves washing back and forth at her feet the garments she has snatched up and then, in her frantic horror, unconsciously dropped.

This suggests at once the question, how far is the realism of the shorter poems retained in the epyllion? The first impulse is to say, hardly at all. The subject of the longer poem is a story of the mythical past when the gods mingled with men and there was an aura of romance in the world. But this is not the whole story. There is no place, of course, for the vulgarity and vituperation of the short hendecasyllables. But these comprise only one minor phase of realism. The realism of the epyllion is relative. One small detail is that Catullus does not invoke the Muse but drives directly to the heart of his story. The motives too of hero and heroine are realistically human and understandable. With all its mythological setting, with its superhuman characters, we are dealing with human men and women, their human joys and tragedies. The atmosphere is romantic but the emotion is realistic, and at the very end, as if to show that this was the result of conscious purpose, the poet shocks us with his picture of what realism may be without the dream.

For since our world, embracing impious crime,
Has banished justice from its covetous heart,
Brother sheds brother's blood incontinent
And children mourn no more a parent's death.
The father prays to lose his elder son
To lie untroubled in his marriage bed.
Mothers, seducing sons with treacherous guile,
Fear not the anger of avenging gods.
Our madness that knows nought of right and wrong
Has turned the gods against our guilty race
Till they consort no more with human kind
Nor share their glory in the light of day.   (64.397–408)

It is indeed rather shocking, this deliberate introduction of
sordid detail which might be appropriate in satire or in hendecasyllables but which offends us in its romantic setting. We
are not called on to judge Catullus but to understand him, and
this I think we can do. The new poet was surely Alexandrian
to this extent, that he delighted in contrast and in vivid effect.
The descent to the vulgar serves sharply to emphasize the
contrast which has been implicit all the while between human
and divine love. We must remember that Hellenistic art
produced not only the Apollo Belvedere but also the wrinkled
old hag and the ugly fisherman.

It would seem perhaps unnecessary to say anything about
the variety displayed in the "Peleus and Thetis" after what has
already appeared in our discussion of pattern and realism. But
all has not been said. It has been noted that each of the two
central panels contains a central recital, one the lament of
Ariadne, the other the song of the Parcae. The first would
seem to follow a conventional pattern with individual application. Direct vituperation of Theseus is followed by self-pity,
reminiscence, reminder of Ariadne's impossible position, and
finally a bitter curse against Theseus. The symmetrical pattern
is evident. The song of the Parcae is wholly different, stanzaic
in form with a recurrent refrain. It is a unique wedding hymn
with a pastoral refrain: "Run on, ye spindles, weaving the

thread, run on." It hails the happy bridegroom, reminds him of his good fortune, prophesies in some detail the achievements of his hero son, Achilles, and ends by returning to the happy wedding night. Epic tags are scrupulously avoided and everything is done to escape the monotony of the epic as felt by the new poets. Nor should it be overlooked that romantic love is the main theme of the poem, not a subsidiary one, and that the central figure is a woman.

Finally, and this has been hinted at already, there is in the poem a pervading lyric quality, not only in the wedding hymn, not only in the similes, but in many a pregnant phrase and haunting expression throughout. The tone is set when, in the first lines, the pines of Pelion swim the sea. The chill sobs which rise from Ariadne's moist lips and the prayer kindled like a sacrifice on those lips are not simple narrative expressions. The picture conjured up by a few perfectly chosen words of the maiden princess in her fragrant chamber, the injunctions which fly from the careless mind of Theseus like clouds on the mountain peak before the breeze, old Aegeus straining his eyes to see the returning ship—everywhere the imaginative choice of the right word betrays the sensitive lyric poet. A new type has been established in Latin poetry and a poem created which has appealed to countless readers but even more to the poets who succeeded its creator.

The variety of the longer poems would be incomplete without some failures. Catullus' example of a conventional Greek type, the "Address to the Closed Door," serves this function well. It belongs with the erotic trifles and may have had some interest for the social circles of Brixia and Verona because of its gossip and innuendo. For us, its only interest lies in the fact that Catullus experiments here with another type new to Latin literature. This type consists of an imaginary conversation between a lover and the door which bars him from his love and the plaintive protest of the door at being always made the scapegoat.

Scarcely more important are the extended epistles to Ortalus and Allius. These two poems come to us in poor shape textually. The first accompanied a translation of Callimachus (very likely "The Lock"). The other seems to be a manuscript confusion of two poems, one a letter, the other an elaborate expression of gratitude for help in his affair with Lesbia. Both poems contain tributes to his brother, set in the epistolary frame, and the second includes the story of Laodamia after the fashion of an epyllion.

Two other long poems are more congenial to Catullus' temperament, experiments in truly lyric poetry. They are wedding hymns, both showing meticulous care in construction but each having its own individual pattern. One is in hexameters and has a suggestion of introduction and conclusion but not in the nature of a framework like that of the epyllion. The opening lines present the situation. First (1–5), the boys of the wedding party see Vesper, the evening star, and leap from the banquet table for the wedding hymn.

> Vesper is come; rise up oh youths, Vesper is here;
> Its light, so long awaited, lifts o'er Olympus' height.
> 'Tis time to rise, 'tis time to leave the festive cheer:
> The bride is coming; sing, sing, to the god's delight.
>   Hymen, oh Hymenaeus, come, Hymen, oh Hymenaeus.
>   (62.1–5)

A group of girls across the room see the boys rise and guess the reason (6–12) and then (13–19) the boys spur themselves on to the singing which develops into a contest between boys and girls. At the end of the poem, in the last eight lines, the boys address the bride and commend her to her husband. Within this setting there are three pairs of lyric stanzas sung responsively by the boys and girls. The girls sing of the cruel side of Hesperus and present the simile of the hyacinth shorn of its beauty when plucked; the boys hail the kindly Hesperus and develop the simile of the ivy, useless until wedded to the elm. The stanzas vary in length but each is concluded with the same refrain as in the opening five-line stanza.

The other wedding hymn, in glyconics, is more lyric in quality, much gayer. It was written for a particular wedding, that of Vinia and Manlius, and has a much more realistic atmosphere. The pattern is set by loosely approximating the order of the Roman marriage rites. Hymen is invoked and invited to the wedding.

> Lord of the heights of Helicon,
> Child of Urania, hastening,
> Tender bride to her bridegroom bring
> Bride to be—Hymenaeus, come.
>   Hymen, oh Hymenaeus, come.
> Wreathe thy locks with flowers sweet
> Born of spring's delight,
> Come with wedding garment meet
> And upon thy snow-white feet
> Golden sandals bright.   (61.1–10)

The occasion is defined: after a hymn to Hymen, the bride is summoned; the boys, scattering nuts, suggest with a covert and gracefully concealed realism, the fescennine jokes of the wedding procession; the bride enters her new home; the bridegroom is called; good wishes are expressed and, with a prophecy of future happiness, the door is closed on the happy pair. Both hyacinth and ivy appear once more, and three different refrains are employed.

It might seem that, in a book of a hundred and sixteen poems, the maximum of variety had now been attained. But there is one more poem to consider, another variety, and this one perhaps the most original, certainly one of the most moving of all the poems and the greatest challenge to the traditionalists. For the "Attis" (poem 63) as it is called, abandons all the restraint of Roman dignity, assuming the wild frenzy of the eastern cult of Cybele. The young Greek who is the subject of the poem has, in a moment of mad devotion, consecrated himself by emasculation to the service of the Great Mother. From the shore of Phrygia, the scene of his sacrifice, he wildly leads a band of initiate followers through the forests and up the slopes of Ida. Before the palace of the goddess he falls exhausted into a profound sleep. Awakening, he realizes the

horror and the finality of his mad act. He rushes back to
the shore and, looking hopelessly toward the coast of Athens,
bemoans the madness which has forever bereft him of home
and humanity. Cybele has seen his revulsion and turns loose
her raging lions. At her order, they drive the devotee back
to the wild haunts of his new mistress.

ATTIS

Over the deep in swiftly moving ship
Sailed Attis. When he reached the Phrygian grove,
Eagerly landing in the darkling woods
Of Cybele and maddened by her goad,
He severed with the knife his manhood's pride.

So as he sensed his members sexless now,
Even as the fresh blood stained the forest floor
With snow-white hands he seized the tambourine
Dedicate to the rites of Cybele,
With slender fingers struck the hollow hide
And quivering called his comrades to the rout.

"Up, up, ye Gallae, with me to the groves,
The lofty groves, ye flocks of Dindymene,
That follow to strange pastures at my call.
With me to lead, ye traversed the salt sea,
Unmanned your bodies in despite of Love:
Rejoice, join with me in the furious dance.
No more delay: up, up and follow me
Where rears the Phrygian home of Cybele,
The goddess' Phrygian groves, where sounds the cry
Of cymbal and the frantic tambourine,
Where echoes Phrygian pipe and raucous horn,
Where maenads toss their ivy-wreathed heads
Following the holy rites with shrill acclaim,
Where we shall join them in the frenzied dance."

So at the call of Attis—woman now—
The troupe gave tongue in shrill abandonment.

The tambourines boomed out, the cymbals crashed
As swiftly up the sacred slopes they rushed
Of greening Ida, Attis in the lead
Panting in frenzy, rushing blindly on,
Leading his followers through the forest ways
As some unbroken heifer leads the herd.
The Gallae followed in one swift ascent.

So came they weary to the goddess' house
And fell exhausted, without nourishment.
When with sweet languor sleep had closed their eyes
In sudden peace the madness left their hearts.

And when the glorious Sun in radiance
Looked forth upon the heavens, the earth, the sea
And with his champing steeds dispersed the dark
Then Sleep deserting Attis took his flight
To where Pasithea waited to welcome him.
From soothing sleep aroused, his madness gone,
Attis remembered all that had transpired,
With sinking heart realized what he had lost
And where he was: so in his black despair
He sought again the shore, with streaming eyes
Beheld the unending ocean and cried out
In broken accents to his fatherland.

"Oh home that bore me, home that nurtured me,
With such mad folly could I run from you
As slave from master, to the far-off woods
Of Ida there to make a furtive home
Amidst the snow and haunts of wild beasts?
Where may I look to you my country now?
My eyes would turn to you while yet there be
Some moments free from that mad ecstasy.
Can it be true I left my home for this?
Have I forever lost them—parents, friends,
My country? Shall I never see again
The public square, the wrestling field, the course?

Oh wretched heart, to bleed forevermore.
What can life give that I might not have been?
I—woman now—but then a youth, a boy—
I was the flower of all our playing fields.
My door was thronged, my threshold ever warm
And festive garlands ever decked my home
When day returning roused me from my bed.
Shall I be now the slave of Cybele?
A maenad I? A fragment of myself?
A man unmanned? Shall I forever dwell
Upon the snowclad slopes of Ida, pass
My wretched life 'neath Phrygia's towering peaks
Where feed the deer and mountain-ranging boar?
Now, now I know my sin, now, now repent."

So as the cries died on his rosy lips
Bearing their message to the listening gods
Cybele loosed her lions from the yoke
And goading to action spake the fiercest thus:
"Up, up in fury, bring the madness back;
Drive him again back to the forest depth
That would escape too easily my power.
Up, lash thy tail and make the land resound
With thy fierce roar and toss thy tawny mane."

So spake great Cybele and loosed the beast
Who lashed himself to fury as he went
Trampling with frightful roars the underbrush.
But when he came to the white sandy shore
And saw the frail young Attis by the sea
He charged and Attis fled to the wild woods
Forever there to be the goddess' slave.

Oh mighty goddess, mistress of Dindymene,
Far from my home, I pray, thy madness turn.
Elsewhere bestow thy frenzied ecstasy.

Consistent with the exotic subject, the meter employed is
the galliambic, unique in the corpus of Latin poetry and bril-

liantly expressive of the passion and pathos of Attis' emotional tragedy. Nevertheless, behind the wildly disordered effect of theme and meter, the form of the poem is as carefully ordered as that of the "Peleus and Thetis." The first five lines give briefly and vividly the facts of the situation; the last three lines are the poet's reaction to his own creation. Within this slender framework there are two panels presenting the contrasting phases of Attis' fanatic madness.

1–5, Exposition of Subject
6–11, Rousing of Attis to Fury
12–26, Song of Ecstasy
27–34, Frenzied Rout to the Mountain
35–38, Interlude of Relaxation
39–47, Reawakening: Return to Shore
48–73, Song of Despair
74–90, Recapture of Attis; Return to Mountain
91–93, Prayer of the Poet

The transitions are smoothly concealed, the emotional pictures continuous. The realism consists in the brilliantly vivid portrayal of human emotions at their extremes. The lyric quality of both setting and passion presents, in maturity seasoned by experience, the poet of the political invective and Lesbia's sparrow.

IV · TRANSITION

he pioneer work was done before the battle of Actium ushered in Augustus' era of reconciliation and peace, the era which gave favored poets the opportunity of perfecting their art at leisure, free from the alarms of civil strife. Without any pretense of poetic skill, Lucilius had opened the way for the expression in verse of a wide range of personal opinion. Lucretius had battled the state control of personal belief and presented with passionate conviction, in didactic hexameters, the philosophy of individualism. Catullus had brought into Latin literature a whole galaxy of new modes: the hendecasyllable, the epigram, the wedding hymn, the elegy, the epyllion. It would be a mistake, of course, to think of these men as isolated pioneers. There is every indication that the passion for writing verse was widespread. We know of some of the writers: Varro of Atax (satire, epic, and elegy), Cicero, Calvus, Valerius Cato, Cinna, and Caecilius (epyllia), Cassius of Parma (epigram and elegy), Ticidas and Laevius (elegy). Calvus also wrote epigrams and Cicero a verse translation of the didactic poem of Aratus. Furius Bibaculus wrote epics in the new style.

Some of the new poetry had developed into fairly fixed types, such as the erotic elegy and the epyllion, but in general the real contribution of this body of poetry derived from Alexandria lay in the variety, the personal expression, the use of both commonplace realism and carefully elaborated ornamentation, and the insistence on artistic form. Each of these elements was susceptible of exaggerated misuse, but each also could be and was of inestimable value to all later poets.

After the battle of Actium, as Octavian the conqueror in civil war became Augustus the apostle of peace and founder of a new Rome, there developed with surprising speed and apparent spontaneity a literary circle in some ways comparable with that of Scipio and Laelius a century earlier. It centered around Maecenas, a man of startling contrasts and extraordinary personal influence, an aristocrat of ancient pedigree, wealthy and socially distinguished. He was Augustus' close friend, apparently devoting his life to the interests of his chief. He held practically none of the public offices, remained an eques, but represented Augustus in important negotiations and, in the absence of the first citizen, administered for him the affairs of the city. Chiefly, however, he contributed to the imperial program by encouraging such literary men as might add to the luster of the regime. Horace was probably the closest of his protégés, but Vergil, Varius, and Propertius were also bound to him by ties of friendship and obligation. The so-called Circle of Maecenas differed in one great essential from the earlier Scipionic Circle. The group which gathered about Laelius and Scipio consisted entirely of private citizens in a free republic, interested in developing a literature scarcely out of its swaddling clothes. They were all devoted patriots but there was nothing remotely official about their activities. The national emphasis of early Roman literature came from the patriotic enthusiasm of its makers and supporters. Of the Circle of Maecenas, the same cannot be said without certain important reservations. Maecenas and his chief were wholly engrossed in the politics of the new Rome. Their literary associates were mainly men who had been of the opposite camp. Horace had actually fought in the ranks of Brutus' army and was living in Rome on sufferance. Vergil's family had suffered by the confiscations perpetrated by the victors to reward their veterans. So had the family of Propertius. Messalla, who was on friendly terms with the members of the Circle though he had a less official salon of his own, had fought with distinction under Cassius and had written a history of the civil war with at least exaggerated objectivity if not actual republican bias.

It seems clear that the literary patronage extended by

Maecenas was, originally at least, part of a conciliatory policy by which the new government hoped to win general support and maintain both the domestic peace and the imperial security which it was striving to establish. There is ample evidence that the favored writers were encouraged if not urged to celebrate the deeds and character of Augustus and his party and to lend glamor to the new regime. There is no evidence of compulsion. We find the poets excusing themselves with grace and shrewdness from a task which they find unsuited to their particular abilities and which only Vergil accomplished in anything approaching the expected form. But all of them in their own various ways contributed to the glorification of Augustus and his government. It is true that, like the members of the Scipionic Circle, Horace and the other beneficiaries of Maecenas' patronage showed a strong national devotion in their poetry, and also that they all celebrated with heartfelt enthusiasm the virtues and traditions of early Rome. But all of this was in a new spirit. It was the glorification of a new movement, centering around an individual hero, and the deliberate but sincere effort to reconcile the new regime with the old. Fortunately the members of the group were poets first and partisans only incidentally. But in all of them there was a devotion to Rome that permeated much of their work. The earlier circle had been primarily devoted to prose, the later was a group of poets. Both were inspired by the optimistic spirit of their day, for in each case Rome was embarking on a new and exciting phase of its history. In both cases the old Roman characteristic of simple living and honorable thinking emerged in warnings against luxury and false pride. The Stoicism of Scipio's friends is not so obvious or dominant in the group around Maecenas. The basic morality of Stoicism is congenial to Horace and Vergil, but both men were eclectics who had listened to Lucretius and his Epicureanism and had developed their own philosophy of human understanding. Stoicism in the age of Augustus was marked neither by the enthusiasm of the novice nor by the belligerence of the rebellious reactionary of a later day.

[62]

Another characteristic of the Augustan situation must be borne in mind. Maecenas and Augustus did not represent the really old aristocracy of Rome, in spite of the insistence of the poets on the Etruscan ancestry of Maecenas and on the divine origin of the Julian line. They do represent the top rung of the ladder of official society, where a Vergil or a Horace, if accepted by the leaders, might feel himself socially made. They and their fellow poets held their social position by virtue of their ability, of the power of their genius to add to the glory of the new regime. They were persuaded that the glory of that regime was one with the glory of ancient Rome, and so what they wrote has the ring of real sincerity. Most, if not all, of them were converts from the republican camp. None of them seems to have been of an important family. Unfortunately many of them are only names to us apart from this association: Varius, Plotius, Valgius, Octavius, Fuscus Aristius. Two men whom Horace mentions frequently with respect and even affection are in a wholly different category. Messalla was a member of one of the old Roman families. Pollio, while perhaps of less distinguished lineage, had enjoyed high public prestige in the late republic and was a man of distinction and importance. Messalla had been definitely against Octavian; Pollio, although a friend of Antony, had maintained a certain neutrality after the death of Caesar. Both were on terms of friendliness with Maecenas and Augustus. Both gathered about themselves numerous young literary lights who either were not attracted by the official group or were not invited to join it. They do not represent an opposition to Maecenas and his circle, but they seem to have had poetic aspirations entirely independent of political enthusiasm.

Such opposition as there was came from the grammatici, the scholar-teacher professionals—the schoolteachers, as Horace insisted on classifying them. Here we run into more foreign names, even less distinguished than those of the protégés of Maecenas: Demetrius, Pitholaus, Furius Bibaculus, Fannius, Tigellius, Crispinus. Their poetic ancestor and revered model was Valerius Cato. Here is perhaps the key to the situation. Cato, a favorite of the young fashionables of the fifties, had enthused a notable group of poets that included Calvus, Catullus, and Cinna and, with less happy results, Catullus, Memmius, and Hortensius. His independent and in many cases brilliant students had brought new life into the tradition of Roman poetry. His professional and probably less brilliant followers had carried on the more obvious and more easily imitated phases of his poetic innovation. But these same professionals had the "academic" prestige behind them; they were the successors of Cato and had the power to make (or break?) poets. From this number came no doubt the literary arbiter Tarpa, whom Horace scorned to please. Horace's quarrel with the grammarians was an early one, conducted before his position was wholly secure, but it marks the beginning of his career as a critic. Pollio too was something of a critic. It was he who established the custom of literary readings, so fatal eventually but at first a healthy center of mutual criticism. It may well be that under the influence of Horace's attacks and the popularity of Pollio's recitations the prestige of the professional critics was broken.

This prestige had not been broken when Horace, the son of a freedman and an ex-republican officer in the army of Brutus, began writing his satires and epodes or when Vergil was composing his pastoral eclogues. Vergil, the earlier starter, intrigued by the glamor of the new poetry, followed its star in his juvenile poems, and Horace too showed no aversion to the new poetry in such trivialities as his army skit on Brutus and Rex or his more ambitious early epodes. Tibullus may seem to have wavered before he settled down to the matter approved by the grammatici, but Propertius consistently pursued the erotic elegy which Horace came to condemn.

The transition of Horace and Vergil to the camp of the imperialists was made easy for them by the policies of Augustus aimed at restoring the traditional simplicity of Roman life, eliminating the evils of extravagant living, and fostering the agricultural strength of Italy as a whole. In spite of a certain amount of philandering with Epicurean quietism, both poets could embrace these policies without embarrassment and with enthusiasm. Tibullus too was tempted but probably found, like the rich young man of the gospel, that the world was too much with him. At any rate, the new Augustan policies, subtly supported by Maecenas, gradually but inevitably produced and soon widened the breach between the poets of the Circle and the grammatici of the schoolroom. The best of the officially recognized poetry survived, as did also, in all probability, the best of the erotic elegy, which was officially frowned upon. But there must have been much of the school-sponsored poetry —elegy, epyllion, and epigram—which disappeared under what came near to being an official censorship. Perhaps it was the independence of Pollio and Messalla that protected the surviving remnant.

What is of more interest at the moment is an understanding of what was actually the contribution of the neoterics to the work of the poets of the new orthodoxy and what part of their contribution the latter rejected.

It was certainly not the newness of the new poets which offended Horace. His own proud boast was that he was the first to bring the Aeolian song into Latin measures, as he also claimed to be the first to introduce Parian iambics into Latin. In satire he grants Lucilius the position of pioneer but clearly implies that it was he himself who gave the type standing and stature. Horace, like Lucretius, claimed openly and proudly the laurels of the pathfinder.

It may throw some light on Horace's violent disapproval of Valerius Cato and his followers, the neoterics, to note the grounds which he himself specifies for his dislike. First and foremost, the introduction of Greek words into Latin verse. This, as Hendrickson has shown, may be extended to other Greekizing practices, including metrical softening. Carelessness of workmanship he criticizes, too, but this largely in satire, and it is more a specific and individual criticism than a general one. He reverts frequently to the striving for popular applause which, he gives us to understand, comes as the result of showy appeal, public reading, and the attempt to satisfy the

current critics, who are, in his opinion, the grammatici, oc-
cupants of an entrenched position.

More emphasis must be given, I think, to the last detail,
Horace's distaste for the grammatici. It is, on the surface at
least, Horace's most unattractive quality. Himself a wage
earner of humble origin, he speaks constantly with scorn and
arrogant superiority of the members of the guild. Obviously
he resents their importance in the public estimation, and, scorn
them as he will, he cannot hide the fact that they do worry
him. His attitude toward them becomes an unlovely snobbishness. His repeated reference to his own acceptance by the
leaders of the state is part of the same pattern as his scathing
dismissal of the schoolteachers laying down the law to their
female child pupils. Fortunately this attitude does not affect
the real artistic output of Horace the poet. It does however
suggest a reason for his vigorous attacks on the rival school of
his day. It recalls the hostility between Terence, patronized
by the Scipionic Circle, and the professionals in the guild. But
now the aristocracy-supported poets were writing drama, lyric,
epic, and satire while the professionals were backing the elegy,
the epyllion, and the epigram. The former pretended, at least,
to go back to Ennius and Accius, the latter, we know, did go
back to Calvus and Catullus.

There was some measure of consistency in Horace's position
when he chose to base his criticism of the rival school on its
Greekizing characteristic. For, strictly limited, the Greek
influence which he attacked was the influence of the late Greek
poets of Alexandria, and the familiar traits of that school were
learned allusion and the artificial pursuit of love as these appeared in the epyllion and the erotic elegy. It is significant that
Tibullus, accounted always one of the four great elegiac poets,
was a friend of Horace and that he showed enough of the
qualities which Horace respected to induce the latter to try to
keep him from writing elegies.

V · VERGIL

f the two great Augustan poets, Vergil was born in 70 B.C., Horace in 65. The difference is slight, but if, as seems probable, we must bring down the date of Catullus' death to the early fifties, then the short span of five years may be most significant. For Horace, having spent his childhood in rugged Venusia, could have had no experience of the poetry of Calvus and Catullus as it first startled the literary circles of Rome. But Vergil, five years older and a fellow countryman of Catullus in Cisalpine Gaul, may well have gotten his first poetic thrills from the cadences of the new poets while their songs were still novelties.

At any rate we know that the young Vergil was a devotee of the new school. In the early poetry which Vergil would have suppressed but which his friends preserved, Catullus is the strongest single influence. There is a sustained parody of Catullus' poem to his boat, a Catullan line is directly quoted in another poem, and the opening of "Ciris" is deliberately reminiscent of the earlier poet. Also, and much more fundamentally, we find the young Vergil pursuing the same variety of production, writing short poems of vituperation or compliment, incidental, humorous, and epigrammatic verses, as well as an elegy and two epyllia in sharp contrast with each other. We find, too, the mixture of realism and artificiality and the contrast of lyric beauty and plain prosaic bluntness, even a rather futile effort to use brazen indecency. We are vividly and constantly reminded of Catullus.

From Mantua, his birthplace, and after an elementary schooling at Milan, Vergil moved to Rome at about the age of eighteen. His father was an undistinguished but presumably successful farmer and perhaps a manufacturer of pottery.

Vergil seems at no time to have been pressed for money and at
Rome was taken under the protection of men of wealth and
prominence. Like all the young men of his class he studied
rhetoric under the popular lecturers, but he was more interested in the new poetry popular with the group of his
younger friends that included Cornelius Gallus, Quintilius
Varus, Octavius Musa, and Varius.

As Catullus acknowledged Callimachus as his master by
translating "The Lock," so, with a more Catullan whimsey,
Vergil bowed to his Roman master with a clever parody, a
poem addressed not to a much-loved boat but to a very dubious
politician who, starting as a Gallic mule driver, wound up with
changed name in the curule chair of a Roman official.

That man Sabinus whom you see, my friends,
Insists he was the swiftest muleteer ever.
No hurrying dump cart e'er surpassed his speed
Whether his business called to Mantua
Or Brixia. And this, he claims, the home
Of jealous Tryphon, noble and sedate,
Will not deny nor yet the tenement
Caerulius owns, where he, Sabinus now
But Quinctius in those days, with two-pronged shears
Cropped his mule's hairy neck so that the mane
Should wear no sores beneath the Cytorian yoke.
Cremona cool and mud-enveloped Gaul,
You know these facts, Sabinus says, and well
Remember. For 'twas in your dreary wastes
He made life's start and in your treacherous swamp
Spilled his first cargo. Thence through rolling miles
He bore the yoke whether to left or right
The mule broke wind or oftener dead astern.
No vows he paid to crossroad deities,
So says Sabinus, save this final one:
Ancestral reins and newest currycomb.
But this was long ago: aloft he sits

Today on ivory throne and dedicates
Himself to Castor and to Castor's twin.   (10)

This skit appears in a collection of miscellaneous short poems under the general title of *Catalepton*, or *Trifles*, corresponding roughly to Catullus' characterization of his own shorter efforts as *Nugae*. The newer poets had extended the Greekizing tendency, and Vergil at least preferred to borrow a Greek title. It is a small collection of only fourteen pieces to which is added an editorial tribute to the author by the unknown editor.

> More winsome than the bard of Syracuse,
> Greater than Hesiod, Homer's counterpart.
> Lo, these first offerings of that poet divine
> Reveal in motley measure his untaught Muse.
>
> (*Cat.* 14a)

Most immediately striking in this group of poems is the variety, in content, tone, and form, after the fashion of Callimachus and Catullus. The young Vergil was not an adept at vituperation but he attempted it, acknowledging, by quotation, his master in the field.

> Father-in-law, your own curse and the world's,
> And Noctuinus, son-in-law besot,
> By *your* lust and by *yours* has such a maid
> Departed from us pregnant? Woe is me,
> How universal is that famous line:
> "Father and son-in-law, you've ruined all."   (*Cat.* 6)

More allusive and enigmatic is his attack on some unknown scholar-murderer. Vergil is striking a blow against the affectation of the archaic. Corinthian words are old rarities like old bronzes.

> Behold that lover of Corinthian words,
> That rhetorician there, who, in his role
> Thucydidean—lord of the Attic plague—

> Compounding Gallic *tau* with *min* and *sphin,*
> For his own brother mixed a fatal brew. (*Cat.* 2)

In the friendlier trifles Vergil was more at ease, although the Catullan echoes still sound clearly in the following tribute to Octavius Musa.

> Where'er the seasons of our life shall lead,
> Whatever lands, whatever men we know,
> Straight may I perish if I have a friend
> Dearer than thou. How could it ever be
> Else when to thee, Musa, the gods above,
> The Graces too, have rightly given all
> That Phoebus loves and Phoebus' choristers?
> Who is there, Musa, with thy gift of song?
> Who in our world can speak so winsomely?
> Clio herself has no such eloquence.
> So if I may but love thee, 'tis enough:
> For what have I, that thou shouldst love me too?
> (*Cat.* 4)

One more effort must suffice for quotation before I attempt to relate these juvenilia with Vergil's life and literary activities previous to the composition of the major works on which his fame depends. It is perhaps a note of gratitude for the gift to him of the former home of the philosopher Siro.

> Cot that once sheltered Siro, tiny farm,
> (And yet the treasure of your master too)
> To thee myself and all my dearest kin,
> If to my fatherland shall come the worst,
> I now commend, my father first: to him
> Mantua and Cremona thou shalt be. (*Cat.* 8)

We left Vergil for a look at the *Catalepton,* which is from the time when he had just come to Rome and joined the group of young intellectuals in the study of rhetoric. The chronology of his life is clear in the major outline and we need not be too much disappointed when we find no general agreement on

the minor details. In the readjustments after the civil wars,
the family property in Cisalpine Gaul was confiscated, but
Vergil already had friends in the new government and suffered only sentimentally. He was comfortably maintained by
his powerful friends at Rome so that he could continue his
studies in rhetoric and poetry. From these however he was
soon distracted by the appeal of philosophy, very likely by
the pleasure which he drew from the poem of Lucretius. For
it was not to the austere doctrine of the Stoics that he was
drawn but to the more urbane principles of Epicurus. This
was natural for one with so little of the spirit of contention
and also for one of the new poets, all of whom turned in-
stinctively from the somewhat evangelical code which tended
to make man his brother's keeper and also maintained the
obligation to serve the state and hearken to the call of duty.
So it is not surprising to find Vergil turning away from the
pursuit of that rhetoric which was primarily intended to prepare the young man for active political oratory and, with his
group of young poet friends, migrating to Naples to sit at the
feet of the philosopher Siro. The *Catalepton* has a short poem
expressing his farewell to the life he was leaving.

> Begone ye empty paint-pots of the school—
> Words, pompous words of tawdry pedigree—
> You, Selius, too, Varro and Tarquitius,
> And all your greasy colleagues of the bench,
> The tinkling cymbals that misled our youth.
> And you that I loved best, Sextus, farewell,
> Farewell to all the whole dear specious lot.
> My sail is set for harbors of the blest
> To hear great Siro's wisdom-laden words
> And claim life's freedom from devouring care.
> Begone ye Muses too—a long farewell,
> Sweet muses: for the truth will out, full sweet
> Ye were. So come anon to visit me
> With seemly interval and modestly.   (5)

Naples became his favorite home in spite of occasional nos-

talgic memories of Mantua and in spite of a compelling dream
of the Roman empire and its mission, which grew steadily in
his mind as the years advanced. Both the Bay of Naples with
its beach at Sorrento and the dream of empire appear in a
somewhat later poem, and in the *Catalepton*.

> If I should live to embody my soul's dream,
> Goddess of Paphos and Idalia,
> Till with you in becoming song of mine
> Trojan Aeneas triumphs through Roman towns,
> Not with rich incense only or the gift
> Of painted tablet shall your temples glow
> Or garlands gratefully proffered by pure hands,
> But blood of humble ram and haughty bull
> Shall stain your hearth and, with his quiver bright
> Of myriad hues, shall winged Cupid deck
> Your shrine in living marble radiant.
> Come to my aid, oh Cytheria, come:
> Your Caesar calls you—from Olympus come—
> And my plain altar by Sorrento's shore.   (14)

Meanwhile Siro had died and philosophy had yielded to
poetry. Vergil cherished the home of Siro, which may well
have been left to him by the philosopher or, if it was a grant
from Augustus to Siro, it may have gone to Vergil in partial
recompense for his lost farm. Since Vergil was buried at
Naples, it seems likely that he had made it his home for the
rest of his life.

The experimentation which we have noted in the poems
of the *Catalepton* was much more extensive than the items
selected for translation suggest. There were three Priapus
poems in three different meters. One, in the proper elegiacs,
is an inscription for a Priapus statue; one, in iambics, is a
mildly invective threat by the garden god against trespassers;
the third, in Priapean meter, is a more friendly appeal against
intrusion with a warmly appreciative thumbnail sketch of the
simple farm which the god protects. In time to come the
Priapus poem, centering around the scarecrow god, became

a popular conveyer of indecent wit. Vergil seems to have had
no liking for indecency but it is not improbable that the type
had its fountainhead in these mild beginnings. One poem of
the *Catalepton* is an ambiguous play on words on a local incident, another a conventional epigram on Alexander or some
equally ambitious conqueror; one of the shortest is an attempt to follow custom by dealing with unnatural love and the
longest is an encomium on Messalla; Noctuinus is favored
with a second mild invective, an unidentified Octavius is ral-
lied for his careless drinking, and a comparatively long epode,
in the style which Horace made famous, attacks some unknown Lucius.

Here is variety in minor verse, but like Catullus, Vergil
was more ambitious in his experimentation. Apart from the
Catalepton, several longer poems have survived in spite of
Vergil's desire to suppress them. One, which would have been
perhaps the greatest loss had Vergil's editors strictly followed
his wishes, is the realistic picture of a poor dirt farmer starting the day in his cold and dreary cottage in the depressing
dusk of the early morning.

> Now had the night unrolled ten wintry hours,
> The cock had crowed his watchman's canticle
> When Simychus, the meager farmer, turned
> To meet the threatening hunger of the day;
> Grudgingly put one foot on the cold earth
> And then the other, rolled from his squalid cot
> To feel his stumbling way across the dark
> And lifeless shadows to the chilly hearth.
> From off the few warm coals he sweeps the ash,
> Opens his lantern, lights the ragged wick,
> And puffs the embers into languid flame.
> The fire halfhearted takes reluctant life
> While he, guarding his little flame with hand
> That shakes, opens the closet door and from
> The slender pile of corn upon the floor
> Fills up his half-peck measure. Then he turns

To put his lantern on the bracket fixed
Fast in the wall beside his home-made mill.
He frees his arms from out his goat-skin coat,
Brushes the dust thick settled on the mill,
And sets to work: one hand supplies the corn,
The other turns the mill; with weary round,
As on hand spells the other, grinds the stone.
The ground meal issues forth the while he sings
A tuneless ditty to beguile the time.
At last he calls for Scybale, his one
And only helper. African her birth
And every feature speaks her origin:
The kinky hair, broad lips, and dusky hue,
Her wide, expansive bosom, wrinkled breasts
Down-hanging, belly pinched, thin legs, and wide
Prodigious feet that show through ragged shoes.
On her he calls to rouse the dejected fire
And boil the water.   (1–38)

There is too much to quote in full. Simychus makes a flat
loaf of bread from his corn and Scybale buries it in the ashes
to bake. Then the farmer proceeds to concoct the dish which
gives its name to the poem—"Moretum." Happily there is
no exact equivalent in English. From his kitchen garden he
brings in four bulbs of garlic, some parsley, rue, and coriander.
These he dumps into a mortar with some water, salt, and
grated cheese and crushes the mess together with his pestle.

Then as his left hand pulls his ragged cloak
Between his shaggy legs, his right hand wields
The pestle, crushing apace the fragrant garlic,
Mixing it with the rue and cheese and salt
Into a juicy mess. Round goes his hand
And by degrees the various elements
Lose their identity, the colors merge
From many into one.
   (*E pluribus unum* is the phrase for this conglomeration.)
On goes the stirring none the less, but now

With even course and slow the pestle moves
In dreary circles. So to the stiffening mass
He adds some drops of oil, Minerva's gift,
And vinegar in frugal stream, then stirs again,
Drawing the whole together. Finally
Two fingers wipe the edges of the bowl
Forming at last the pudding of his dream.
   Meanwhile from out its ashen sepulcher
Scybale, ever busy, draws the bread.
It joins the finished pasty. Simychus,
The fear of hunger banished for the day,
Pulls on his boots, dons cap, then trudging forth
Yokes up the patient oxen and at last
Deep in the earth plunges his wooden plow.   (100–24)

Something new sounds in these simple lines. Here is stark realism with no touch of academic learning, no patronizing condescension. Here is understanding and appreciation of the simplest possible independent human lot; no maudlin sentimentalizing, no complaint, no touch of moralizing or satire. It is grim, but it is realism at its best. Vergil, who knew farming from the easier angle, was poet enough and had sufficient greatness of heart to understand and feel with the poor peasant who was farmer perforce. At the same time, his heart responded just as spontaneously to another character of the Roman scene, leagues removed from the dirt farmer: a Syrian tavern hostess crying her wares by the side of the highway.

> The sparkling hostess stands before
>   Her tavern black with soot,
> She beats her merry castanets
>   And shakes a wicked foot.
>
> "Why wait without the door," she cries,
>   "Aweary with the dust?
> Come one, come all, where bowers wait
>   And tankards cool with must.

There's music too, the dancing pipes,
    Old wine and cheeses new,
Bacchus and Cupid, roses red,
    And flowers of every hue.

Come in, old priest, thy weary ass
    Is sweating with the heat
Our Vesta loves an honest ass
    Come, spare his aching feet.

The thickets sing with katydids,
    The lizards seek the shade:
Come, lay thee down and take thy rest:
    For what were goblets made?

Beneath yon overhanging vine
    Weave chaplets for thy hair:
The wine is bubbling in the cup,
    The maid that brings it fair.

Away with him that frowns on joy
    And prates of virtue dour:
Death plucks his ear and whispers low:
    'I follow, seize the hour.' "   ("Copa")

This is a foreshortened adaptation but gives, I believe, the feeling of the poem better than any attempt at more literal rendering. The scene is realistic and the emotions human. At the same time there is something more of poetic coloring than in "Moretum." This is possibly due merely to the lighter atmosphere and merrier tone. Certainly there is no academic pedantry.

When, however, Vergil turned to the epyllion, as he did in two of his youthful pieces, he, like Catullus and their Alexandrian forebears, applied all the erudition of which he was master. The first of these that I shall consider is probably a goodnatured parody of the learned type. It is by no means a casual production like the Sabinus skit but is carefully and even elaborately constructed and contains many notable lines,

[76]

some of which, suggested by Lucretius, Vergil thought good enough to rework in his *Georgics*. The poem is called "Culex" and is the tale of a gnat or mosquito which saved a farmer from the attack of a great snake and was rewarded by a fatal slap. From the lower world he comes back to disturb the sleep of his slayer with a long account of that realm and a complaint of his misfortune. On waking, the repentant farmer builds a fine funeral monument for the mosquito and writes for it a worthy epitaph. The workmanship is painstaking and the poet prefixes to the story a short prologue to forestall exactly what has too often happened, the acceptance of the poem by incautious readers as a serious epyllion.

> I have been trifling (with Thalia's help),
> Octavius, and spiderlike have spun
> A tenuous web. For from my trifling's born
> This ballad of the Gnat, so that the world
> May know, in lighter vein yet fittingly,
> His history. Art, take thy leave, and thou,
> Envy, depart. Whoever carps at fun
> Or scorns my muse, his name and fame shall be
> Considered lighter even than a gnat's.
> Anon my Muse shall speak in weightier tones
> When time shall yield the fruit of confidence
> To polish verses worthy of thy taste.   (1–10)

With this warning Vergil launches into an invocation to Apollo which involves the muses and Pales and much geography and mythology in the best Alexandrian manner. This is followed by a dedication to a young Octavius, listing many conventional subjects which are spurned for "gentler songs that run on slender feet." The transition to the subject matter of the poem is abrupt—"but I must proceed to my undertaking"—and suggestive of the orator with whom this phrase or its like was almost a commonplace. It also serves to keep the speaker in view. The poet has occupied with personal address 41 lines of a poem of 410 lines. (This becomes 100 out of 541 in the second and more serious epyllion.) The new poets, with their interest in their own emotions, might be expected perhaps to play the showman in presenting their more pretentious offerings. But Catullus did not set such an example. His "Peleus and Thetis" opened with a story—"Once on a time"—and not with a speech by the master of ceremonies. The opening of "Culex" recalls the prologue which Lucretius prefixes to his didactic poem, *De rerum natura*, with both invocation and dedication. It comes as no great surprise therefore when in line 34 Vergil recasts the ringing line of Lucretius, "When Carthage to the conflict hurled her might." The echoes of Lucretius are numerous throughout the poem, those of Catullus very few indeed. It would seem probable that "Culex" was written soon after Vergil had begun to study philosophy and that his real fascination with Epicureanism was for the poetry of its great Roman protagonist. At any rate the prologue, for better or worse, had come to stay. It was to be an unhappy part of the imperial epic, though Vergil himself discarded it. His first published work was a collection of pastorals which, largely dramatic in character, gave little chance for the author to intrude. The book opened directly with the remark of one countryman to another: "Thou Tityrus, beneath the spreading beech, / Piping on slender reed thy sylvan muse." The *Georgics*, Vergil's second publication, was written by request and quite naturally has a dedication to Maecenas and Augustus, and has an invocation also. A new element appears at the end of the last book, a sort of signature.

> So did I sing of how to till the earth,
> Care for the herds, the woods, while Caesar led
> His thundering chargers past Euphrates' stream,
> Gave laws to peoples, paved his way to Heaven.
> This Vergil then by fair Parthenope
> Dwelt in ignoble peace the while he piped
> The shepherds' songs and, flushed with fearless youth,
> Sang "Tityrus beneath the spreading beech."   (IV.559–66)

Years later when he left the *Aeneid* unfinished, he had written as the opening lines the following:

> I am the poet who once on slender reed
> Piped my new song, then from the woods emerged
> To make the earth produce at man's desire,
> A boon to farmers; now of dreadful Mars,
> Arms and the man I sing who came from Troy.

It may have been his editors; more probably it was Vergil himself who decided to delete the personal record and begin with "Arms and the man . . ."

The personal tone of the prologue to "Culex" is quite out of line with the spirit of "Peleus and Thetis," which plunged directly into the subject in the first line. The same was probably true of Catullus' Greek models although we have no direct evidence to prove this. The Greek classical epic had only a short appeal to the Muse to give the poet her assistance. The discursive prologue with a dedication appears to be a Roman addition. The didactic poem may have been the source. Lucretius prefixed a prologue to *De rerum natura* containing an appeal to Venus, a dedication to Memmius, and a discussion of his subject matter. But literary terms are particularly striking in the opening lines of "Culex." *Gracilis* and *tenuis* are opposed to *gravis,* a light tone as against a dignified, serious one. *Lusimus* (we have played), *per ludum* (in sport), *iocos* (trifles), *poliantur carmina* (let our songs be polished)—the whole smacks of a literary attempt to win and hold attention. The rules of the rhetor's school are behind this effort and the same is true of the forswearing of hackneyed subjects which follows after the florid invocation. The orator was taught to show that his case was either new or extraordinarily important and interesting in order to hold the attention of the court. The poet had the same education, which would seem to have been effective. In addition, the poet had the precedent of the prologue in comedy, which the Romans had stretched to include self-defense and attack on the level of literary criticism. It is difficult to absolve Vergil from some share of responsibility for the monotonous line of personal prologues which follow from the author of "Aetna" down at least to Statius, even though Vergil himself showed some restraint in the *Georgics* and much more in the *Aeneid*. His two youthful epyllia carry the personal prologue to an extreme, perhaps justified in "Culex" if we accept it as a parody.

The first section of narrative consists of sixteen lines and takes the old herdsman with his goats, shortly after dawn, out to the higher meadows and distributes the animals picturesquely over the landscape. Thereupon 40 lines eulogize the blessings of the country life, its contrast with civilized luxury, its simplicity, repose, and freedom from care—an unrealistic and poetic picture. It carries us unconsciously to noontime, and again the narrative is resumed and the herdsman collects the goats around the stream which is shaded and cool and provides an excuse for further poetic extravagance—the gods and sprites that once frequented the grove with their songs and dances, the various trees which compose the grove, each with its mythological connotation. There are 11 lines of narrative, 44 of decoration. Now comes the climax of the tale. The herdsman lies down and falls asleep, when Fortune brings to threaten him a horrid snake, actually a mighty serpent of the poetic imagination. A benevolent gnat sees the serpent, recognizes the danger, and wakens the farmer by stinging him between the eyes. In a natural human reaction, the old man slaps the gnat and kills it, then sees the snake and dispatches it with a club. All this has occupied 45 lines. We are kept informed of the time schedule by the arrival of night, attended by Vesper; the flock is driven home, and the farmer goes to bed and to sleep. This requires but five lines. No sooner has he begun to sleep than the spirit of the gnat appears to him and reproaches him for his ingratitude, describing his dreadful state in the lower world. For this he requires no less than 174 lines. He covers not only the familiar tortures of the lower world, including Tityus and Tantalus, Sisyphus and the Danaids, but proceeds to Elysium to report on the heroines, from Alcestis to Eurydice, and heroes, from Hector to Scipio.

His story told, he vanishes. The old farmer, grief-stricken, gets up and prepares a funeral mound circled by marble slabs. A long list is given of the flowers that shall grow to adorn the mound, and then the old man carves the gnat's epitaph:

> Small Gnat, to thee the guardian of the flock
> For gift of life brings tribute due to death.   (413–14)

The poem as a poem scarcely deserves the space we have given it, but it has significance in Vergil's development as a poet. The structure is noteworthy. The main narrative forms a framework about a central picture which occupies nearly half of the whole work. This central core is not a concrete picture like the tapestry of Catullus, but it has the same character of separateness by virtue of being a dream description. Vergil's study of earlier poetry, from Homer and Hesiod to Catullus and Lucretius, is obvious throughout, as are the traits of the new poetry that we have noted—variety, realism compounded with poetic imagination, learned allusion, and meticulous attention to form. The idealization of the country, the sympathetic understanding of the old farmer's simple character, the embryonic interest in the heroes of Roman history —all this and much more is suggestive of the Vergil of the major works.

The second epyllion, which was probably written first, "Ciris," need not be considered at length. If "Culex" reflected Vergil's study of Lucretius, "Ciris" indicates a close attention to the poems of Catullus. The opening words, *Etsi me vario iactatum laudis amore* (Though beset by yearnings for praise), could hardly fail to recall the earlier poet's *Etsi me adsiduo confectum cura dolore* (Though beset by constant sorrow), and the Catullan echoes throughout are constant. The prologue occupies a hundred lines and has personal apology, definition of subject, dedication to Messalla, and invocation of the muses. The story is the tragedy of Scylla, daughter of Nisus, King of Megara, which was under attack by Cretan Minos. Nisus had one red lock in his shock of white hair and Fate had decreed that Megara should be secure as long as he retained this lock. Scylla, looking out from the walls of the beleaguered city, saw and fell in love with Minos and to win him determined to cut the fatal lock. She is discovered in her first attempt by her old nurse Carme and the opportunity is thus offered the poet to introduce the story of Carme and her daughter Britomartis and their misfortunes at the hand of Minos. When she fails to dissuade Scylla, Carme proceeds to help her. They fail in their attempt to persuade Nisus to make peace with Minos and a second assault on the lock succeeds. In four lines we learn of the cutting of the lock, the fall of Megara, and the punishment of Scylla, whom Minos spurns and drags through the sea, roped to the stern of his ship. Sixty-eight lines are given to the description of the surprise of all the sea gods at the horrid sight and to the lament of Scylla. The conclusion of the poem is unexpectedly drawn-out —an account of the course toward Crete with a catalogue of islands passed, the final sympathy of Amphitrite, who turns Scylla into the bird Ciris and sets her free, the details of the metamorphosis, and the reaction of Zeus, who turns Nisus into a sea hawk that forever pursues the fleeing Ciris.

This is by no means a great poem. The self-conscious erudition is burdensome, the compression of the action and the expansion of description and allusive suggestion make for hard reading, and no great sympathy is aroused by any of the characters. The inset story is too vague and unimpressive, and the lament is not comparable with Ariadne's either in its own compelling force or in its setting. But we have in the Ciris another bit of experimentation on the part of a "new" poet. True to the tenets of the clan, Vergil chose an unfamiliar theme—perhaps too much so in this case—a heroine in a tragic situation, and told her story with a minimum of narrative and a maximum of description and protestation. If he had died at thirty, we should have had a small volume of "new poetry" with all the variety of Catullus' book, lacking, to be sure, its fire of love and hate as well as the artistic perfection of "Peleus and Thetis" and "Attis," but with some promising indication of a maturity mellower than one would have expected from Catullus. Vergil's early ambition, whch he outgrew, was to win such praise as Callimachus won with a new poetry that was not for the popular consumption of the mob but for the cultivated appreciation of the elite.

> Mine are the songs that I have sung with you,
> Taught by Apollo and the Muses nine,
> By Bacchus and Aglaia. Should my song
> Though humble rise to match Cyrene's bard,
> Echoing in native strain the Grecian wit,
> Then would I soar beyond my farthest hope.
> That were enough—I scorn the multitude.
>
> (*Catalepton* 9.59–64)

The miscellaneous poems which we have been considering would seem to have been written for the most part when Vergil was still a young man, but one or two of later date were included by the editors. About 37 B.C. Vergil himself published a collection of pastoral poems. Early editors gave them the name *Eclogues,* or selected poems; what Vergil called them we do not know. The unity of the group lies in the convention, sustained throughout, of a countryside setting with shepherds and goatherds speaking and singing, a type which, if not invented by Theocritus, at least was best represented in Greek poetry by him. It represents one of the extremes of Alexandrian artificiality. The country which Vergil presents is itself a never-never land, and nature is remodeled to fit it. There are reminiscences of the district around Mantua, where the poet spent his boyhood, but completely commingled with these are echoes of Theocritus' Sicily and imaginary pictures of an idealized Arcadia, conceived as the happy home of singing shepherds, more skilled in conventional poetry than in the care of animals. In their ideal setting, the shepherds sing of their loves or compete for a rustic prize with alternate songs. Realistic details appear only for artistic contrast and to give some sanction to the rustic convention. Vergil, in spite of attempts to prove otherwise, was no dirt farmer. His father, like Horace's, gave him the best education available, and he was only eighteen when he went to Rome to study rhetoric and then on to Naples for his pursuit of philosophy under Siro. This question of Vergil's farming experience and knowledge has been greatly complicated by the stories in the ancient lives concerning the confiscation of his farm and his part in it, as touched on in two of the eclogues. The triumvirs were seizing land in Cisalpine Gaul in 41 B.C. and the family farm was in the district unfortunately affected. Tradition has it that Vergil's friendship with Varus or Asinius Pollio, both of them governors of the province, helped to save his property and that he went to Rome and, introduced to Octavian by Gallus, obtained the restitution of the farm. But Vergil had first gone to Rome eleven years before, and there is no sound evidence that he ever settled down again in the north. The details of the ancient lives are largely drawn from the *Eclogues* to make more vivid the story of the confiscation. This brings us squarely to the consideration of the evidence of the poems. One of the conventional practices which Vergil inherited from the Greek pastoral was that of introducing real characters, including the poet himself, in the guise of shepherds. When this is done, a new element of unreality and confusion enters into the poem, already highly artificial with its conventional setting and unrealistic shepherds. (This masquerading of real characters as shepherds became a major characteristic of English pastoral.) We can hardly question, therefore, the accepted interpretation of the first and ninth eclogues as representing Vergil himself and some friend discussing the tragic land seizures of 41. The danger of misinterpretation lies in a possible failure to accept wholeheartedly the convention which utterly confuses the shepherds and their ways with the masquerading characters and theirs. Everything is fanciful and allusive. The tone and manner are vividly exemplified in the first eclogue: the scholar poet from the school of Siro is represented as the shepherd Tityrus, piping under a beech tree, telling how he gaped in awe at seeing Rome (where he went to gain his freedom), then retiring to his humble cot with its supply of apples, chestnuts, and cheese. If we try to save the situation by making Tityrus one of Vergil's slaves, the literal interpretation is just as difficult. The fact is that Vergil, already at home with the distinguished group closely associated with the future emperor, is drawing, with the conventional machinery of the pastoral poem, a fanciful picture of a possible situation.

It serves to express by allusion his gratitude to the powers of state for, probably, providing restitution of his property, and possibly some compensating assignment. Such a thrice confused source is not safe evidence for drawing the conclusion from the ninth eclogue that a second ejection took place and this time with an undignified and painful scene of personal violence. What was important to the poet was less his own loss or threatened loss than the pity of a situation in which the real peasant suffered real disaster. If he treats this somewhat lightly in an almost fantastic setting, that is because he chose a somewhat fantastic medium. It is hard to associate tragedy with a Dresden china shepherdess, but it is not impossible, and such success as Vergil has in suggesting the realities of life beneath the furbelows is all the more striking.

In spite of the fact that this first published collection of Vergil's work contains only poems of one general category, the pastoral, it also contains the same desire for variety and the same fear of monotony that are strongly evident in all the new poets. The first eclogue, as we have seen, deals with a personal experience, but it opens with two lines which immediately certify the medium to be used: "Thou Tityrus beneath the spreading beech / On slender reed dost pipe thy sylvan muse." A title like *Pastoral Poems* would not have been any clearer. The tenth, and last, poem is again personal but otherwise wholly different. The first line marks it as the final poem of the collection but also removes it slightly from the category of the first by the direct personal address of the poet: "This last strain, Arethusa, grant me now; / To Gallus I must sing." The whole poem is a tribute to his friend, but Gallus too was a poet and probably wrote pastorals, and the convention of the pastoral is lightly maintained throughout. The final line vouches for the type and suitably closes the collection: "Off, home, my well-fed goats, for Hesperus comes."

Between these introductory and closing lines variety is perhaps the most noticeable characteristic of the collection. The poems alternate throughout between a dramatic construction, with direct conversation free of external manipulation, and a type in which the poet speaks directly to the reader in explanatory address. Within the two groups, each poem is also unique in form, with the exception of the two personal reminiscences which we have discussed—the first and ninth. In form the two are much alike: two shepherds discuss the sad situation; but in the ninth a little of the pastoral competitive singing furnishes a touch of variety. Of the remaining dramatic eclogues, one has a contest with two shepherds and a judge. They sing a succession of short stanzas, and there is no decision. The second is a competition with no judge, in which each competitor has a single long song. The third is told by a shepherd outside the contest, the competitive pieces are short, and there is a judge and a decision.

In the same way the nondramatic pieces show variety of form as well as subject. Eclogue 2 is Corydon's song for Alexis told with a five-line introduction without use of first person. Number four is the poet's tribute to Pollio consisting of the prophecy of a child to come who will bring Rome back to the days of gold. There are three lines of introduction in the first person plural. The sixth eclogue has a twelve-line introduction in the first person singular, dedicating to Varus the story of the captured Silenus and his song. In eight there is an elaborate sixteen-line introduction, dedicating to Pollio two stanzaic songs with refrains by two shepherds, the songs separated by two lines of explanation. Finally the tenth has an eight-line introduction in the first person leading to a direct tribute to Gallus.

The obvious effort to arrange the collection with symmetry and variety is Callimachean if not generally Alexandrian. Without forcing the argument we can go a step further to note the tendency toward artistic form in the individual poems. The

third is quite simple. There are 59 lines of conversation between two shepherds, leading up to a friendly contest in which
they sing matched couplets alternately for 48 lines while a
third shepherd acts as judge. At the end, the judge, in four
concluding lines, refuses to give verdict. The notion of a
framework is clear enough but the interest in the setting is such
that the framework somewhat overbalances the central core of
the shepherd songs. This is to a certain extent compensated
by the brevity of the concluding half of the framework. The
fifth eclogue, without a third character, is rather more elaborate. After 19 lines of introductory conversation between two
shepherds, the body of the poem consists of two songs to
Daphnis, one by each shepherd, of 24 and 25 lines. These are
divided by eleven lines of conversation and followed by ten
more that form the concluding framework to the poem as a
whole. The close but inexact correspondences are noteworthy,
and even more the contrast between the two songs: one, the
mourning of all nature for the death of Daphnis, the other, the
gladness of all men and gods at Daphnis' reception in heaven,
the honors which will be joyfully paid him. Eclogue 7 presents
a third type of framework construction. One shepherd recounts the situation directly with just a bit of quoted conversation. This takes twenty lines as against the two lines with
which the same shepherd concludes the poem to complete the
framework. Within this frame he quotes six pairs of four-
line stanzas sung alternately by two other shepherds. The
eighth eclogue consists of two songs introduced directly by
the poet, stating his subject, dedicating the eclogue to an unnamed friend, and briefly giving the setting. The songs are
elaborate, in stanzaic form with refrain, the first shepherd
mourning his unhappy love for a fickle shepherdess, the second winning back his favorite boy with rustic sorcery. The
poem ends abruptly with the return of the boy, Daphnis, with
no resumption of the framework. In the two personal eclogues,
1 and 9, there is practically no formal framework. Tityrus,
piping under the beech tree and finally inviting Meliboeus into
his cottage for the night, furnishes a beginning and an end.

So, in the ninth, the opening gambit of the conversation—"Where to, Moeris?"—is taken up in the last—"Let's be on with our business."

In the four remaining eclogues, those which do not present any singing contest or responsive songs, there is always discernible, in spite of the light touch of the pastoral poem, something of the formal structure. Each is in essence a single song introduced in a few lines by the poet. Eclogue 2 is the song of Corydon for his faithless favorite, Alexis. He begins by picturing his mad love driving him in search of the boy and ends by chiding himself and reminding himself that he can find another love. Within this slight frame is another. In the first half he boasts of his country wealth and handsome appearance as a lure to Alexis. In the latter half he calls himself a fool for this pride—a richer rival has outbid him. At the heart of the poem are the offerings which he would have Alexis consider—his own of song and simple gifts, then nature's of abundant flowers and fruits. The sixth poem, dedicated to Varus in lieu of a formal eulogy, is the story of two shepherd boys who find Silenus asleep, bind him, and win from him a song. The setting is long and the final half of the framework correspondingly short—merely the last line, indicating the coming of night. The song itself begins with the story of creation and ends with the story of Gallus recognized as poet by the spirit of Linus. Between these two sections come stories of mythology amongst which Pasiphae occupies 16 lines with a mere mention of Prometheus and Hylas preceding and of Atalanta and the sisters of Phaethon following. Eclogue 10 is introduced as a tribute to Gallus and his love for Lycoris. Surely the commentators are right and Vergil is really doing homage to the elegies of his friend in which Lycoris is the heroine. This is the only one of these poems in which the poet appears at the end to complete the external framework, and in the last lines of the pastoral collection he completes the confusion of reality and convention; they carry out the similar confusion in the opening lines. For in both groups, Vergil the poet speaks in his own person, but in the first speaks of singing to Gallus while the goats graze and in the last bids the goats, now thoroughly fed, be off for home as Hesperus rises to end the day. The song of Gallus is introduced, as was the song of Silenus, at some length. His central song is the apotheosis of Love—*omnia vincit amor.*

There remains the fourth eclogue, which is unique in every way. Its three introductory lines recognize this fact and are the only touch of pastoral in the poem,

> Sicilian Muses, sing we of higher themes.
> The country's not for all. If woods we sing,
> Let them be worthy of a consul's ear. (IV.1–3)

The higher theme is the coming birth of a child who will usher in the final period of Cumaean prophecy, bringing to Rome a second golden age—unto us a child is born. Interpretation has run wild in its attempt to explain the allusions. Vergil was simply rewriting Isaiah; the child is the Jewish Messiah or the Christian Savior; he (or she) is Asinius Gallus or the notorious Julia. The framework consists of an opening description of the first golden age and a closing appeal to the child to bring on the new age of gold. The heart of the poem recounts the beneficence with which nature will bless his childhood, his youth, and his manhood.

The eclogues were welcomed by the literary world of Rome as the triumphant establishment of a new type in Latin literature. Slight and artificial as they seem to us, their delicacy and even their sentimentality was a significant contribution. The new poetry had made romantic love a reputable subject for verse and it had also recognized the appeal of nature. For the first time these are combined as leading themes worthy of independent development. The confusion of art and nature, of imagination and realism, of rustic innocence and urban sophistication, is wholly contrary to the traditional spirit of early Roman poetry, but it was completely within the spirit of the new. Into this confusion Vergil injected enough of the personal appeal to his friends and patrons, enough of his own feeling for his native land and treated the whole flight of fancy with enough technical mastery to win the approval even of the opponents of the new poetry.

It is traditionally stated that Vergil, with the *Eclogues* finished and published, was requested by Maecenas to write the *Georgics;* in fact he himself in the third book speaks of the "orders of Maecenas." Undoubtedly the government was inclined to encourage agriculture, and a poem which idealized and eulogized the life of the farmer was welcome support. But Vergil was not the man to write on an uncongenial subject under orders. His interest in the country and the people of the country was certainly not that of a practical dirt farmer, but this does not mean that it was not deep and sincere. His boyhood in Mantua was never far from his mind, and its memories mingled with the literary landscapes of Arcadia and Sicily in the *Eclogues.* Even so in the *Georgics,* they merge unconsciously with the matter of the many books Vergil had read about farming. But there was a more effective motive for the new composition. The one great field of Alexandrian poetry which Vergil had not as yet essayed was the didactic: his poetic ambition was more important than the call of the farm. The latter (plus official pressure) merely determined the field of the effort. The result is no farmer's manual: it is a literary tour de force, a work of art, created from material, both realistic and literary, dealing with certain phases of the farmer's life. Didactic poetry was first written in Greek before the development of prose composition. Whether in the field of philosophy, agriculture, or astronomy the serious didactic essay in verse gave way without a struggle to the more practical prose treatise. Only the academic literary clique maintained the poetic version, which thus became an artificial exhibition rather than a practical guide. It is therefore not untrue but misleading to say that Vergil modeled his *Georgics* on Hesiod, the first didactic poet of Greece, who in his *Works and Days* expounded the contemporary doctrine of the farmer. Like his other works in the field of the new poetry, the *Georgics* have a touch of reality in that they deal with the plain people of the country and the drudgery of their daily lives. But this

[90]

realism, such as it is, assumes a minor role in comparison with the artistic selection and arrangement, the imaginative and highly poetic modes of expression, and the constant departure from the matter in hand to embrace ideas and digressions dear to the poet but utterly foreign to the farmer.

It will be worthwhile to quote at length the prologue to the *Georgics,* for in turning to the longer and more serious type of poetry, Vergil follows not so much a Greek model as that of a Roman predecessor. To the educated Roman, trained always as a public speaker, no matter what pursuits he might be destined to follow, the rules of rhetoric required a preliminary appeasement of the audience. The textbooks gave elaborate instruction as to how to win the listener's attention and sympathetic interest, and such an effort was almost instinctive for a Roman writer. But, more than this, Vergil looked directly to Lucretius as his congenial master in the didactic field. Here was a poet boldly preempting a new territory in Latin poetry, teaching the philosophy that would free suffering humanity from the fear of death and doing so in the most impressive and imaginative poetry that Rome had yet known. Vergil not only pays specific tribute to Lucretius in the *Georgics* but echoes, throughout the work, cadences and turns of expression that are clearly Lucretian.

With all the similarity, however, the differences between the *De rerum natura* and the *Georgics* are more important still. Lucretius was both teacher and poet, and the two characters appear clearly in his work but are rarely merged. In the *Georgics,* poet and teacher are inextricable, with the poet the stronger, and both are at the service of the state. Lucretius strove to deliver the individual from the fear of death. Vergil was, personally, just as sympathetic with the individual man, but the object of the *Georgics* was to further the well-being and the glory of the new Italian empire that should be the culmination of the old Rome. The prologue has therefore no tone of contentious argument. Otherwise it has much in common with that of its predecessor.

What makes rich harvests, under what star to plow,
Or when, Maecenas, vines are wed to elms,
The care of cattle, how to foster flocks,
The wisdom that preserves the thrifty bees:
From these my song. You, then, oh glorious orbs
That rule from heaven the gently gliding year,
And Liber too and Ceres, giver of life,
If by your benefice our earth renounced
Chaonian acorns for the richer grain
And mixed the Aetolian streams with newfound grapes,
Ye Fauns, the farmer's ever present gods,
(Come hither, Fauns, and all ye Dryad maids)
Your gifts I sing. And thou, oh Neptune, come,
That with the trident's blow gave earth the horse,
And thou, preserver of Cean groves, for whom
Three hundred cattle, snowy white, crop clean
The thickets; leave, oh Pan, thy native woods,
Lycean glades, thou guardian of the sheep:
If aught to thee is thy Maenalian song,
Tegean, come to my aid; Minerva too
That gave mankind the olive and that boy
Who fashioned first the plow; Silvanus, come,
The cypress in thy hand; come all ye gods
And goddesses who gladly guard the fields,
Ye who produce new harvests without seed
And ye who send abundant rain from heaven.   (I.1–23)

The clarity and directness of the first four lines and a half,
which state the subject of the poem, are lost in what follows.
The farmer who was lured by them to read on would perhaps
recognize the sun and moon as the glorious orbs of heaven,
and Liber and Ceres might be reasonably familiar to him.
Their functions however, confused by the allusions to Chaonian
acorns and Aetolian streams, would surely elude him, and he
would not be enlightened by the trident blow, the Cean groves
(even if he had heard of Aristaeus), the Lycean glades, the
Maenalian song, or even the cypress symbol of Silvanus. This

appeal is not to the farmer but to the new school of poets, as is
the extravagant flattery of Augustus which follows.

> Come thou too, Caesar, who in years to be
> Shalt join the council of the gods above
> Whether to rule our cities, governing
> The lands while earth accepts thee as the lord
> Of harvests and of seasons, on thy brow
> Thy mother's myrtle, or, as ocean's god,
> To accept the sailors' eager homage paid
> Even by farthest Thule (by the gift
> Of all her waters Tethys shall call thee son),
> Or wilt thou, in the revolving zodiac,
> Be a new star where, 'twixt Erigone
> And following Chelas, opens a welcoming space
> Where Scorpion draws his claws to give thee room.
> Whate'er thou'lt be—for surely Tartarus
> May never hope to have thee as its king,
> Nor would such lust of empire still be thine,
> However Greece may praise the Elysian Fields
> Whence no appeal can win Proserpine—
> Grant me an easy course, smile on my bold
> Emprise: in pity for the farmer folk
> Ignorant of the way, attend me now,
> Learning while still on earth to hear our prayers.
>
> (I.24–42)

The artificiality of this conceit of leaving to Augustus the
choice of his function in heaven when his career on earth is
over, is made very clear by Lucan's exaggerated version when
he bids Nero choose the center of heaven, since, otherwise,
the whole universe will be thrown completely out of balance.

The prologue, then, informs us directly that Vergil's poem
is to be a didactic poem dealing with tillage, training of vines,
care of cattle and sheep, and bee culture. As a matter of fact
these are in general the subjects of the four books. It tells us
indirectly that the book will not be a practical manual but a
product appropriate to an Alexandrian poet. And such it ac-

tually is, but the emphasis must be put on "poet" rather than on "Alexandrian." For Vergil learned much from many sources about the affairs of the farm and, carefully selecting those activities which would appeal to the general curiosity of educated men, he treated them not too professionally but with the touch of a wise amateur. He presented even the most prosaic drudgery with his finest poetic expression and kept the whole from being monotonous by constant digressions, both interesting and charming. The whole poem ends with a 250-line digression telling the story of Aristaeus and his bees, constituting almost an eighth of the entire work.

This story of Aristaeus requires consideration. There is a traditional explanation which seems to be largely apocryphal that this is a substitution, that when his poem was finished it ended with a tribute to Gallus, but that, Gallus having died in disgrace while the poem was being written, the tribute was removed at the suggestion of the emperor and that Vergil substituted the Aristaeus myth. The tribute to Gallus, even if it had been appropirate, could have been but a fraction in length of the Aristaeus story, and, as all four books are of approximately the same length, much more material must have been subtracted with it. Considering Vergil's careful methods of construction and the presence of Aristaeus in the preface to the poem, this last-minute major change seems most improbable. Furthermore, the Aristaeus myth is germane to the subject, and even the insertion in it of the tale of Orpheus and Eurydice is not without its meaning for a poet who has made the power of song triumph over the mundane subject of agriculture.

This digression has a further interest of its own. We have seen Vergil in his younger days experimenting in "Culex" and "Ciris" with the Alexandrian epyllion and, in these as in the *Eclogues,* have noted his preoccupation with artistic forms. Now the Aristaeus tale is a short but perfect epyllion. It plunges directly into the narrative, like Catullus' "Peleus and Thetis."

The shepherd Aristaeus abandoning
Peneian Tempe where, the story goes,
His bees had died of hunger and disease,
Stopped, sorrowing, by a river's sacred source
And prayed his mother thus with loud complaint:
Mother, Cyrene, mother that now dost dwell
Beneath these waters, why by divine descent,
If as thou sayest Apollo be my sire,
Didst thou then bear me to be damned of fate?
Where is thy love for me? Why didst thou hold
Before my eyes hope of immortal life?

(Georgics IV.317–25)

The goddess hears her son's plaints as she sits with her attendant nymphs in a grotto beneath the water. The scene is pictured at some length and the Greek names are introduced with great relish. Clymene sings to them as they all sit spinning. When Aristaeus' lament reaches their ears, Arethusa rises and looks out from the surface and reports the facts. She is dispatched to bring Aristaeus, who is instructed how to find Proteus, who, if captured and bound, will tell him how to recover his bees. Aristaeus surprises Proteus asleep and binds him fast. Proteus gives him his answer but not directly—only by recounting how Eurydice died by a serpent's bite as she fled to escape the sight of unwitting Aristaeus. He tells the whole tale of Orpheus and Eurydice and then escapes. But Cyrene shows Aristaeus what he is to do to appease Eurydice and regain his bees, and the story ends with the successful carrying out of her directions.

The framework story is not concerned with a romantic affair, but it should be remembered that the same was true of Callimachus' "Hekale." The general tone and manner of narrative is thoroughly characteristic of the epyllion, with much use of the visual image, considerable description, and extensive employment of decorative names.

While the Aristaeus story is the longest digression and the most elaborately constructed, each of the four books contains two major digressions and the amount of space taken from the main subject increases with each book. Each of them is at least loosely connected with the topic under discussion at the time and seems to grow naturally out of it. For example, the difficulty of plowing and the attendant hardship leads naturally in Book I to the somewhat philosophical discussion of the theory that God has made everything that once was easy difficult of accomplishment in order to develop man's ingenuity. Out of the discourse on stars and seasons rises the account of omens at the death of Caesar and a prayer for Augustus' preservation. The second book has digressions on the glories of Italy and the joys of country life, the third on shepherd life in other countries and on the great pestilence. In the last book there are a digression on gardens with reminiscences of an old gardener in southern Italy and the final story of Aristaeus.

The variety attained by these digressions is part of the poet's purpose, evident in the plan of the poem as a whole, which is clearly Alexandrian in its elaborate construction. The first two books form a unit, as do the last two. Each unit has a long prologue (42 and 48 lines) with invocation and dedication, the first invocation introducing the whole as well as its part. Books II and IV end with a brief framework (two and eight lines), the latter including a conclusion for the whole poem with the identification of the poet as the writer of the *Eclogues*. These two books have short introductions only (eight and 17 lines), largely to state the subject, the second seeking also to renew the reader's interest if it be waning. The whole forms a unit with two clearly marked panels, the first panel deals with the earth and its products, the second with animals and bees. The didactic manual has become a work of conscious literary art and Vergil has tried his hand at the construction of a longer poem on a single subject with various devices of form and content to save it from monotony.

By 27 B.C., when the *Georgics* were finished and published, Vergil had experimented with nearly all of the poetic vehicles which the Hellenistic poets and their Roman successors had produced. He had applied his art to their realism and their romanticism, their simple directness and their extreme artificiality. All the while, in spite of their general abhorrence of the long poem, he seems to have kept in mind his desire to write the great epic poem of Rome. That Augustus had, as we know, keenly desired to have one of the poets of the day write up his own achievements, was both incentive and discouragement for Vergil in carrying out his long-standing ambition. Augustus' accomplishments, much as he admired them, did not furnish the material and scope for the poem as he conceived it. At the same time, the glory of Rome visualized by his imagination did culminate in the reign of order and peace that his sovereign had established. His solution of the problem lay in a dramatic epic of the origin of Rome within which was foreshadowed the greatness to be. This conception precluded the *Aeneid* from being a chronicle or an epic of adventure. That is why it is the wrong critical approach to compare it with the wholly different products of Homer, Apollonius, Naevius, and Ennius. The extreme in this line of criticism is the old characterization of the first six books as Vergil's *Odyssey,* the last six as his *Iliad.* This idea has long since been abandoned, but there still lingers the tendency to show how the *Aeneid* diverges from the Homeric plan instead of accepting the fact that it is a wholly different kind of poem. Vergil knew thoroughly his Homer and all the other epic poets, as he did the writers of tragedy and Lucretius and Catullus. And he borrowed from each what fitted his special purpose, remolding each borrowed device to make it his own. But the great pattern of the whole, the conception of his epic poem, was modeled on no other. We shall see presently that the construction of Catullus' "Peleus and Thetis" had a strong influence on the architecture of the *Aeneid.* I shall admit freely that incidents in Homer and Apollonius inspired similar incidents in Vergil's epic and that happy phrases from all his forerunners were freely appropriated without concealment—a tribute to them by an ardent and grateful pupil.

It may be helpful to consider one major incident of the *Aeneid* before looking at the structure as a whole: the story of Dido. It might be more accurate to speak of the tragedy of Dido, for she is a tragic character not only in the manner of her death but throughout her story. Furthermore the treatment of the story is to a great degree dramatic.

To begin with, there is no parallel to Dido in Homer. Nausicaa makes a pleasant impression on weary Ulysses but nothing comes of it. Circe and Calypso are colorful digressions in his adventurous wandering. The faithful wife that waits at Ithaca is little more than a static device to give a sort of unity to the chronicle of adventure. But Dido dominates a third of the *Aeneid,* is a fully drawn character, definitely not passive, and plays a major role in the main story of the epic.

To take this last point first: the Aeneas who occupies Italy and founds Rome is a different Aeneas from the man who left Troy with his family and his gods. Even by his own account his actions on the night of Troy's disaster were not strikingly heroic or brilliant. One quality he had—*pietas*—and that stubborn loyalty to his own people and his country's gods plus the guidance of his father Anchises carried him through the crisis. Anchises was the real leader throughout the voyage to Sicily. Aeneas had to be trained by hard experience. He learned while still in Troy the futility of standing heroically on the burning deck; he learned to forgo revenge for the sake of gaining a higher end. And on the voyage, through one experience after another, he grew in wisdom and patience. In Sicily Anchises dies and Aeneas is left to lead the Trojans by his own devices. The storm that leaves them shipwrecked on the coast of Africa emphasizes the solitary position of the leader who rises, in spite of very human fits of despair, to the demands of the situation. But in this most desperate of crises comes the greatest of the tests which will determine his fitness to lead the final assault on Italy: the possibility of an easier solution, the personal ease and power of a city already built for his command and to be shared with an incomparable heroine who has won his heart. It is from the rejection of this

greatest of temptations that he emerges, not merely the *pius
Aeneas* of the early books, but the confident and heroic leader
of the invasion. Such would seem to be the function of the
Dido incident in the plan of Vergil, but it is hardly so that it
has been thought of by centuries of readers. For Vergil, the
new poet, could not make Dido a mere Circe or even a lotus-
eating Siren. Her side of the picture was the kind of subject
dear to the heart of the new poet, and so well did he develop
it that thoughtless readers have always sympathized with Dido
and condemned Aeneas as a faithless lover. And even the
greater critics have felt the need of a word of defense for the
hero. What Vergil really does is not to justify Dido or make
Aeneas a scoundrel. He creates a real tragedy in which we
must sympathize with both Dido and Aeneas but in which we
must also recognize the inevitable fate that brings about the
tragedy. This can be demonstrated, but first a glance at the
mechanics of the story.

Vergil, we know, had planned to begin his epic with what
is now Book III, then following the story of the voyage chrono-
logically down to the landing in Africa (Book I). Then
Aeneas would have told of the fall of Troy (Book II) and the
tale would have continued with Book IV. In a change of plan
he produced a four-book epyllion in the familiar form of
"Peleus and Thetis"—Books I and IV the framework story
of Dido and Aeneas and Books II and III the insert story of
the defeated Trojans. (Actually, the relation of the parts
comes closer to "Hekale" than to "Peleus and Thetis," but
the latter was in the mind of Vergil as he wrote. The evidence
lies in the constant verbal reminiscences, and the fatal result
has been the popular conception of Dido as the deserted victim, another Ariadne.) With the Alexandrian model in mind,
it was not unnatural that Vergil should develop the character
of his heroine. Every romantic device is used to produce a
story of true love. But in spite of the strong influence of the
epyllion, this story is but an incident in the long epic.

With Book IV the tragic element becomes dominant. At
the very opening, Dido admits to Anna not only her love for

Aeneas but her vow of fidelity to Sychaeus and her determination to keep her faith inviolate even if it means death to herself. Later, she repeatedly admits to herself that she has broken her faith and finally bids herself to die "as she has deserved." This by no means protects her from tragic suffering or from the human desire for vengeance on the man who has caused her suffering. But in his case also we are too apt to forget that his simple defense is true: he has made her no pledge, there was no true marriage (as she tries to pretend there was) and he goes, heartbroken and unwilling, to fulfill his destiny. Vergil undoubtedly, with his sensitive sympathy for human suffering, makes Dido too appealing or, perhaps more accurately, presents too lightly Aeneas' position in this particular book. For the moment, he was writing the tragedy of Dido. Fate lay behind the action, but the efficient instruments of fate are human characters, emotions, and reactions. Anna is the confidential slave of tragedy with her specious advice. Dido, like Phaedra, follows the specious advice in her own way and to her own destruction and in so doing brings suffering to all concerned. Vergil was closely akin to one aspect of Euripides. Neither of them, as philosophers, believed in the personal gods of Homer with their human frailties and personal intrusion into human affairs. "Can gods feel such anger," asks Vergil, and Euripides says, "The gods should be kinder than men." Both recognized a compelling fate and both, as poets, freely used the symbolism of the gods to make vivid the interplay of fate and human character.

At the risk of stressing the Dido episode too heavily, a word should be said about the relation of Dido to the Medea of Apollonius. Medea in the *Argonautica* is surely the first heroine to loom large in an epic story, and there is no question that Vergil knew her and to some extent used her in creating his Dido. But Medea and Dido are not equally important characters. Medea is a useful instrument and the Alexandrian poet devotes enthusiastic artistry in presenting a picture of her barbaric passion. But, her function performed, she has no continuing influence nor is she given the dignity of a tragic exit.

Dido may be better compared with the Medea of Euripides' tragedy.

We are now in a position to consider the episode in relation to the whole poem. If these first four books contain the story of the hero's preparation, the events leading up to and making possible the conquest of Italy and the inception of Roman power, the last four are just as surely the tale of that accomplishment. What of the four that are framed between these two blocks of four? Books V and VI may be said more properly to belong to the first group, for in his handling of the games and the final organization of the fleet, Aeneas is at last establishing his unquestioned leadership. But both books represent pauses in the action, relaxation of the tension, and, to a considerable degree, suspense. The fifth, in a practical way, and the sixth, in a spiritual way, give to Aeneas his supreme confidence. Similarly, Books VII and VIII belong more properly to the final group. They are part of the story of conquest, but they too represent a pause in the action: the suspense grows and the fighting does not really begin. But in these four central books is to be found what to Vergil was perhaps the greatest significance of the poem. In the first performance of the *lusus Troiae* at the games, in the founding of the kindred city in Sicily, in Anchises' prophetic picture of Rome's greatness, in Aeneas' visit to the future site of Rome, in the preview of Roman history on the shield of Vulcan, and in the roll of Italian cities in the catalogue, we are given the significance and meaning of the whole career of Aeneas. It is from such a point of view that the adventures of the Trojan hero became more than a romantic epic or even a national chronicle. They are sanctioned by the decrees of fate, they are made to interpret the ways of god to man.

Consistent with the self-conscous patterning of the *Aeneid* is the fact that each of the individual books has its own unity and its own pattern. In two cases Vergil would seem to have left the transition between books unsettled, but these are at most details for revision and do not affect the fact that each book is a unit in respect to subject matter and form, in sharp contrast with Homer as we have it and as, presumably, Vergil had it. (How Homer himself may have divided his epics we do not know.) It will be sufficient to examine one book which Vergil left in a less finished state than the rest, thus giving indication of his working method. This is Book IX, the first of the real battle books. The first lines are a deliberate transition from the eighth book, which dealt with Aeneas far from the scene of the war.

> The while such deeds were happening far away,
> Saturnian Juno from the heavens above
> Sent Iris to bold Turnus. Turnus by chance
> Was sitting in Pilumnus' sacred vale.   (IX.1–4)

This is extremely concise and factual, perhaps to be expanded before publication, but it serves to make the transition and to emphasize Turnus, the central figure of the following two books. Turn to the last four lines of Book IX.

> Then headlong in his armor with a leap
> He plunged at last into the yellow stream
> Which bore him on still waters joyously,
> Washed clean of battle, to his waiting troops.
> (IX.815–18)

It has been a book of Turnus' exploits. These are presented in two panels. The first 138 lines show Turnus alerted by Iris, gathering his forces while the Trojans man their walls and swinging into action with a rousing speech to his troops. Lines 503–814 present the second panel, Turnus in action: the resumption of battle after an intervening night, a series of valiant deeds culminating in the battle at the gates of the Trojan camp, and Turnus' adventures within the camp. The 314 lines between these two scenes of action are concerned with the story of Nisus and Euryalus and their attempt to break through the Rutulian lines to bring news of the crisis to Aeneas. This story is in itself a carefully constructed epyllion. There is clear indication that Vergil had worked it up independently to be integrated later with the rest of the book, for preceding it and following it are two blocks of lines which can be looked on only as unfinished sketches for the setting of the story. They show a lack of clarity and force quite uncharacteristic of Vergil. Each group contains an unfinished line; the second group seems even to have been misplaced by the editors. But each group sketches the situation first in the Rutulian, then in the Trojan, camp.

Such is the central feature of Book IX. Each of the flanking panels has its own construction with a general parallelism between the two. In the first, Juno alerts Turnus in the absence of Aeneas. The troops gather on both sides. Then follows a full-size picture of Turnus in two sections, swinging into action in the first and in the second haranguing his troops. Between the two is the story of the ships turned into sea-nymphs. Similarly in the second panel, the battle is resumed with a new invocation, this time to Calliope. Then we have the battle at the Trojan camp in two sections, first various Rutulian deeds of valor, second Turnus at and within the gates. Framed between these two sections is the story of Ascanius shooting his deadly missile of war. The story has always been considered a rather feeble effort to emphasize the position of Ascanius and his emergence into a position of leadership. It is not an impressive incident, but it should not be forgotten that it was an arrow shot in sport by Ascanius that precipitated the whole war, just as now his arrow shot in anger precipitates the critical battle in the camp. The general symmetry of the book may be seen in the following outline:

1–24, Turnus Alerted by Juno
25–46, Latin Forces Gather. Trojans Man the Walls
    47–76, Turnus Swings into Action
        77–125, Story of Ships to Nymphs
    126–58, Turnus Harangues His Forces
        159–75, Notes for Introduction
           176–502, Nisus and
                Euryalus

459–72, Misplaced Notes for
Conclusion
503–24, Battle Renewed
525–29, Invocation of Calliope
530–89, Latin Deeds of Valor
590–671, Ascanius Incident
672–818, Battle at the Gate. Escape of Turnus

There is much of Book IX that was left to be polished in the final revision, but most striking in this regard is the story of Nisus and Euryalus, or rather its lack of integration with the main narrative. A similar story left without perfect integration with the main text appears in the second book, the story of Sinon and the wooden horse. This is framed by the two parts of the Laocoön incident, in the second of which Laocoön is introduced as if he had not previously appeared. The first half is not necessary to the understanding of the second, which is complete in itself, but it adds greatly to the dramatic effect as well as to the artistic structure of the Sinon story. On revision it would surely have been retained, but its inconsistency and partial irrelevance would have been corrected.

The Misenus episodes in Book VI also show evidence of having been inserted. Perhaps the most striking single episode, in some respects, is the Cacus story inserted in Book VIII in the account of Evander's banquet in honor of Heracles. It would seem at first glance to have no role in the main narrative, to be a merely decorative feature. But it must be remembered that this book is one of the four in which Vergil developed the theme of Rome's future greatness, and this story redounds to the glory of Rome's greatest traditional hero and gives meaning to some of her most treasured and perhaps least understood rites. Livy found it of sufficient importance and interest to relate it in full, and it must have had no slight significance in the eyes of Vergil's contemporaries.

There are many other episodes throughout the *Aeneid* which form interesting digressions, but the striking thing about them is the way in which they are integrated into the main narrative. They are not isolated episodes, like so many in the Homeric epics: each has its function in the larger unity of the whole, and—of importance in the present discussion—each has an artistic structure characteristic of the new poetry.

It should now be clear, I think, that if, in a sense, Vergil goes back to Homer as the great writer of epic, it is only in the sense that, in the *Georgics,* he goes back to Hesiod. The *Aeneid* is an utterly different poem from either the *Iliad* or *Odyssey.* From the *Odyssey* came the suggestion of organic unity, but only a suggestion. The idea of talking with the departed heroes may have come to Vergil from the *Odyssey,* but how different from the bald necromancy of the Greek epic is Aeneas' visit to the underworld, beginning with the golden bough and ending at the gates of ivory and horn. In the battle details, too, unfamiliar and unsympathetic to Vergil, he relies on what he has read, but even these scenes are transformed: they are no longer glorious deeds of heroes but the dramatic struggles toward the final achievement. The games, the catalogues, the divinely given shield are more than decorative details. The epic moves from the first lines inevitably to the last. The sword, hero, Troy, Fate, and Italy of the first two lines reappear in the last three as the Trojan hero fulfills his fate by plunging the sword into the heart of the last opponent to the unity of Italian conquest.

This dramatic unity, maintained through twelve books, might easily have produced a fatal monotony, but Vergil, with his feeling for the new poetry and its fetish of variety, prevented this by countless devices. One critic has gone so far as to insist that Vergil alternated the tragic and the comic in successive books. He did not succumb to any such pitfall of systematic variation, but it takes only a cursory review of the twelve books to convince even the skeptic that the variations are deliberate. Book I is almost a preview of the variety to come. Plunging into the heart of the story, the first half is filled with the realistic thrills of the great storm and shipwreck and the forgathering of survivors on the shore of Africa. Then comes the interlude in which realism is mixed with mysticism as Aeneas meets his divine mother masquerading as a local huntress. Finally romance takes over with the discovery of Carthage and Dido. Books II and III, dramatically put into the mouth of Aeneas himself, present two types of narrative story, the epic tale of the fall of Troy and the discursive sea chronicle. Book IV is sheer dramatic romance. Then comes the relaxation of the book of the games (V) and the mysticism and philosophy, the picturesque pageantry of the visit to the Lower World (VI). Books VII and VIII again present two different types of narrative, illumined for the Roman reader by constant reminders of his local traditions. Then come finally the four battle books and the greatest challenge to the new poet. Not only are IX and X set off against XI and XII, the first pair belonging primarily to Turnus and the Rutulians, the second to Aeneas, but it is in these books that the writer applies his art most assiduously to the introduction of colorful relief: the fairy tale of the ships transformed into sea-nymphs; the story of Nisus and Euryalus; the first essay in warfare of the young Ascanius (Book IX); the council of the gods; the voyage of Aeneas from Caere to Ostia; the Etruscan roll call; the heroic deaths of the two young heroes, Pallas and Lausus (Book X); the funeral rites for the fallen; the dramatic council at Latinus' palace; the romantic story of Camilla (Book XI). With XII the approach of the great climax is sufficient to hold interest throughout and the story becomes more closely knit. Juturna may be considered an incidental decoration, but she could not be readily removed without destroying the narrative texture.

Apart from matters of constructional form, the new poetry is evident throughout the *Aeneid* in many a characteristic of style and feeling. These require too much analysis and exposition to receive more than mention here: expressions of sentiment approaching sentimentality, the merging of simile into symbolism, the acceptance of romantic love as legitimate epic subject matter and hence the increased role of the heroine, the (very rare) intrusion of the poet, speaking in his own person, the frank and purposeful use of quotation from and allusion to previous poets and their writings. This last point is so typical of Vergil and his fellow poets of Rome as to require a further word.

The ninth book again serves best to illustrate Vergil's method: because of the lack of final revision, the borrowings are more conspicuous. In lines 263 ff. Ascanius, with almost boyish enthusiasm, is accepting the offer of Nisus and Euryalus to attempt the recall of Aeneas. They have themselves suggested the adventure and freely offered their services, but the boy lists a profusion of gifts which have the definite sound of inducements: two engraved cups, two tripods, two talents of gold, an antique mixing bowl, the horse of Turnus, and twelve captive women. The tripods and the women are unexpected to say the least—even Ascanius promises the women as the gift of his father. But the explanation is clear when we recall that Agammemnon, goaded by Nestor, enumerated as the gifts that he would offer to win back Achilles' aid (*Iliad* 9.122 ff.) seven tripods, six talents of gold, twenty caldrons, twelve horses, and seven women, with twenty more to be added when Troy fell. There is similar wholesale borrowing from Ennius: lines 806–14 are only partially adapted from lines 401–08 of the earlier poet. Vergil had already indicated that he had Ennius before him when he plunged into the battle scene at 503 with *At tuba terribilem,* which every contemporary reader would recognize; and numerous other Ennian phrases could hardly fail of detection. In the same way reminiscences of Catullus and Lucretius are more numerous and obvious than in the more polished books.

Vergil felt no compunction in borrowing from his predecessors. As a rule, in the finished version, he changed the phrase sufficiently to make it his own but not to conceal its origin, which not infrequently gave a desired tone to the situation he himself was developing. Thus he enhances the tone of depression in Aeneas' speech to his mother Venus in line 390 of Book I by echoing the words of abandoned Ariadne in Catullus, 64.125. In the same way, the tone of grief in line 376 of the same book is made stronger by the recall of a phrase from Catullus' lament for his brother (101.1). Again, to enhance the effect of richness in his description of Dido's palace (I.639) he borrows liberally from Catullus' brilliant picture of Peleus' palace in 64.43,44. Such procedure was not considered plagiarism but flattery.

This reworking of phrases from former poets becomes prominent in Augustan times and would seem to have been a trait of the new poetry. It later received a further impetus from the practice of the rhetorical schools but probably was due in the first place to the meticulousness of the neoterics in the creation of the perfect phrase. The practice is too familiar to require extensive illustration here: one instance will be enough. Catullus in "Peleus and Thetis" pictured Ariadne, deserted on the shore of Dia, looking out over the sea and suffering great waves of emotion: *Prospicit et magnis curarum fluctuat undis* (As she looks forth, her body heaves with mighty waves of woe). It was a suitable and effective figure of speech. Vergil echoes it when he wishes to present *his* heroine Dido in the throes of passion (IV.532): *Saevit amor magnoque irarum fluctuat aestu* (Love rages and heaves with mighty tides of wrath). In spite of the change from *magnis curarum undis* to *magno irarum aestu,* the source of Vergil's figure and phraseology is clear. In IV.564 he varies the wording with *variosque irarum concitat aestus* (and rouses varying tides of wrath), in VIII.19 gives another variation, *magno curarum fluctuat aestu* (and heaves with mighty tides of woe), and, finally, in XII.831, retains the figure without a single word of the Catullan version: *Irarum tantos volvis sub pectore fluctus* (You nurse such floods of wrath within your breast).

It would be unforgivable to leave the impression that Vergil was a mechanical manipulator of phrases or in any sense a copyist of the inspired creations of others. These echoes of Catullus are no furtive pilferings but rather the recognition of Vergil's appreciation of his debt to his predecessor. It has become clear that this debt was far-reaching. With the *Aeneid,* Vergil emerged the national poet of Rome as Homer was the national poet of Greece. But the hero of the *Aeneid* became merged as a symbol with the glory of Rome as neither Achilles nor Ulysses with that of Greece. In the accomplishment of this end, the personality of the author emerges so vitally that Vergil, with his sense of the pity in the world, is as real to us as Homer is indistinct and impersonal. No small part in the achievement of this result must be credited to those adventurous young poets who dared commit to their poems their inmost thoughts and emotions and who at the same time wrought patiently to create a body of poetry, self-conscious, yes, but intricate in pattern, rich in traditional allusion, combining tentatively the best of realism and artificiality. To Vergil's sympathetic genius it was given to build on sturdier foundations than theirs but also to use and perfect what they had had the courage to produce.

VI · HORACE

T HE SATIRES · Horace was born five years after Vergil in 65 B.C. in the remote village of Venusia. There can be little doubt that his father, a freedman, was a dirt farmer, attaining perhaps to the modest dignity of tax collector in his native district. The farming in the neighborhood of Venusia, high on the spine of Italy on the road from Capua to Brindisi, must have been as hard as that in the stoniest hills of New England. Venusia had once been a frontier community and seems to have retained something of the crudity as well as the vigor of a garrison town. It had none of the lushness of the Po valley or the amenities of Mantua and Verona. Horace himself had little enough experience on the farm although the memory of it stayed with him always. While he was still a boy, his father took him to Rome for a better schooling than could be had at Venusia. We have no evidence as to whether the farm was sold to make this possible or how soon afterward his father died. At any rate, Horace had enough money to go to Athens for the completion of his education and there is no further information about his father. Horace's devotion to him is indicated in the sixth satire of the first book.

> Yet, if my character
> Rings true, with faults not many or too black
> (As one might cavil at disfiguring moles
> On a fair complexion), if no serious charge
> Of greed or meanness can be justly brought
> Against me, if my friends think well of me—
> The credit is my father's. With no wealth,
> A poor man on a lean and hungry farm,
> He would not send me off to Flavius' school
> With hulking sons of tough centurions,

Lunchbox and slate in hand, and every Ides
Paying eight asses to be taught. Himself
He took me off to Rome to learn the skills
That every knight and senator provides
For his own sons.

       .   .   .

Unless I lose my mind, I'll never be
Ashamed of such a father. I'll not claim
As many do that 'tis no fault of mine
My parents were not free-born and renowned.
No such defense for me. Far otherwise
My deep conviction. If some turn of fate
Should bid the years roll back and ask of us
To choose new parents, each to his own taste,
Content with mine, I would not take instead
Those honored with the fasces or a throne.
(I.6.65–78, 89–97)

It was while Horace was reading philosophy in Greece that
Julius Caesar was assassinated, and some months later Brutus
came to Athens recruiting young Romans for his army. Horace
was evidently won by his eloquence and joined the republican
forces, being commissioned tribune in spite of an unwarlike
nature and a complete ignorance of military affairs. There
followed an unhappy period ending in the defeat at Philippi.
The young student was evidently considered harmless enough
not to be punished for his rebellious behavior, and we next find
him, in 41 B.C., back at Rome with a job as clerk in the
treasury department, almost as distasteful to Horace as the
life of a soldier. Better times were ahead. In some way he
met Vergil and Varius, who must have found promise in the
somewhat crude and bitter verse that he wrote from time to
time. They introduced him to Maecenas, who presently accepted him into the circle of his friends. This meant a semiofficial endowment for Horace and before long the friendship
of Octavian. Eventually Maecenas gave him (in 33 B.C.) the

small villa in the Sabine hills which was his favorite home for the rest of his life.

Horace published his first volume of verse in 35 B.C., at approximately the age at which Catullus died. One would not, then, expect to find in it the youthful, exuberant emotion so marked in much of the work of the earlier poet. Furthermore, Horace's life had been far different from that of a well-to-do young blade at home in the frivolous society of Rome. He had a serious upbringing and his experience as a defeated revolutionary and a wage earner were sobering to say the least. But he did have a contemplative mind and, as something of an outsider, a good chance to study the life around him. In addition he was a shrewd observer with little rancor and a rare vein of humor. Only later was his fine sense of the poetic to make itself evident; his first attempts at writing were of a more pedestrian variety. They consisted of what he called *sermones,* or conversations, short essays in hexameter verse about almost any topic of timely interest. Later on he explained his early choice of vehicle in lines to be taken with some reservation.

> The while Alpinus in a turgid flow
> Murders his Memnon or befouls the source
> Of the great Rhine, these trifles give me sport
> That never shall resound to win the praise
> Of Tarpa as their critic or survive
> To meet return engagements on the stage.
> Of all that write of courtesans and slaves
> Fooling old men, the cleverest today
> Is our Favonius; Pollio writes the deeds
> Of kings in triple meter; epic verse
> Varius with his high spirit rules alone;
> The country-loving muses give the palm
> To Vergil for his tender elegance.
> This only was there left, by Varro tried
> And other few, which I could write perchance
> Better than they though far behind the man

Who tried it first: I never would attempt
To wrest from him the crown he wore so well.
(I.10.36–49)

In other words, comedy, tragedy, epic, and pastoral were all being written by poets, great or at least competent, and so Horace took up the type which Lucilius had created but which had no successful contemporary representative and as yet no name. These lines may not be completely serious, and they may have been written partly as introduction to the compliment to Fundanius, Pollio, Varius, and Vergil, but they are still significant. Horace recognizes the drama and the epic as legitimate fields of poetry. He goes beyond them to include not only the pastoral of his friend Vergil but also "what Lucilius wrote" and at this point he opens up a field of argument with the new poets. For Lucilius was a subject of contention. He had been a friend of the conservatives in the circle of Scipio and Laelius but he was also claimed by the neoterics as the first of their school. What he wrote was so much of an innovation that it had no traditional name. It was highly personal, expressing the author's point of view on a wide range of subjects. It gloried in the insertion of Greek words. To this extent it was certainly new. On the other hand, Lucilius was a vigorous exponent of stoicism and virtue and, although each of his essays was longer than any of the casual pieces of the new poets, none of them had the perfection and polish or the decoration of poetic conceit and learned allusion of their longer efforts. It was as though Lucilius had adopted the independence and realistic contemporary outlook which the new poets were to claim but had gone no further in the direction they were to take. So both sides could with some show of justice claim him as their own.

It is quite probable that Horace had little interest, as a young man, in any quarrel between poetic schools. He chose Lucilius as a model because his was a fairly easy type of verse to write and because, by virtue of its timeliness, it offered the opportunity for a young writer to make himself heard. The earliest products of Horace's pen give every appearance of having been written for this purpose.

Satires 7, 2, 8, and 4 are generally accepted as the earliest, probably in that order. The seventh is an army skit built around a poor pun, an appeal to Brutus, the king-slayer, to get rid of a barracks pest named King.

> The pus and venom of Rupilius Rex,
> The refugee; how half-breed Persius
> Took his revenge, a tale of barber shops,
> Still goes the round of drugstore gossipers.
>
> (I.7.1–3)

This rather brutish and certainly coarse manner of expression is obviously intentional and is maintained consistently throughout. The mock heroic touches only emphasize it. P. Rupilius Rex was a political exile who had been praetor and whom Brutus had accepted as one of his officers. It is hard enough to believe that the scene depicted could have actually taken place in the court room of Brutus, but even harder to find any excuse for publishing this ribald account of it except a desire for notoriety.

In its opening lines, which attack the musician Tigellius, the second satire has something of the same low bid for attention. Other individuals are also given rough handling, but the chief bid for attention lies in the salacious subject matter and in its forthright presentation. The piece shows, however, real ability in construction and expression, indications of possible genius, which to some extent redeem the satire.

Satire 8 is a violent attack on one Canidia, a reputed poisoner presented as a loathsome witch. There is here a more definite attempt to give artistic form to the work as a whole. The speaker is Priapus, or rather his effigy, in an abandoned cemetery which has been converted (none too successfully) into a garden. He introduces himself in the opening lines and his unconventional behavior drives off the witches at the end of the satire. Canidia and her confederates, with their collection of gruesome materials for a witches' brew, form the body of the piece.

By now Horace would seem to have felt that he had succeeded in drawing attention to himself, and either he had been criticized for his vicious attacks or, as seems more likely, saw fit to pretend that he had aroused more resentment than he really had. Attacks on a little-known singer and on other obscure persons and on a suspected female poisoner of no social standing can hardly have stirred the influential men of Rome. But it pleases Horace to defend himself, to give to his poetic vehicle a respectable if doubtful pedigree and to put himself on record as a writer familiar with the best literary tradition.

This he does in the fourth satire. He aligns himself with the Old Comedy of Athens and with Lucilius, and he pays passing tribute to Ennius, thus making his appeal to the more conservative group of poets and patrons. But, in criticism of both Lucilius and Ennius, he perhaps seeks to avoid giving too much offense to either school. In both ways he might hope to attract the attention of the semiofficial group gathered around Maecenas. He has certainly not yet been accepted by them or he would surely have made capital of their acquaintance, as he does later in satires 9 and 10.

In these earlier satires, 2, 4, 7, and 8, Horace does not think of himself as a poet. In fact, he repudiates the title and claims to be writing prose in meter.

> First, I exclude myself from those I grant
> The name of poet; for you could never say
> It is enough to round a verse, and if
> One writes as I do, nearer to the talk
> Of every day, you would not call him poet.
> For he who wins that name must have at least
> Inspired imagination, noble style.
>
> .   .   .
>
> If from these skits which I now perpetrate,
> As did Lucilius once, you take away

The quantities and meter, putting the words
In different order, you will never find,
As in that famous line, "When dire Discord
Had battered down the iron-shod gates of War,"
The scattered remnants of a dismembered poet.

(I.4.39–44, 56–62)

He does, however, claim to write with care and correctness in contrast with Crispinus, who, here as elsewhere, is accused of verbosity and carelessness. This reference to Crispinus is of particular interest because, while it is implied here that he wrote verses, he is otherwise assumed by Horace to be a stoic philosopher of the duller sort. Horace seems in this fourth, his first critical, satire, to suggest some relation between his own satires and stoic philosophy, but he proceeds to a further definition: what he writes is not the refined theory of the professional philosopher but the homely good sense of the traditional Roman of the old stock.

With Satire 5, Horace provides evidence to support his claim to be a follower of Lucilius: he imitates a Lucilian subject. It is a dull affair dealing with a trip to Brundisium in the train of Maecenas, but it has interest as containing his first allusion to his friendship with Vergil and Varius and to any acceptance by Maecenas. He is certainly not close to Maecenas, and his protestations of friendship with the others do not indicate any great intimacy. He does, however, show the beginning of a new confidence in his new environment, enough at least to speak ironically of the high position of a scribe.

This confidence is definitely greater in the sixth satire, in which Horace pays his respects to Maecenas primarily on the ground of his disregard of birth as opposed to quality even though his own lineage is most distinguished. He is sufficiently confident to emphasize the fact that his own father was a freedman, almost making a boast of it and declaring his satisfaction with his humble origin and simple life.

With Satire 3, Horace seems to be taking more thought for the orderly arrangement of the subject matter. He creates a situation and an atmosphere by drawing a brief picture of the inconsistency of Tigellius. By the introduction of an imaginary interlocutor he gives a certain dramatic form to the satire, which develops into a discussion of the human tendency toward carping criticism and a plea for tolerance. This involves a criticism of the Stoic doctrine that all faults are equally grave. With a fairly clever transition to the Stoic paradox that the philosopher is by logic a king, Horace winds up with the conclusion that he is happier with his toleration than the king with his sovereignty. The structure is not closely knit, but it is there and obvious. The subject matter no longer consists of crude personalities. The tone is less defensive and more urbane.

The variety already shown is extended in the ninth satire, and equally there is a striking advance in geniality of tone and urbanity of expression. The subject is a single character familiar to every reader: the social bore. The scene, the familiar road through the forum, and the meeting of Horace and the bore are developed simply and realistically and without haste. The direct discourse gives dramatic life to the satire, and the swift conclusion, reminiscent of the stage god from the machine, is wholly satisfying.

> I strolled the other day in aimless thought
> Along the Via Sacra, lost to the world.
> Up ran a fellow whom I scarcely knew
> Who grasped my hand and cried effusively,
> "My dear old man, how are you?" "Not too bad,"
> I said, and seeing him set to join me, added,
> "Glad to have seen you." He ignored the hint,
> Saying, "We ought to know each other well:
> I'm a poet too." "I shall," said I, "for that
> Remember you more kindly." Eager to shake him
> I first rushed quickly on, then, stopping short,

Whispered some nothing in my slave boy's ear,
The while the sweat coursed downward to my shoes.

. . .

But no: it chanced, thanks to our short delay,
The prosecutor in his suit rushed up
Shouting, "Where to, you villain?" And to me:
"You'll witness this?" I fairly stretched my ear.
He dragged the bore away. Great shouts all round.
Gathering crowds. 'Twas so Apollo saved me.

(I.9.1–11, 74–78)

At the heart of the satire there is an indirect tribute to Maecenas naturally introduced and given a serious tone in a natural
and realistic fashion. The intent was evidently to make this
bit of conversation the high spot of the satire, framed by the
dramatic dialogue, but the framework was too well done to
permit this result: the satire will always be thought of as
"The Bore."

I followed after. He began again:
"How goes your progress with the great Maecenas?
A man of few friends, that; discriminating.
You've played it well, but 'twould not hurt your case
To have support like mine to back you up.
If you would introduce yours truly—" "There,"
Said I, "We do not live on terms like that.
No house is freer of such venal vice.
It does not hurt my pride if someone else
Is richer or more learned. Everyone
Has his own place." "A lovely tale," said he,
"That I can scarce believe." "And yet, 'tis true."

(I.9.43–53)

Probably the latest of the satires of Book I is the first,
written with great care for that position. There are no caustic
personalities; the subject is of a general philosophical character
like that of the third. It deals with the general dissatisfaction
of man with his lot, ascribing this state of mind to too great a

concern for wealth. There is a more personal framework. The opening and closing sections deal with the thesis in general, the central part with details presented by means of half-developed conversation between Horace and an imaginary objector. The conclusion is noteworthy for two things in particular: the epigrammatic *est modus in rebus* ("There is a decent mean and limits set / On neither side of which the right can stand") and the borrowing from Lucretius of the figure of the contented guest leaving the banquet of life ("And so it comes about that in this world / You rarely find a man who willingly / Confesses to have lived a happy life / And, like a well-fed guest, withdraws content"). Finally, a slender outside frame is furnished by the opening address to Maecenas, which makes the satire an introduction to the volume, and the abrupt ending, in which Horace pulls himself up sharply with a glancing thrust at the loquacity of Crispinus.

Enough and more. You'll think that I have robbed
Crispinus' notebook. Not another word.

There remains the tenth satire, Horace's defense of his criticisms of Lucilius. It is also his most extended discussion of satire and, by implication, of the poetry of the day, a summary of his position as a literary critic at about 35 B.C. In supporting his claim that Lucilius was a careless writer, he extends his criticism to other characteristics of Lucilius, and with the phrase *neque simius iste* ("nor yet that ape, trained only to sing Calvus and Catullus") goes beyond the field of satire into that of lyric poetry. The suggestion of the vice of Greekizing applies to the poets criticized and they turn out to be for the most part grammatici. Over against them, Horace picks out a group of poets and a group of men at court whom he prefers to please. By the use of the word *equitum* in one of his illustrations he includes Maecenas in the second group. By implication, Homer, Ennius, and Accius are his ideal poets and to a limited extent Lucilius too, but all of them have a venerable crudity or, at worst, human defects which give the modern poet room for advance and improvement. Very definitely Horace repudiates the grammatici. The use of *plorare* in his repudiation ("Go, wail before the benches of your female pupils") at least suggests that he chiefly deplores the elegy. In the last five lines, the use of *qualiacumque* and *libello* gives the impression of another side thrust at Catullus. Vergil is included among the elect even as the writer of pastorals, but there, I suggest, is where Horace would draw the line, excluding from the ranks of the respectable all writers of elegy and epigram.

The first book of satires shows an advance from the crude, vindictive character of the earliest skits to essays with a certain amount of artistic construction and considerable evidence of shrewd observation as well as responsible judgment. They are extremely varied in both content and form. At first glance it seems curious that Horace should revert in the first satire of the second book to a defense of the literary type as he conceived it in I.4, the vehicle of direct and sharp criticism of individuals after the manner of Lucilius. But the approach is now wholly different. The poet would establish his right to criticize just as firmly as he did before but with a more gracious address and in a more artistic form. Established as a writer and assured by his new security in life, mellowed by his association with the circle of Maecenas, Horace speaks out with confidence and good humor. His defense is now specious and gay. He needs no defense, he is master of his art. The form has developed from implied to real dialogue, the dramatic setting is carefully chosen and skillfully executed. Horace, consulting his friend, the eminent lawyer Trebatius, is advised drily and dogmatically, until in the end the authority is forced to yield to Horace's indomitable assurance.

> *Horace.* There are who think my satire goes beyond
> The limit with its punch. Others believe
> That all I write is flat; a thousand lines
> Like mine, they say, one day might well produce.
> Advise me please, Trebatius, what to do.
> *Trebatius.* Be silent. *Hor.* What! Write nothing more
>   you mean?

Treb. I do. *Hor.* I'm blessed if that would not be wise,
But I can't sleep.

. . .

Treb. I cannot find a flaw in what you say.
But be advised and watch your step, or else
You'll be in trouble from your ignorance
Of sacred law. If any man compose
Against another evil verses, then
There's right of action, legal remedy.
Hor. Oh, evil verses, yes. But if one writes
Good verses praised by Caesar as the judge?
If one, his conscience clear, assails but those
Worthy of such abuse? *Treb.* The papers, then,
Will be torn up: you'll leave the court scot-free.

(II.1.1–7, 79–86)

Much the same is true of most of the satires of Book II.
The Stoic teachings of the third satire are the basic doctrines
in which Horace firmly believes, but, in the mouth of an excited
convert quoting a professional fanatic, they serve equally as
the basis for a merry burlesque of the over-solemn preacher.
So too in the fourth satire, Catius, the apprentice gourmet,
quotes the precepts of his mysterious master in the art of
overrefined gastronomy. The burlesque is not obscured in this
case by any underlying elements of belief. The fifth satire,
perhaps the most brilliant of all, deals in the same light manner
with the practice of legacy hunting. The burlesque effect is
heightened by making the chief speaker Tiresias, his consultant
Ulysses. Horace does not appear. The opening dialogue is
strictly dramatic; the closing dialogue is curtailed by the abrupt
and undignified departure of the ancient seer at the call of
Proserpina.

Ulys. Answer me this, Tiresias, adding to
All you have told me: by what arts and wiles
To build again my squandered capital.
Why do you laugh? *Tir.* Is it then not enough
For one so wily to return at last
To Ithaca and his ancestral hearth?

Ulys. Oh thou who never lied to any man,
Thou seest how naked and in want I come
Back to my home with you as prophet guide.
There neither herds nor produce have survived
The greedy suitors. But, divorced from wealth,
Virtue and ancestry are worthless weeds.
Tir. Since, then, quibbling aside, 'tis poverty
You fear, listen and hear the way to wealth.

         .   .   .

                         But I must go.
Proserpina imperious summons me.
Good luck—farewell.   (II.5.1–10, 109–10)

The ninth satire is much like the fourth in artistic form. Fundanius reports a dinner given by a man of newly acquired wealth and no taste, a precursor of Trimalchio. Here again the concluding framework is dispensed with and the satire ends with the flight of the guests from the banquet. In Satire 7 the framework is complete. The humor of the situation is secured by making the interlocutor Horace's own slave, Davus, who reads him a lecture on his own derelictions.

There are two more satires in Book II. Neither of them is in true dialogue form, a fact which sets them apart from the other satires, as does also their less boisterous type of wit. They are not burlesque or farce. They are serious expressions on the part of the poet. Satire 2 is a discussion put into the mouth of an old dirt farmer, Ofellus, lecturing his sons on the subject of plain living. Such dialogue as there is consists of hypothetical interruptions, and Horace intrudes a first-person guarantee of Ofellus' integrity. Finally, Satire 6 is another direct expression of the poet's gratitude for and appreciation of his Sabine farm. Framed within the two parts of this is a vivid picture of the contrasting city life from which the farm is his refuge. A third of the whole consists of the story of the city mouse and the country mouse with which the satire ends, summarizing the whole essay. The fable, in its simplicity, has a charm greatly enhanced by the art that is

never intrusive but always effective and by the lyric touches
that make vivid the succession of pictures. It illustrates well
the development of Horace's skill as a poet up to the time when
he was thirty-five years old.

> Then Cervius very likely will produce
> Some old wives' tale to embroider well his point.
> There may be envious praise of weary wealth
> That haunts Arrelius. Cervius takes his cue.
> Once on a time, says he, a country mouse,
> Tradition has it, in his meager hole
> Was entertaining for old friendship's sake
> A city mouse. Close-fisted and perforce
> Guarding his savings, still he could relax
> In hospitality. Forth from his hoard
> He brought, unsparing, cherished bits of corn,
> A few hard peas, and fragments half consumed
> Of bacon rind, seeking to overcome
> The jaded appetite of his city guest
> That with fastidious tooth suspiciously
> Touched each new offering, while the country host,
> Stretched on a thorny couch of new-cut chaff,
> Ate spelt and darnel uncomplainingly.
> Finally in despair the city mouse
> Burst forth: "My friend, how can you bear to live
> Forever in this god-forsaken hole?
> Won't you set forth with me and learn to know
> Cities and men rather than these wild wastes?
> Take to the road nor let yourself forget
> That we who tread the earth have mortal souls:
> Nor great nor small can miss the call of death.
> Live while you can, get pleasure, nor forget
> That life is short." This urbane argument
> Persuaded in a trice the country mouse.
> Out of his hole he sprang. The two set forth
> Eager to reach the city walls by dark.
> Already Night had traversed half its course

When they two crept into the wealthy house
Where ivory couches stood with coverlets
Of Tyrian purple, and upon the board
Heaping remains of yester evening's feast.
The city mouse, turned host, bade his rude guest
Recline upon a couch. Gaily himself
He played the part of slave, dispensing food
And dainties, stealing a taste of each before
Serving his rustic friend who, well content,
Lolled there in pleasure at his changed estate.
Sudden, the mighty din of opening doors
Drove host and guest from off the banquet couch.
Hither and yon they rushed while rising howls
Of watchdogs added to their frenzied fright.
Then spake the country mouse: "No life for me
Is this. Farewell; my simple country hole
Will comfort me with safety and plain fare.

(II.6.77–117)

The satires were written between 41 and 30 B.C. The same year that saw the publication of the second book also produced a volume of *Epodes* which represented, along with the *Satires* but in different form, Horace's early efforts in poetic composition.

THE EPODES · It is in the *Epodes* that Horace begins to show an interest in the lyric poetry that was to be his lasting monument. The type however is not primarily lyric. To Horace the epodes were "iambics" and his model Archilochus, significantly not Alexandrian but early Greek. The connotation of iambics, in the Greek, is clear from the verb, to iambize, meaning to attack violently in verse. The repute of Archilochus furnished Horace with a decent poetic pedigree and sanction for his vindictive iambics, which were scarcely in the character of their author but which served to attract attention in the same way as did the contemporary early satires. In Epode 6, Horace presents himself in the role of violent poet. He chal-

[124]

lenges a malicious contemporary to stop picking on nobodies
and to face up to a real fight.

> Why, like a craven cur, do you attack
> Innocent visitors while turning tail
> Before a wolf? Will you not rather howl
> Your empty threats at me, attacking one
> Who'll battle back? For, like Molossian hound
> Or tawny Spartan, shepherds' mightiest friend,
> I'll follow after through the deepest snow
> Whatever beast molests. You fill the woods
> With horrid bark—then take the proffered bribe.
> Beware, beware: against malicious souls
> I'm full of venom, armed with ready horns
> Like him whom treacherous Lycambes scorned
> As son-in-law or Bupalus' fierce foe.
> Or, if I be attacked with venemous tooth,
> Think you I'll take revenge in childish tears?   (VI)

The earlier epodes are vicious indeed and wholly unre-
strained by any sense of kindliness or decency. The eighth is
a thoroughly scurrilous attack on an unidentified old woman
who has sought Horace's favor and whom he repels with the
frankest enumeration of all her physical deficiences. Number
12 is closely similar. The sixth has been quoted. It has vigor
and directness and no indecency but also it has no great distinction in spite of an evident effort in that direction. The use
made of two figures, the dog and the bull, is a trifle disturbing
and the somewhat learned allusion to Archilochus and Hip-
ponax in the closing lines is inappropriate to this type of incidental verse. There is something of the same straining for
effect in Epode 10, which is a propempticon in the iambic
spirit for one Maevius, wishing him an unsuccessful voyage.
The winds are all invoked to harass his ship and, if they
comply and Maevius is tossed onto the shore, a corpse to be
devoured by the gulls, Horace promises a kid and a lamb in
sacrifice to the weather gods. All that we know of Maevius is
that he was one of the pair of poets whom even the kindly

[125]

Vergil used as symbols of bad verse (*Eclogues*.3.90). The whole tone of the poem is one of exaggeration, perhaps with humorous intent, though this can hardly be proven. At any rate we have here, if only in a sort of parody, experimentation with a form which Horace was to use with better grace in his odes of later date.

In this group of earlier epodes, there is one, the fourth which attacks an upstart freedman for his ostentatious bearing in his new position of wealth and distinction. This is a perfectly sound use of the iambic even if it is not in the best of taste coming from the inconspicuous son of a freedman. To a certain extent it is an experiment in form. *Superbus ambules* (you walk about proudly) seems to echo the *superbus et superfluens / perambulabit* (proud and arrogant / he will walk about) of Catullus' famous attack on Caesar (29), which Vergil knew and quoted. The epode ends with the supposed remarks of the indignant populace, suggestive of the technique used in some of the odes.

There are two epodes (5 and 17) which attack one Canidia. She is represented in the fifth as a gruesome witch who, with her companion witches, tortures and murders a young boy in order to use part of his vital organs to create a charm. It is the same Canidia whom Horace attacked in Satire I.8, but there is greater bitterness here. The seventeenth masks this bitterness under the mockery of a pretended recantation. Both of these epodes are partially dramatic and have a suggestion of framework construction: the fifth begins with the victim and ends with him, the witches occupying the main body of the epode; in the seventeenth the opening consists of Horace's pretended surrender and plea for mercy, the conclusion of Canidia's rejection of the plea. In the fifth Horace creates an atmosphere of deep sincerity and real hatred; the picture is realistic and the only literary allusions are familiar and suitable ones to Medea and Thyestes. The seventeenth with its elaborate irony has not the same direct force and is definitely more literary. Catullus' device (42) of calling the girl he has vilified *pudica et proba* (modest and pure) is borrowed directly. If we were tempted to doubt the fact of borrowing, the use of *perambulabis* in the next line would dissipate any doubt. Some twenty names from Greek mythology appear in the epode, not obscure ones but still conspicuous.

These seven epodes seem to be early ones, corresponding in time and tone with the second satire of Book I. They indicate an author still immature but showing definite signs of marked ability, striving for attention, a student of Catullus as well as of Archilochus, as in the satires he was a student of Lucretius as well as of Lucilius. They show some personal as well as literary bitterness. And finally they give no indication of any acquaintance with Maecenas or his circle.

Two of the epodes have political reference. The first, number 7, is a protest to his fellow citizens against some new outbreak of civil war. Horace plunges dramatically into direct appeal to them: *Quo, quo scelesti ruitis?* (Whither, whither are you running, traitors?) They will ruin in fratricidal war the city which escaped from Hannibal, and only Parthia will rejoice. The epode is brief and ends with a reference to the fatal strife of Romulus and Remus, familiar to every Roman schoolboy, a strife which has left its curse on divided Rome. In Epode 16, the same subject is treated but in a much more literary or academic manner. The opening *Altera jam teritur* (Another age is beginning) sets a calmer pace and the main body of the poem is an appeal to the better citizens to sail off with the poet to the fabled Islands of the Blest. The more mature Horace, the disillusioned republican, the rebel appeased perhaps by the wise Maecenas, can see the danger of civil war and yet sit down and write his Golden Age as elaborately and calmly as Vergil and the others did theirs. It is almost an exercise in contemporary pastoral.

Nor did Horace stop there. In Epode 15, to the faithless Neaera, he flirted with the elegy. The opening lines produce a lyrical atmosphere: " 'Twas night and in the quiet vault of heaven / The moon shone bright." Ovid borrowed more than once the opening device, *Nox erat et caelo*. Eleven is actually a fragmentary elegy in all but meter, and the second epode

is no true iambic. With its surprise ending, it has something
of the character of an extended epigram, but it is really bucolic,
the city man's dream of the country, idealized like so much of
the country in the eclogues of Theocritus and Vergil—pretty
and pure art—but Horace showed by the surprise ending that
he knew what he was doing.

Happy the man who far from business cares
Like earth's first innocent inhabitants
Ploughs his ancestral acres with his steers
Nor knows the bane of interest and loans.
For him no bugle blast, no storm at sea
Rouses to fear; he shuns the market square
And all the portals of the city's great.

And so betimes he trains his tender vines
To climb their cedar posts or, stretching out
In the far meadow, watches lazily
The lowing cattle munching as they go,
Or prunes the dead wood from his apple trees
And grafts new shoots to win a happier crop,
Presses the honey into well washed jars
Or shears his wobbly, uncomplaining sheep.
When autumn rears its head with apple crown
He picks his fruit and gathers in his grapes
With grateful offerings to his simple gods.
Oh, then what joy to lay him down in peace
Beneath an aged oak or in the grass
Along the murmuring brook that gaily bursts
From bubbling springs whose softly plashing notes
Mingling with bird songs lure him to kindly sleep.
Or when the revolving year brings wintery storms
Forth with his dogs he hunts the boar or snares
The quail or rabbit for his evening meal.
And if, beside, a frugal country wife
Kin to the sunburned Sabines keep his house
Stocking the hearth against her man's return,
Spreading the table with good country fare

Washed down with his own wine, he will not miss
The Lucrine oyster or the foreign grouse.
Better the produce of his homely farm
Enjoyed in peace, far from the madding crowd.

So spake the banker Alfius, poised to move
Into the country—sold his stocks and bonds
On March 15th, but then, on second thought,
Bought them all back again on April 1st.   (II)

In the remaining epodes Maecenas figures in one way or
another. This does not prove that all of the epodes which we
have considered are earlier than this final group but it does
indicate that most of them probably are, that they come from
the period when Horace was a little-known poet experimenting with various types of verse, possibly exchanging ideas with
Varius and Vergil, but not as yet sure in his own mind what
he really wanted to do.

Of the four epodes addressed to Maecenas, two, the third
and the fourteenth, deal with comparatively slight incidents,
like so many of the poems of Catullus. Horace's reaction in
Epode 3 to a dish overseasoned with garlic that was served
at Maecenas' table and the poet's mock-serious wish for
Maecenas' appropriate suffering should he ever serve it again,
indicate some advance in the intimacy between the two men.
The fourteenth shows about the same degree of intimacy.
Horace extricates himself by a frivolous excuse from the
necessity of writing more diligently and makes just enough
fun of Maecenas to be amusing but not annoying.

> Your frank complaints, Maecenas,
>   Are boring me to death.
> You ask why nerveless lassitude
>   Has hushed my poet's breath,
>
> As though I'd quaffed the hemlock
>   And tasted Lethe's sleep.
> 'Tis no such thing. By god's behest
>   My word I fail to keep.

Anacreon of Teos
Loved with a love divine
Bathyllus—and the poems he wrote
Collapsed, the same as mine.

You love a modern Helen
Who worships no one more.
My Phryne's but a onetime slave
With lovers by the score.

There is enough classical allusion in both poems to give the necessary literary touch, which contrasts well with the down-to-earth basis of each, but the allusions are familiar rather than learned.

The other two Maecenas episodes are surely among the latest, for both deal with the battle of Actium, the first composed just before, the ninth immediately after, the victory of Octavian. The first does not present Horace in a particularly pleasant light. Maecenas is departing, presumably on a dangerous mission (generally taken to be the campaign leading to Actium), and he does not plan to take his literary dependents with him. Horace rather extravagantly protests that he will go, for he must be near Maecenas in danger. But he insists overmuch that it is not for mercenary reasons that he would go, and more than a third of the epode is occupied with the assurance that Maecenas has already given him ample rewards and that he desires no more. It is a somewhat formal composition with several Catullan reminiscences and entirely without the characteristic tone of iambic verse.

The ninth epode has much more spontaneous fire. Six lines each, at the beginning and end, call on Maecenas for a celebration in his palace of the battle of Actium. They feature a rather reckless drinking party, which befits the situation. Within this framework, largely in exclamatory phrases, certainly in lyric rather than iambic spirit, sounds the battle and the victory. Literary allusions and reminiscence are forgotten. It is the younger Horace who speaks, but in the manner of his later maturity.

One epode is left for consideration, the thirteenth, a winter piece which might well be one of Horace's later lyrics. The stormy weather is welcomed by the poet as sound reason for a happy gathering of friends, forgetful of all troubles and following the advice of Chiron to Achilles. With this advice the poem trails to a finish in the manner of some of Horace's best odes.

Foul weather lowers and hides the heaven above
While rain and snow bring Jupiter to earth.
The sea, the woods resound with Thracian blasts:
Come, seize a moment from the day, my friends,
While yet 'tis seemly and our youth is strong
Without the cloud of age. Bring out the wine
That knew my friend Torquatus' consulship.
No serious talk be here: the kindlier gods
Perchance may solve our woes. The present calls
For spikenard and Cyllene's lyre to soothe
Our breasts and free us of corroding cares.
So sang the noble Chiron to his ward:
"Spirit unconquered, mortal though goddess-born,
Thy fate, the land of great Assaracus,
Coursed by Scamander's stream and Simois,
Whence the gray Fates, weaving their changeless web,
Shall never bring thee home. So, while thou mayst,
Banish each threatening ill with wine and song,
The saving solace of life's grim despair.

It is not easy to find in Horace's early ventures, the satires and the epodes, any general hostility to the new poets. He was certainly not averse to variety. He adopted the traditional forms of satire and iambic but, within the general categories, he experimented with all sorts of types: the propempticon, topical verse, elegiac, lyric, pastoral. He was not, like the young Vergil, strictly imitative of any of them and he evidently came to the conclusion that, in line with his strong preference for the older Greek poets, he did not like the complaining elegy, the smart epigram, or the learned epyllion.

[131]

These he would leave gladly to the grammatici, whom at the same time he was abandoning to their frugal living while he felt his way into the circle of the favored. By the time he was coming to be at ease in his new environment and enjoying the comfort of the Sabine farm, he had found his own medium of poetic expression and was on his way to being the lyric voice of Augustan Rome.

THE ODES · It was in 30 B.C. that Horace published his second book of *Satires* and turned definitely to the writing of lyric verse. That was the year in which Vergil finished the *Georgics* and began his long struggle with the *Aeneid*. The Battle of Actium had gotten rid of Antony and Cleopatra the year before, but Octavian did not return to Rome until 29. The Horace of the *Odes* is of course the same man as the Horace of the *Satires* and *Epodes* but a little more mature, much more sure of himself, more independent, more secure and settled, socially, economically, and politically. He, like Vergil, is prepared to forget the revolutionary past and to join in hearty support of the new dictator, whose platform, already hinted at, was to be reconciliation and peace.

But he is the same Horace, always interested in creating something new. When, in 23 B.C., he published in one volume the first three books of *Odes*, the first nine poems were in nine different meters and as varied in subject matter as in form. In a sense they are a preview of the collection as a whole, containing the poet's acknowledgment of Maecenas as his patron, his formal and patriotic tribute to Augustus, a less formal one to his friend, Vergil, and, with these, lighter poems of life and love, full of laughter and tears and with a delicate touch, the poet's own mature philosophy of life. All this was of real concern to Horace, but primarily as a lyric poet. Of this he leaves no doubt in the introductory ode.

The first ode is definitely transitional as well as introductory. Unlike the rest, it is written not in stanzas but in a continuous series of asclepiads, a meter used by him only here and in the final ode of Book III, an envoi to the volume. It contains his dedication of the collection to Maecenas, a curiously slight dedication, for it consists merely of the address in the first two lines and a second address in the last two.

> Maecenas, scion of royal stock, to me
> A bulwark and a cherished source of pride.

> .   .   .

> So, if you'll count me with the lyric bards,
> My uplifted head shall strike the very stars.
>
> (I.1–2, 35–36)

Both pairs are detachable from the poem itself and seem almost like an afterthought, for the ode is artistically complete without them and the *quodsi* of the next to final line is prosaic, a favorite word with Cicero for introducing the summary of an argument. This does not indicate any lack of respect for Maecenas. He had been amply praised and thanked in the *Satires,* and he and Horace were now on a basis of intimate friendship as evidenced by many a warm personal ode in the volume now dedicated to him.

Our interest for the moment is not in this dedication but in the poem to which it is attached and in its implications with regard to the volume which it introduces. It begins abruptly, like so many of the satires: "Some men the racecourse thrills." Eight types of mankind are indicated by a concise characterization of their chief concerns in life: the politically ambitious, the devoted farmer, the merchant, the military hero, and so on. At line 29 comes the abrupt and all-important contrast to which these characterizations have been leading.

> For *me* the ivy which rewards the brow
> Of poets uplifts me till I walk a god.
> For me the cool grove and the tripping dance
> Of nymphs and satyrs purge me of the world
> If but Euterpe silence not her pipes
> Nor Polyhymnia still her Lesbian lute.
>
> (I.1.29–34)

If the ode had been written in hexameters and expanded with

dramtic setting, with homely illustration and urbane wit, we would have had another typical Horatian satire. But it is not. The metrical form is simple but it is traditionally lyric. Horace did not use it again save for the concluding ode of the volume, a short ode, rich in poetic figure and phraseology, expressing his proud claim to have accomplished what was only a hope in the opening ode. He had become a lyric poet.

The meter of these two odes is not really lyric in Horace's strict use of the word. To him lyric poetry was first and foremost the poetry of Alcaeus and Sappho. This was the Aeolian song which he subdued to Roman numbers. It was basically stanzaic and, in spite of two experiments by Catullus, Horace was justified (granted his definition) in considering himself the first lyric poet of Rome. Apart from the meter, however, the introductory poem gives ample indication of the lyric impulse behind the odes to which it is an introduction. Each favorite occupation is indicated by a brief characterization, not a description but a suggestive list of concrete details that make vivid the quality of the occupation. The soldier, for instance, and the hunter:

> Many there be to whom the camp life calls,
> The blare of trumpet and the bugle blast,
> And war, hated of mothers. Under an icy Jove
> The hunter stays, forgetful of his wife,
> If once the deer be raised by faithful hound.
>
> (I.1.23–27)

The Olympic contests are represented by the dust raised by the chariots, the hot axles, the palm of victory; and politics by the fickle populace and the triple honors. Such phrases as *evehit ad deos* (exalts to the gods), *trabe Cypria* (Cyprian barque), *bellaque matribus / detestata* (war loathed by mothers), and *sub Iove frigido* (under icy Jove) are notable but hardly conspicuous in a poem nearly every line of which is marked by imaginative suggestion. It is so that Horace declares his departure from satire and his entry into the ranks of the lyric poets.

Two more details are to be noted in this first ode. The return to himself in the lines which present his own ideal indicates that his lyrics are to be personal: he is going to avail himself of the door opened by Catullus and the new poets. But, just as clearly, he hints at the difference which separates him from the neoterics: it is the Lesbian lute to which he aspires. His models are to be the lyric poets of the earlier, classic Greece, not the scholar poets of Alexandria. At first glance, the *Myrtoan* Sea, the *Cyprian* barque, or the *Icarian* waves may seem a trifle academic, but they were not so to the informed Roman reader. To him the stories of sudden marine disaster were wholly familiar, as was the wealth of Attalus, which yielded the phrase "on Attalid terms," and its suggestions. Finally, the pictures are thoroughly Roman and contemporary. Even if the Olympic victory does offer a passing bow to Pindar, it is in reality won on the dusty course of the Roman circus.

The Horace of the *Odes* is, then, the same man as the Horace of the *Satires*. But he has resigned something of his rebellious quarrel with life. Philosophically he has reacted both from the superficial Stoicism of Roman proverbs and also from the superficial Epicureanism of the younger intellectuals to turn toward an eclecticism more nearly allied to serious orthodox Stoicism. But always, it must never be forgotten, he is poet first and philosopher afterwards. From this conflict arises some of the perplexity engendered by Ode I.34.

A careless and infrequent worshiper,
I scorned the gods to wander willfully
The way of mad philosophy till now
Perforce I trim my sails, retrace my course.
For Jupiter, who with his flashing fire
Ever disrupts the clouds, has driven now
Through cloudless blue of heaven his thundering team
And that swift chariot whose passage shakes
The sullen earth, the wandering streams, the Styx,
The Atlantic Sea, and horrid Taenarus.

He can bring down the mighty from their seats,
Exalt the lowly. Fortune, at his behest,
Rapacious ever, on shrill wing, removes
The kingly crown to place it where she will.

The poem will always arouse argument but, whatever the bolt
from the blue, it was enough to convince Horace that the
philosophy of crass materialism was not for him. From politics, too, after bitter experience, he was content to withdraw
to the harbor of peace and poetry.

> Ship of mine, new tempests breaking
>   Soon will bear thee back to sea;
> Quickly now, all else forsaking,
>   Seize the harbor valiantly.
>
> Seest thou not thine oarage shattered,
>   Masts dismantled, canvas torn?
> Scarce the quivering hull, wave-battered,
>   Lifts toward heaven its wreck forlorn.
>
> Rigging gone, by gods forsaken,
>   What avails thy Pontic pride?
> Never sailor more mistaken:
>   Painted poops no safety hide.
>
> Once the source of all my bitter
>   Torture o'er the storm-swept seas,
> Still my care, forget the glitter
>   Of the gleaming Cyclades.   (I.14)

I am aware that this interpretation of the poem is far from
being generally accepted. But the traditional belief that
Horace is addressing the ship of state misrepresents the Horace
of the *Odes*. At a much earlier stage of his experience he
might have pictured the state as a battered wreck, but not after
Actium and his own wholehearted acceptance of the new regime. He could, however, with complete propriety, recall his
own disastrous experiment in the storm of war and warn himself against any repetition of such an error of enthusiasm. The

figure of the ship of state was of course not unfamiliar but much less common than the figure of the ship of life with its harbor of peace, philosophy, old age, or death. Two quotations will suffice to indicate that Horace readily turned to the ship as a symbol of his own life. The first is *Odes* III.29.57–64.

> Not mine, if groans the mast 'neath Afric blasts,
> To turn to whining prayers or deal in vows
> To save my Tyrian wares and Cyprian
> From adding to the wealth of Ocean's greed.
> Nay, safe within my humble little craft,
> The kindly breeze and Pollux, kindly twin,
> Shall bear me safely through the Aegean storms.

The second was written near the end of his days when, as the accepted poet laureate of Rome, he still thought of his life as a voyage (*Epistles.* II.2.199–204).

> Whether my ship be great or small, I'll sail
> The selfsame character: I may not voyage
> With swelling sail before a favoring breeze
> But I fare not through life with adverse winds,
> In strength, in mind, in virtue, rank, and wealth
> The last among the foremost, still in front
> Of them who close the rear.

The Horace of 30 B.C. was, then, a man conditioned by experience to enjoy a life of moderate comfort undisturbed by ambition, passion, or greed for wealth. The golden mean was for him not a mere happy phrase but a realized fact. He expresses his own state of mind in one of his few intimate personal revelations, I.31. It would seem to have been written when Horace had gone home to his Sabine farm after the great day of celebration when Augustus dedicated the temple of Apollo, his monument to culture. The pomp and ceremony undoubtedly included a public and official prayer for the greater glory of Rome. Horace, at peace again in his beloved hills, makes his own prayer to the god of light and song.

What is *my* prayer? What can Apollo give
　　Now to his bard that pours
Libation from his simple bowl? To live
　　Mid rich Sardinian stores?

Nay, nor to own the herds Calabria breeds
　　Nor India's cherished gold
Nor that fair land where silent Liris leads
　　By many a quiet fold.

(Let him who will prune the Calenian vine,
　　Proud Fortune's child,
Or from rare goblets drain the rarer wine,
　　On whom the gods have smiled.

For surely he has won the smile of Fate
　　Who, undismayed, each year
Braves the Atlantic. Mine be the simple state
　　That knows no haunting fear.)

Grant me contentment; child of Leto, give
　　Sound mind and body whole
And, with the ripening years, let me still live
　　With music in my soul.

When Horace bade himself avoid the gleaming Cyclades
and make for the peaceful harbor, he was in part applying
to himself his familiar and kindly irony, in part generalizing
a personal theme into a more universal philosophy. It was
pointless indeed for him, the freedman's son, the ex-clerk, to
renounce a life of political glory and danger. His withdrawal
from politics is merely a dedication to a life of poetry and
philosophy with a renunciation of those misguided theories
and enthusiasms of youth which had proved so nearly fatal.
He did not renounce his poet's privilege of supporting the new
regime of Augustus and so serving the state, but, whether he
was writing to please Maecenas or to satisfy his own changing
moods, it was not as an active performer in the ranks but as
the servant and spokesman of the Muse.

Both his early enthusiasm and his sincere change of heart

are quite understandable. Given a father proud of his newly acquired citizenship and ambitious for his son's success, enthusiasm may be taken for granted. Most of the father's life and the formative years of the boy's were spent in a remote village where the old beliefs and customs were undoubtedly less disturbed by civil conflicts than at Rome and where the Republic was still a name to conjure with. The traditional concept of sturdy Roman solidarity that Horace learned from his father had little in common with the degenerate state that was already crumbling under the impact of corruption and revolution. But, to the simple folk of Venusia, the political, social, and economic forces which made the situation possible were utterly remote. The concrete fact which stood out clearly was that one man, Julius Caesar, had defied the rule of senate and people to seize the power which they associated with the traditionally hated name of king. So, when Brutus' call reached Horace, aloof at his studies in Athens, he responded with wholehearted enthusiasm. The results were appalling. With the failure of the Republican cause, Horace was stranded. Left to his own devices, a man of his intelligence must have realized that the side on which he had been fighting did not represent with complete integrity the ideals in which he believed. New friends, above his own station in life and far more experienced, must have prepared his mind for new hopes. Augustus, when he had eliminated all opposition, showed extraordinary wisdom in presenting a platform which would make it easy for one from the losing side to join the new movement. The platform proposed the restoration, as far as possible, of republican forms of government, the revival of agricultural Italy, the restoration of traditional religion and morals and, above all, the establishment of peace and security. To such a program Horace could subscribe with sincerity and enthusiasm.

Furthermore, men of letters were to be given an honorable place in the new regime, their role, to spread the gospel of toleration, their reward, ample recognition and support. The kindly interpretation of Horace's response is that he was grateful for his timely rescue, that he was sincere in his allegiance, and that he liked his new friends better than the clerks in the guild of scribes. A less charitable view makes the poet a sycophant and mere social climber. Everything in his behavior through life makes the second view untenable. He had more than a trace of snobbery and he overidealized his princeps, but he never forfeited his independent spirit or his robust self-respect.

After the dedicatory poem, Horace presents what is almost a program: nine poems displaying the eight metrical schemes which appear almost exclusively in the volume and embracing the variety of content which characterizes it. That he intended these odes to stand as a sample group is indicated first by the succession of eight different meters and second by the fact that the first and last of the nine are not merely the only two in the same meter (Sapphic stanzas) but also by the relation of the two. The first, a tribute to Augustus, leads up to the presentation of the princeps as Mercury in human guise; the last is a graceful hymn to Mercury, the god beloved of all the gods. These are formal productions. The tribute to Augustus, while it expresses by implication Horace's renunciation of his early opposition and his declaration of allegiance to the new regime, has the rhetorical ring of a public ode. The hymn to Mercury, a study of Alcaeus, is the simpler tribute of a lyric poet to the patron of the humanities.

The intervening odes cover the range of Horace's muse from semiformal and strictly serious to light and almost frivolous personal poems. The persons addressed are as far apart as Augustus and Lyde or Thaliarchus. In the really formal poems and in some that might be called semiformal, Horace goes back to the early Greek poets Pindar and Bacchylides, especially the former. In these odes there is nothing to suggest even remotely the Alexandrians or the neoterics. The old insistence on virtue and religion and on the fundamental tenets of Stoicism are strongly in evidence, and the tone is one of intense but dignified patriotism. At first, Horace assumed a certain apologetic diffidence when he approached the more elevated style. In his address to Pollio (II.1), as his enthusiasm grows and his style becomes heroic, he checks himself with a deprecatory smile.

> What ocean or what river has not seen
> Our grievous warfare? What far distant sea
> Is not discolored with our Daunian blood?
> What shores know not our carnage?

> But stay, my headstrong Muse, leave not thy trifles
> To sound the phrases of the Cean dirge.
> With me, within Dione's grotto here,
> Strike measures of a lighter vein.   (II.1.33–40)

But by the time he wrote the so-called Public Odes (III.1–6) he was full of confidence:

> I scorn the common herd and warn them hence.
> Be silent all. Songs never heard before,
> Priest of the Muses, I now sing for all
> Our youths and maidens.

These odes form a very definite group within the collection. Horace made a practice throughout the three books of separating poems in one meter from each other by poems in a different meter. This practice he rarely varied, and then with the obvious purpose of showing a close relation between the poems in the same meter. The six public odes are all in alcaic stanzas. Furthermore, except for numbers five and six, there is a careful continuity which joins ode to ode. As a group they form a continuous and powerful defense of Augustus' policies and an appeal to the younger generation to return to the integrity of earlier days. After expounding the futility of luxury he pleads for the validity of strength and justice, intellectual power, and loyalty. The sixth ode is not closely welded to its predecessor. It gives almost the impression of having been written at an earlier date and then utilized as a competent summary of the group of odes. It sums up and concludes the appeal but in a furiously pessimistic tone. This is not a wholly fair statement of the case. It needs amplification.

Carried away by his magnificent picture of Regulus calmly departing to meet his death in Carthage, Horace closed the fifth ode on a note of deep tranquillity.

> Yet even so,
> He pushed aside his kinsfolk and the press
> Of commoners that barred his way and passed
> As though, the business of his clients done,
> The case decided, he were going home
> At evening to his loved Venafran farm.   (III.5.50–55)

The lyric poet has for the moment relaxed the tension of the patriotic ode but only to return to his public function with the trumpet blast of the sixth and final poem.

> Crimes of our fathers shall be visited
> On you, my Romans, till you build again
> The crumbling temples of your gods and purge
> Their statues of the grimy soil of time.   (III.6.1–4)

Augustus' building program is made symbolic of a true and more extensive reformation.

> Because you walked humbly before your gods
> You hold your empire. So it began and so
> Must be again. The gods neglected bring
> Disaster manifold to suffering Rome.   (III.6.5–8)

And so he develops this theme, which opened the whole series, the inescapable punishment of the guilt of a decadent state that has all but destroyed the Rome of a glorious past. And he brings this to the terrifying conclusion of the final stanza.

> What is there that our years have not debased?
> Our fathers' age, worse than our grandsires' day,
> Produced us baser yet who now bring forth
> A generation fouler than ourselves.   (III.6.45–48)

So speaks Horace the public orator. We may prefer the relaxed conclusion of the fifth ode, more in the character of the private Horace, but it is not a question of what *we* may like; what we are looking for is *his* way of writing, of which this is one definite type. The whole series breathes an intensity of patriotic fervor wholly alien to the neoteric poets and the Alexandrian egoists.

It is of interest to note that the last two odes of Book II, directly preceding this group of formal, patriotic poems, are both in alcaic stanzas, suggesting a possible connection with the group. They have been thought to be introductory, or rather preparatory, to the public odes. This theory, if we keep in mind the fact that these two odes are written in a lighter vein and are prevented by the book division from being formally united with the public odes, is convincing and enlightening. Ode II.19 tells how the poet came upon Bacchus while strolling through the woods and how the god's exalted inspiration was to some extent imparted to him. Ode II.20 is a flight of fancy in which the poet is transformed (almost too literally) into a swan which traverses the world on strong new wings. Elsewhere (Ode IV.2) Horace, in eulogizing Pindar, calls him the Dircaean swan (as opposed to himself, the Matinian bee, modest and busy). It is tempting to believe that for the moment, while writing the public odes, he conceived of himself as the Roman Pindar and that the concluding odes of Book II fancifully prepare the reader for this assumption. At any rate we can be sure that Pindar was his model.

Horace's formal poetry reaches its climax in the "Saecular Hymn," the official ode for Augustus' great celebration of the founding of Rome. The assignment to write this hymn was equivalent to an appointment as poet laureate and was the source of great pride and satisfaction to Horace. The only time that he ever mentions his own name is in the ode that tells of training the boys and girls whose future pride would be that they were in the choir which sang the hymn by the poet Horace.

Horace was sincere in his admiration of Pindar, who represented for him the higher range of poetry, and in this admiration may well be found part of the ground for his scorn of the neoteric poets. Calvus and Catullus had had no national ideal to support. Personal ambition and civil war had destroyed the old Roman Republic. Their successors in Horace's day had not developed his enthusiasm for the Augustan regime and continued what was to him a frivolous line of poetic creation. They, like Catullus, were therefore akin to the Alexandrian poets and not to Pindar.

Horace was not only or even primarily the public spokesman. He gave his highest respect to the Pindaric ode, but his heart's devotion belonged to the Lesbian muse, and his most congenial undertaking was to develop seriously a line of lyric verse of which he was justly proud and for which he is chiefly loved today. The private odes not only far outnumber the public but were the basis for his own claim to immortality.

Horace was by no means unacquainted with the poems of Catullus. He borrowed from them unusual words and even phrases—from the two stanzaic poems and especially from "Peleus and Thetis." It is in one of his poems generally held to be an early creation that conclusive evidence appears that he had studied with care the epyllion of Catullus. In his propempticon to Galatea (III.27) he incorporates the story of Europa. As in "Peleus and Thetis," the narrative is condensed and rapid, and the lament of the heroine is the core of the poem. That Catullus was his model is clear from the fact that the tale of Europa diverges sharply from the traditional story and conforms closely with that of Ariadne in "Peleus and Thetis" and is characterized throughout by verbal echoes of that poem. The ode is a tour de force, for, while it is in the Alexandrian form of a propempticon, it is in reality an adaptation of the epyllion to the lyric. It was not very satisfactory and, although he experimented with the same idea in telling the story of Helen (I.15) and also that of Hypermnestra (III.11), he did not find the form appealing. He left the epyllion to the neoterics and devoted himself to less artificial types. He did experiment, and more successfully, with the pure propempticon (I.3) and very warily with the elegy (III.10), using the conceit of the closed door and the excluded lover, but he never again approached so closely the Catullan spirit as in the Galatea-Europa ode.

Horace was as eager as Catullus to experiment and as avid of variety, but his character and his whole life interest led him to the writing of poems of a deeper understanding and, with his own concern for a working philosophy of life, he could not avoid the conclusion that the new poets were self-centered and superficial. Perhaps he underestimated what they had done to free the poet from the dead hand of tradition and perhaps he undervalued the emotional depth and artistic integrity of Catullus. It would be nearer the truth, I think, to say that he really extended the scope of the earlier movement. He recalled the poetic explorers to earlier and more profound models and added depth and understanding to their enthusiastic brilliance.

Among the sample poems at the beginning of Book I, Horace's favorite metrical scheme, the alcaic stanza, is represented by one of his best-known odes, a winter piece in the setting of the Sabine hills.

> See how white Soracte stands
>   Bright with drifted snow,
> How the trees are bending down
>   And the frozen streams scarce flow,
>
> Out with the cold, pile high the logs,
>   Fetch a jar of wine;
> Pour me, Thaliarchus, straight
>   Sabine, vintage twenty-nine.
>
> Leave to the gods all else beside:
>   When they stay the gale,
> Roaring across the sea, no more
>   Ash and cypress madly flail.
>
> Ask no more tomorrow's lot:
>   Each day Fate may bring
> Count as gain, nor scorn today
>   Eager youth's tempestuous fling.
>
> Ere old age comes shaking locks
>   Grimly gray and few

Seize the joys of street and square
　And the whispering rendezvous.

Go now where her laughter calls,
　Craftily concealed:
Seize the prize—her fingers strive
　Only that they long to yield.　　　　　　　(I.9)

A fragment of Alcaeus betrays the fact that Horace borrowed at least the opening lines from his Greek predecessor,
but he has made completely Roman both the setting and the
resulting thought. Especially Horatian is the scheme of the
poem as a whole. The poet has discarded the idea of a framework so artistically developed by Catullus and which he
himself used in some of his more formal odes. Here the process
is in sharp contrast: from a picture of winter in the country,
the first reaction is withdrawal to the fireside scene made cheerful by the best of country wine. Then follows the second reaction, which brings in the touch of homely philosophy,
specific in statement but general in application. Leave to the
gods the future which you cannot control; enjoy the days of
your youth while you can. His nostalgic dreaming transports
the poet from the Sabine farm to the Campus Martius and the
street corners of Rome. There he leaves the listener to carry
on the dream.

This is a favorite technique with Horace and wholly characteristic of a frequent mood. Winter leads him to reveries of
summer joys in town and, just as perversely, spring inspires the
more melancholy muse.

Spent is the snow: the grass, the leaves grow green;
The season changes and the brooks spill over:
The nymphs in naked choir welcome their queen.

The turning year, the hour that speeds the day
Warn you that life is short. Spring is soon gone
And summer too shall yield to winter's sway.

Yet *seasons* come again; when *we* are sped
To where Aeneas dwells, all, all is over
And we are dust and shades among the dead.

Who knows if kindly gods shall add one hour
To this day's sun? Then to your own soul's weal
Give what your heir tomorrow might devour.

Once your life's sun has set, the judge of Death
Shall speak; nor race nor eloquence nor faith
Can then avail to ransom life's lost breath.

Not Dian's self could save Hippolytus
Nor Theseus from the dreary underworld
Lead back to life his loved Pirithous.   (IV.7)

Even more striking perhaps, because of the blatant contrast between beginning and end, is the poem (II.13), which takes its start from a casual accident in Horace's country life, his narrow escape from being killed by a falling tree. The incident is made vivid by the angry reaction of the near-victim expressed in strong and unpolished language. The first outburst subsides into a bit of personal philosophizing which merges into a more general moral revery and ends like the spring song with a richly poetic allusion to well-known mythological parallels.

It sure was on a Friday
    He brought you from the wood
Who reared you, tree untidy,
    To curse my neighborhood.

That man would choke his father
    And smear the family stoop
With blood of guests, or rather
    Put poison in their soup

Who, in my family garden,
    Sowed you, foul spawn of hell
That, without price or pardon,
    So near my poor head fell.

[147]

How little in life's hurry
　　We learn what to eschew.
The sailor dreads the flurry
　　Of wind that foils the crew,

The soldier dreads the arrow,
　　The Parthian's bow, while *he*
Fears in his very marrow
　　The Roman infantry.

Yet not the storm at morning
　　Nor long expected fight:
Some fate with never a warning
　　Shall bring the endless night.

How near I came to viewing
　　Thy realm, Proserpine,
Or Aeacus renewing
　　Old judgments endlessly;

The regions of the fearless,
　　The thronging maidens mute
Round Sappho ever peerless
　　Tuning her Lesbian lute;

Or thee, thou mightier master,
　　Sounding with trumpet blast
Perils of old disaster,
　　Torn sails and crashing mast.

The shades fill every hollow
　　Of hell to hear those twain
But most intent they follow
　　Alcaeus' battle strain.

Why not, when at his playing
　　Grim Cerberus amazed
Dropped ears and ceased from baying,
　　While even the Furies gazed

In silent wonder; hearing,
    Prometheus lost his pain;
Orion, homeward veering,
    No longer scoured the plain.

Apart from the overall technique of I.9, with its snow-clad
Soracte, there are in it two other elements which are constantly
present in Horace's personal poetry, his carpe diem philosophy
and his devotion to the country. The latter goes so far as to
inspire poems of a pastoral vein reminiscent of the Vergilian
atmosphere. Some of these are purely incidental odes untinged
by any philosophic thought, such as the much translated
address to Pyrrha.

What scrawny boy bedecked with roses
Whose smell humiliates our noses
Is wooing you, my peerless Pyrrha,
    While you consult your favorite mirror?

For whom that beauty-parlor job?
    Simple? Indeed, at twenty bob!
He'll weep his eyes out when he knows
    The fickle way your fancy goes.

For now the simple idiot's singing
    Of you, pure joy and sunshine bringing,
So true and faithful. Bah, poor fool
    That never studied in your school.

Poseidon's temple on its wall
    Displays the trophies of *my* fall;
I sailed those seas and evermore
    I'll watch in safety from the shore.   (I.5)

Perhaps more obviously pastoral, if less vivacious, is the
ode to Lyde (III.28), which emphasizes its consistent country
outlook by a suggestion, in the closing lines, of the rougher
love-making of the city. More simple on the surface, yet
notable for its symmetry of composition, is the ode to Phidyle.

If, at the rising of the sun, thou'lt lift
Thy hands to heaven, honest Phidyle,
And, offering fruits of simple rustic thrift,
    Shalt bend the knee,

Thy vines shall never know the Afric pest
Nor rust consume thy crops; no autumn breath
Of fever waft into thy sheltered nest
    Untimely death.

The sacrificial victim in the grove
Of Algidus or by the Alban flood
That through the oaks and ilex thickets roves
    Shall give his blood

To stain a wealthier altar; not for thee
The blood of victims, kindlier gods are thine
That welcome myrtle and the rosemary
    To wreathe their shrine.

Bring thou clean hands, thy simple gifts to raise
And all earth's wealth shall ne'er its lord exalt
More than thy offering of homely maize
    Or simple salt.   (III.23)

Perhaps the most successful wedding of simplicity and art
is found in III.28, an invitation to a rustic celebration.

Neptune's festive day is come.
    Lyde, fetch the bottle out,
Lock the door to Stoics glum:
    Here's no place for wisdom's doubt.

Look, the sun is high above
    And the hour expectant stays:
Hurry now and bring me, love,
    Vintage of the rare old days.

Hymns to Neptune I will raise
    And his sea-nymphs chorusing;
You shall sound Diana's praise,
    With your lyre to Leto sing.

Then, when sighs the evening breeze,
    Sing we both to her who sails
Through the gleaming Cyclades,
    Swan-borne to her Paphian vales.

Darkness falls—our last notes sound
    Unto Night and solace found.

The odes chosen for illustration represent but a very small part of the variety of Horace's lyrics. They show, however, what he was striving for. He would make wholly Roman his adaptation of the best Greek lyric. In his artistic integrity he would avoid what was to him specious in the later Greek, in some of the earlier Latin and in the work of some of his contemporaries. But with all his generous ideals he was sufficiently human to be proud of his accomplishment and to hope for a closer approach to immortality than Catullus prayed for.

I have reared a monument to outlive bronze,
More lofty than the royal pyramids,
Which no corroding rain nor Aquilo's
Wild rage can shatter, no, nor countless years
In long procession nor the seasons' flight.
I shall not wholly die: some part of me
Shall outwit Libitina. I shall grow
Still fresh in fame of days to come so long
As Rome's high priest shall mount the Capitol
With silent Vestal. Men shall speak my name
Where sounds the violent Aufidus and where
Waterless Daunus reigned o'er a rustic folk,
Shall tell how, once so lowly, mighty now,
I was the first to lure the Aeolian song
To Italian measures. So, Melpomene,
Assume the pride well earned and graciously
Crown now my locks with Delphi's laurel wreath.

(III.30)

Something has already been said about the casual grouping of poems throughout the volume of *Odes*. A word should be added about the more general arrangement of the odes in the volume as a whole. No one has ever satisfactorily explained the arrangement of poems in Catullus' volume, beyond pointing out the obvious fact that short poems in miscellaneous meters come first, then the long poems and finally short poems in elegiac couplets. This might be the result of a grammarian's handling of the book; it does not suggest arrangement by the poet himself. The introductory poem to Cornelius Nepos does indicate that Catullus himself published either all or some part of the collection. In any case, the conclusion must be that he cared little for artistic arrangement.

Quite the reverse is true of Horace's edition of Books I-III of the *Odes*. The opening ode, with its dedication to Maecenas and its transitional character marking the poet's advance from satires to odes, and the concluding ode in the same meter (never used elsewhere in the volume) expressing the poet's triumph in establishing the Roman lyric, are obvious indications of preparation for publication by the poet himself. It is this fact which, in the first place, justifies a search for some principle of arrangement within the book.

It has long been known that Horace intended a certain formal pattern in the arrangement of odes in his published volume. For example, it has always been recognized that the first six odes of Book III form a unit in subject as well as meter and that the first nine odes of Book I, each in a different meter, might well be looked on as a group of metrical samples. But many scholars go further and see in the first twelve odes of Book II a systematically arranged unit, even going as far as to note that in the three-book volume there are thirty-eight odes preceding this group and thirty-eight following it. This seems a trifle strained, but it is true that the twelve odes do form a roughly symmetrical group. A poem to Pollio opens the series and one to Maecenas closes it. Both are men of high standing in the state, and both are prominent literary patrons. The two odes express in different ways Horace's devotion to lyric poetry while paying tribute to the historical prose of the recipients, but they are wholly unlike in tone and expression, the one to Pollio much more formal, that to Maecenas more intimate and friendly. Between these two odes are five pairs of lighter lyrics, the first of each pair in Sapphics, the second in alcaics. The central pair (Odes 6 and 7) are friendly personal poems to intimates. These are preceded and followed by pairs of amatory odes (4, 5 and 8, 9) and these by poems of philosophic revery (2, 3 and 10, 11), all of these addressed to friends not particularly intimate and on the edge of officialdom. A chiastic arrangement of the love poems (4 and 9 deal with the loves of others, 5 and 8 with Horace's) adds a further touch of conscious artificiality.

There are other similar groupings to be found in all three books but they are never obstrusive or wholly convincing. Far more obvious is an effort to prevent monotony by persistent variety in both form and content. The same meter is used in consecutive poems only to indicate some inner relation. Serious poems of a semipublic character to men of importance are regularly separated by odes in lighter vein to lesser friends of the poet. If two adjacent poems deal in general with the same philosophic thought, they do so in widely different manner and tone. Variety without disorder would seem to be the rule or, perhaps better, reasonable order with great flexibility.

For an understanding of the poet, an analysis of the types of lyric which interested him is more important than the arrangement of poems within the volume. Where the poems of Catullus suggested a division into lengthy and elaborate literary types on the one hand and, on the other, short, simpler types, with sharp divisions in the second group between passionate love poems, vindictive attacks, and amusing or satiric incidental poems, Horace's collection divides itself more obviously into public and private poetry. The public odes have either literary or political content, the private ones are largely love poems or poems with a philosophical content. Horace would seem to have been equally interested in all of these but rarely roused to strong enthusiasm, as was Catullus almost continu-

ously. He was as poised and philosophical as Catullus was
volatile and passionate. What he says of his own attitude
toward love and the lover applies in a general way to all of
his writing.

> *I* sing of banquets and the embattled youths,
> Of furious maidens, nails pared for the fray,
> Immune, I sing—or if not quite immune,
> > Warmed by a tepid flame.   (I.6.17–21)

The fourth book of *Odes* was published some ten years
after the appearance of Books I-III. Horace had in the mean-
time been given the official recognition of appointment to
write the hymn for the great saecular celebration of 17 B.C.,
commemorating the founding of Rome. His position was
secure in spite of the fall from favor of his great friend and
patron. For Maecenas had incurred the wrath of Augustus
and had disappeared from the scene in the interval. Horace
was by no means an old man but he assumes the pose of
age at the very outset of the book. Throughout he speaks
with the authority of age and security. He frequently looks
back upon his earlier days and comments freely on his own
literary production. Book IV is therefore particularly worth
some special attention for the understanding of Horace's
outlook and methods.

Maecenas' departure from the circle of Augustus is immediately felt in the first poem of the volume. In the *Satires,
Epodes,* and *Odes* I-III, Maecenas is directly addressed in
the opening lines, making clear the dedication of these books
to him. It might be expected that, if Horace were to remain,
as he did, in the favored circle, the new volume would be
dedicated to Augustus. We have the testimony of Suetonius
that Augustus wished to have Horace as his intimate secretary
and urged Maecenas to transfer him "from his parasitic table
to the royal board," that Horace excused himself on the
grounds of health, and that Augustus did not as a result abate
in any way his friendship for the poet. It is not, however,
Augustus but Venus who receives the dedication in the first

ode, Venus who was indeed the mythical ancestress of Augustus but whose more familiar role was that of the inspirer of the Lydian lyre. It is to her as such that the dedication is addressed. But this is not the whole story. On further inspection it appears that the first three odes are in fact a composite dedication. One and three are in the same asclepiad stanzas, used only here in Book IV and somewhat sparingly elsewhere, regularly in love lyrics but also in a poem to Vergil and in two consecutive poems intended for Augustus. Between odes one and three is placed a more elaborate renunciation of the grander poetry of epic or Pindaric quality. None of the three is addressed to Augustus, but together they comprise Horace's response to the emperor's strongly expressed wish that he publish more poems, including eulogies of the achievements of the imperial regime. Horace freely recognizes his debt to Augustus, but he will not let it be forgotten that it is the Muse of Lyric Poetry who has made it possible to discharge that debt and that if he is anyone's servant he is servant only to the Muse. It is characteristic of Horace that in deprecating his own power to write as he once wrote, or to write epic at all, he suggests Paulus Maximus as better able than himself to sing of youthful love and Antonius as a better eulogist of the emperor. Both are young protégés of Augustus. In commending them, Horace shows ample evidence of his own preeminence in both fields. And so, in reminiscence of the address to Venus in the first line of the book, the closing line of the last poem presents Augustus as the last scion of the race of Venus.

The twelve odes which constitute the book apart from the three introductory poems are arranged with greater care than appeared for the most part in the earlier publication. The first two present the achievements of Augustus, first through the campaigns of Drusus, then in his own person. Similarly, the last two hail the imperial successes, first in the victories of Tiberius, then in Augustus' own person. Thus did the poet respond to the wishes of his royal patron. The intervening poems are his more direct tribute to the Muse and to two lost friends who had made possible his friendship with Augustus.

Of these two, one (IV.12) is obviously a poem from a much earlier day, for it is an invitation to Vergil, who had died some six years before. The other is an invitation to Phidyle to come to the country to celebrate the birthday of Maecenas. This latter ode is a remarkable example of Horatian tact and loyalty. Maecenas is out of favor, but even Augustus could scarcely object to this recollection of happier days. Both poems are among Horace's finest lyrics.

The remaining poems of Book IV carry out in various ways the intimations of the introductory odes. One, addressed to Apollo, records the training of the chorus to sing the "Saecular Hymn" with the poet's proud and unique introduction of his own name. Three deal directly with the inevitability of death and with immortality derived from poetry. These are addressed to men of considerable importance in the circle of Augustus. By way of variety or contrast (one before and one after the highly poetic poems to Maecenas and Vergil) are two mediocre odes to the highly insignificant Ligurinus and Lyce. Both stress the swift passage of time. The boy is urged to gather rosebuds while he may, Lyce is scoffed at for having failed to do so.

It is possible to go further. Poems 4 and 5 and 14 and 15 are, as we have seen, formal public odes. Between these two pairs are, first, four semiformal odes addressed to Apollo and to three official acquaintances, then four private poems to intimate friends. The first four deal more or less directly with the inevitability of death and with the immortality which may be derived from poetry both by the poet and by the recipients of his verse. The second group consists of the two poems to his most loved and most distinguished intimates, now lost, Maecenas and Vergil, preceded and followed by definitely less pleasant and less important odes to two insignificant characters, Ligurinus and Lyce. The introductory odes had presented Horace as differentiating between the formal type of poem and the lighter lyric. The final poem of the book, to Augustus, forms an interesting conclusion: Phoebus forbids him to write of wars and the heroes of wars but Augustus' greatest achievement, even in war, was the reestablishment of peace and the old Roman virtues. Therefore Horace can and will sing of the line of Venus and Trojan Anchises which culminates in Augustus.

The critics have always recognized the fact that the fourth book of *Odes* has an ordered unity not apparent in the other books. This is obviously true, but it is also quite natural. Book IV was written at the emperor's request for the purpose of glorifying his regime. It is an independent publication, whereas each of the previous books composed a unit in the volume which contained Books I-III. One element which contributes to the impression of unity by developing a climax to the whole has been overlooked. The first two odes in Augustus' honor (4 and 5) are in different meters and in no marked way interrelated. In the first, the achievements of Drusus (the favorite son) are given full and generous praise. The parallel with the early Roman victories under another Claudian Nero serves to enhance the glory of Drusus without emphasizing the share of Augustus in that glory. The ode to Augustus that follows it is wholly independent and to a greater extent personal, urging the return of the emperor to Rome and ending on a lyric note. When we turn to the corresponding pair of odes with which the book reaches its climax (IV.14 and 15) we find a different situation. The two odes are in the same meter, in itself a significant indication of relationship. The first, usually spoken of as a eulogy of Tiberius for his military triumphs, pays small tribute to the elder Nero. Far more space is devoted to a direct address to Augustus, making it very clear that it was he and his wisdom which made possible the glorious victories.

One thing is very noticeable about the ode to Tiberius. It does not have the climactic conclusion of an independent public ode. There is a certain slight reminiscence of the transition between the third and fourth of the Public Odes of Book III. There the rebuke to his straying muse was divided between the two poems, here it is confined to the second. There is a feeling of incompleteness about the closing lines of 14 or, better, a resemblance to the ending of some of the private odes that leaves the reader to dream on with his own unguided imagination. Here, however, his wanderings are brought to an abrupt end if they carry on to the opening of 15. It should also be noted that there are in the fourteenth ode slight reminiscences of the final ode of Book III: the bronze memorial, immortality not only through achievement but through the written record of achievement, and the simile which features the raging Aufidus and the realm of Daunus.

The final ode (15), then, might almost be a second part of this fourteenth. As he had in a previous public ode (III.4), Horace half seriously rebukes himself for attempting the formal eulogy and proceeds to the praise of Augustus for establishing the peace which makes possible a civilized life, the poem ending *progeniem Veneris canamus*. Augustus is, to be sure, the conqueror of the western world, but he is also the descendant of Venus, the patron goddess of lyric poetry or, perhaps more broadly here, of the cultural life which Horace craved for Rome. This reference to Venus not only furnishes the climax for the imperial eulogy but characteristically serves also to lead the reader's thought back to the opening line of the book, where Venus appeared as the inspiration of Horace's poetry.

Two of the personal poems of Book IV call for more comment than I have given them—fortunately, for it would be inappropriate to leave the *Odes* with too much emphasis on the public poems which Horace wrote with skill and elegance but without the same revealing warmth which informs the personal lyrics. The twelfth ode, to Vergilius, is not only intriguing in its own right but is representative of a considerable group of poems which contain invitations to his Sabine Farm. (The farm is not named, but the introductory picture of spring is scarcely the suitable setting for an indoor party in a city apartment.)

> Now harbingers of spring that smooth the sea,
> The Thracian breezes, gently fill the sails.
> No more the fields are stiff with frost, the streams
> No longer roar, swollen with winter's snow.

That ill-starred bird that mourns for Itys' fate
Builds now her nest, herself the living shame
Of Cecrops' house, avenging evermore
The lust barbarian of the royal line.

The guardians of the well-fed sheep begin
With rustic pipes, stretched on the springing grass,
Their songs in honor of the god to whom
The flocks are dear, the dark Arcadian hills.

Vergil, the season brings a healthy thirst
But if, spoiled client of our noble youth,
You crave the Bacchic grape that Cales treads
You'll earn it with a gift of frankincense.

One little jar of scent will buy a keg
Which now is sleeping on Sulpicius' shelves,
Abundant to inspire new hope and strong
To wash away the bitterness of care.

So, if you're eager to embrace these joys
Hasten and come, your offering in your hand.
For I'm no scion of princely marble halls
To let you drain my cups without the price.

Make no delay: put off your lust for gain,
Remember while you may the funeral pyres
And mingle folly with your counsels wise.
Folly in season is a joy to man.   (IV.12)

    It is perhaps essential in the first place to show why I have
assumed that the poem is addressed to the poet Vergil (already
dead) and why it seems to me to be an early poem and a
cheerful one. Recent criticism has tended not only to question
the identity of its recipient but also to disparage its quality and
to ascribe to it a tragic tone of deep despondency (so Fraenkel,
Commager, and Collinge).
    It is a fact that we know of no other Vergilius whom

Horace would have been likely to invite to his farm, but that is perhaps not enough to warrant an ascription to the poet Vergil. However, the implications of the poem and its juxtaposition to one to Maecenas, together with the facts that these two odes are the only ones in Book IV to intimate friends and that both of these friends have been lost to Horace, one through estrangement from Augustus resulting in complete retirement, the other by death, bear out the assumption. But the poem must then be an early one, included here in memory of the poet's closest friend. And, indeed, it bears every mark of being just that. Knowing Vergil's addiction to the poetry of the new poets, to which he himself was not so wholly committed, Horace not only makes the introductory stanzas Alexandrian in their allusiveness (not to say obscurity) but also uses an extraordinary array of Catullan phrases. There is scarcely an important word in the first six lines which is not characteristically Catullan. This is quite sufficient to prepare the way for an invitation which neatly reverses the situation presented in Catullus (13) where the host furnishes the perfume, his invited guest the wine and food. To complete the literary fooling, Horace follows the Catullan reminiscences with equally obvious echoes of Vergil's own early works. Then abruptly all literary allusions stop and the invitation is realistic and down-to-earth. Spring makes us thirsty; come to my party; I have some good wine; you'll have to chip in your share; forget your busy worries and your great friends and come.

Heavy going has been made of the two obvious jibes at the recipient, "client of our noble youth" and "put off your lust for gain." But these are altogether in keeping with the literary teasing of the opening stanzas. They are charges against which Vergil was invulnerable. He did have friends among the young nobles but there is every indication that he was never a social climber and money-making did not enter into his scheme of life. Hence Horace's readiness to tease him with accusations which could not hurt his feelings, since they came from his closest friend. The touch of sentimentality at the close of the ode is not tragic but merely youthful.

The point will be even more clear, I think, if we compare
the invitation to Vergil with that immediately preceding it to
Phyllis to share with the poet his celebration of Maecenas'
birthday. (Unfortunately no agreement has ever been reached
as to the reality, the identity, or the status of the numerous
women whom Horace addressed in his odes, but the Phyllis
of this poem, whether real or vividly imagined, is at home in
the country setting, sympathetic to Horace and his farm, and
more or less of his own earlier social background.) It is an
invitation equally sincere and intimate but adapted to a less
complex and sophisticated nature than that of Vergil. The
poem required more tact, for the great patron of poetry was
now in disgrace with Augustus, at whose behest Book IV
was published. But even the princeps could not take offense at
Horace's tactful introduction of this last tribute to his friend
and former patron.

> A cask I have of good old Alban wine
> Aged for nine years; the garden, Phyllis mine,
> Has parsley for our wreathes and plentiful
>   Supply of ivy too
>
> To make your tresses dazzling fa'r; within,
> My house shines bright with polished silverware;
> The altar, decked with simple greens, invites
>   The sacrificial lamb.
>
> Each household hand is busy. Hither and yon
> Run busily together boys and girls.
> Whirling on high above the excited flames
>   Circles the sooty smoke.
>
> But, to inform you to what joys you're called,
> You come to celebrate the ides that mark
> The midway point of April, sacred month
>   Of Venus, ocean-born,
>
> A day to me more sacred, more revered
> Almost than my own birthday: from that dawn
> My loved Maecenas reckons the passing years
>   Of his life's pilgrimage.

Young Telephus, your heart's desire's obsessed
With a young maiden of a different ilk,
Sprightly and rich; she holds him tightly bound
    In welcome bonds of love.

Scorched Phaethon should chill your greedy hopes
And winged Pegasus must give you pause
Who would not brook his earth-bound cavalier,
    The chaste Bellerophon.

They warn you: seek a mate of your own worth
And, knowing well the fate of hopes too high,
Cease to aspire beyond your fate. Come then,
    Last of my cherished loves,

(For I'll not love another from this day)
And learn from me the measure you shall sing
With that dear voice of yours. Our blackest cares
    Will vanish with our song.   (IV.11)

In spite of the official necessity of winding up the volume with a compliment to Augustus and the Julian family, these two nostalgic poems to Horace's two dearest friends are the true envoi to the *Odes*.

Horace's Sabine farm has become a literary symbol for a peaceful refuge from the city's busy confusion. This is a perfectly sound conception of the small villa in the Sabine hills several miles east of Tivoli and more than twenty-five miles from Rome. But it is not a true picture if we include in it Horace himself working his kitchen garden and pruning his trees and vines. He had not a rustic farm house but a comfortable up-to-date home with a pretty patio and hot and cold baths. The work was done by a small but evidently capable staff of slaves and a resident farmer. Horace knew and liked his neighbors but he was not really one of their community: he did not live on the farm all the year round and, simple as his life there was, his very emphasis on this simplicity marks it as a self-conscious rusticity. He was always trying to lure his friends from the city to visit with him. It cannot have been wholly easy to tempt them. Even today, with paved roads and automobiles, we speak of a "trip to Tivoli," and the Sabine farm was well beyond and above Tivoli and the transportation primitive. We have no record of how many friends, if any, accepted his invitations but we do have a considerable number of the invitations themselves, made as alluring as the lyric poet could make them and always in terms to entice the confirmed city dweller.

There are some dozen odes which, by a generous interpretation, may be called invitations to the farm. No two are alike in form or tone and the recipients vary almost as widely. Of Quinctius Hirpinus we know nothing beyond the suggestions which emerge from Ode II.11. He seems to be a man of some importance seriously concerned with the national situation and especially with the military threats on the distant borders of empire. The ode is really a semiphilosophical comment by Horace on such worries, but it develops into an invitation to the farm with all the stock elements of such an invitation: the roses, the spikenard, the wine, the song, and the dissipation of cares. It combines a formal tone in the opening stanzas with considerable ease and informality in the final ones.

> The threats of war from far Cantabria
> Or Scythia's waste beyond the Adrian surge,
> Forget them now, Hirpinus, cease to fret
>   How best to use a life
>
> That asks so little. So youth's soft-cheeked bloom
> Retreats before the hoary drought of age
> That puts an end to joys of wanton love
>   And swift responsive sleep.
>
> The flowers of spring vaunt not for aye the same
> Fair bloom, the blushing moon one constant phase.
> Why then with counsels of eternity
>   Burden your finite mind?
>
> Rather beneath yon plane tree or this pine
> Let us stretch out with never a solemn thought,
> Our white locks fragrant with the rosy wreath
>   And rare Assyrian nard.

And drink the while we may. The Euheian god
Scatters consuming cares. Come quickly, boy,
Temper the fiery Falernian wine
    With water from the stream.

Call Lyde from the house, that wandering witch,
And bid her hurry with her ivory lyre,
Her hair caught up with casual unconcern
    In truly Spartan style.   (II.11)

    Ode III.21 is not technically an invitation at all. Messalla
Corvinus is coming out to the farm, and the poem is addressed
to a jar of wine which Horace has produced for the occasion,
a jar laid down in the year of the poet's birth. This establishes
a moderately intimate tone which pervades the ode, and the
reference to the days of the Republic is not unsuitable in view
of the fact that both Horace and Messalla, in spite of a wide
difference in social status, were both survivors of the old regime
who fought against the new but, after defeat, espoused with
good grace the Augustan program. Messalla is offered nothing
beyond the wine, no enticing frills, only the wine which
"brings hope to every anxious heart."

    Bottle beloved, in Manlius' consulship
    Born as I too was born, whether to joy
    Thou callest or to strife or maddening love
        Or kindly sleep,

    Whate'er the message of thy Massic wine,
    Worthy libation for a golden day,
    Come forth: Corvinus' self bids thee release
        Thy mellow draught.

    No boor is he to spurn thy precious gift
    Though versed in all the lore of Socrates:
    Even old Cato warmed his virtuous heart,
        'Tis said, with wine.

Often thou dost apply thy kindly goad
To stubborn minds, with gay Lyaeus' aid
Dost solve the cares of wise men, wakening
    Their inmost thoughts.

Thou bringest hope to every anxious heart
And, to the humble, strength and courage too,
Till he no longer fears the tyrant's power
    Or soldier's arms.

Liber shall squire thee and Venus too,
The lovely Graces with their arms entwined,
And festive lights shall shine till Phoebus come
    To rout the stars.

Something more than an invitation is the ode (III.14) which celebrates the safe return of Augustus from Spain. The opening stanzas are as solemn and formal as the so-called public odes. Then Horace turns to his own private celebration of the event at the farm, issuing an invitation to Neaera to join him there. It has something of the "stream of consciousness" quality of *Vides ut alta,* with a nostalgic touch at the close more characteristic of Book IV. The contrast between the formal public ceremony in Rome and Horace's private celebration on the farm gives its essential form to the poem, but within the framework the poet introduced the spikenard, the wreathes, the wine, and the song of his other invitations, including the haunting cares.

Hearken, ye people. Like great Hercules,
Our Caesar, who but yesterday escaped
The laurels bought with death, is come
Safe to his home from far Iberia's shore.

Now let the faithful guardian of his home
Come with her offering to the appointed gods;
Come too the sister of our glorious chief
And come ye too, with suppliant fillets decked,

Ye mothers with your daughters and your sons
So late escaped from death. And come, ye lads
And maidens newly wed. Let now no word
Of evil omen 'scape your guarded lips.

For me the day in very truth dispels
All haunting cares. I shall no longer fear
The clash and tumult or the violence
Of sudden death, while Caesar rules the world.

So go, my boy, bring out the oil and wreathes,
The jar of wine that knew the Marsian wars
If one there be surviving from the days
When wandering Spartacus ravaged the land.

And bid Neaera with her sweet-tuned voice
Bind up her fragrant tresses for the feast.
But if the keeper of her door resist,
Then come away, for with my whitening locks

My temper too is softening; I no more
Delight in quarrels or in lovers' brawls;
Time was, my hot blood would have brooked no stay,
When I was young, in Plancus' consulship.   (III.14)

So we come to three invitations to Maecenas. I.20 is the
earliest, the most formal and by far the longest. It seems as
though the two men were not yet wholly at ease together.
Horace apologizes for his simple offering but turns the apology
into a nice compliment: the wine is plain but I laid it down
the year in which you received your mighty ovation in
Pompey's theater. He then notes Maecenas' heavy responsi-
bilities in the government but reminds him that all is in the
hands of Fortune, that we are responsible only for the present.
Whereupon he develops at length his own philosophy on this
point. Only the wine and the cares to be dispersed by it are
presented; the livelier items of more intimate parties are
omitted.

[166]

Plain Sabine wine you'll drink from rustic bowl,
Wine that I bottled in its Grecian jar
And sealed myself the year the theater rang
    With wild applause

For you, my dear Maecenas, while the banks
Of your ancestral river hailed their knight
With joyous echo of resounding praise
    From Janus' mount.

Rare Caecuban and vintage from the slopes
Of Cales grace your table, my plain wine
Is stranger to Falernian vines or hills
    Of Formii.   (I.20)

Ode III.8 is much more intimate. The tone is lighter. The poem begins with the presentation of the occasion for the party: the anniversary of the day the tree (almost) fell on Horace. Then comes the invitation to wash away the cares of state with a night of drinking. No spikenard or wreathes or music girls.

What this old bachelor is doing here
On this first day of March and what the cause
Of all these flowers and incense lavish, why
These living coals piled on the living sod,

You're wondering, my learned friend adept
In both our tongues? I vowed a noble feast
And a white kid to Liber on the day
When I faced death before that falling tree.

So, as the years roll by, this festive day
Shall always break the pitch-encrusted seal
Of one more amphora laid lovingly
To absorb the smoke in Tullus' consulship.

Drink then, Maecenas, to your rescued friend
A hundred measures and keep bright the lamps

Of evening till the light of day returns:
Begone all clamor of contentious day.

Forget your public worries for the state.
The ranks of Dacian Cotiso are now
A memory, the hostile Persian hordes
Are tangled in the net of civil strife;

Our old Cantabrian foe from Spanish main
Now at long last is bound with captive chains
And now, with every hostile bow unstrung,
The Scythian disheartened leaves the field.

So now become once more your simple self
And, with no thought of where some threat
    may lurk
Against the state, accept with carefree joy
This hour's gifts: forget grim duty's call.

Finally, in III. 29, Horace seems at last to be at ease with
his friend and patron. It makes at once the offer of vintage
wine, spikenard, and roses. Maecenas' surroundings of cloying wealth and the confusion of the city can be relieved by the
peace and comfort of the country, especially during the dog
days which are imminent.

Scion of Etruscan kings, for you I've kept
Long since a jar unbroached of vintage wine;

I've roses too, Maecenas, oil of nard
    To scent your locks.

So tear yourself away nor idly gaze
On dripping Tibur and the sloping fields
Of Aefulae and on the haunted ridge
    Of Tusculum.

Desert your cloying wealth, your palace towers
That reach aloft to touch the clouds of heaven;
Forget the smoke, the splendor, and the din
    Of lordly Rome.

Change may be grateful even to the rich:
The homely meal beneath the poor man's roof,
Bereft of trappings, oft ere now has smoothed
    The troubled brow.

The season comes when Cassiopeia shows
Her brilliant light and Procyon's fierce rage
Ushers in Leo's madness, while the sun
    Brings back the drought.

With spiritless flock, the weary shepherd seeks
The shade beside the brook, the thickets cool
Of rough Silvanus; even the shore is still
    And no breeze blows.

You ponder deep what stand the state should take
And worry for the city, fearing the plots
Of Scythia or of Cyrus' Bactrian realm
    Or Tanais.

God's greater wisdom hides in darkest night
The outcome of the future while he laughs
At timorous mortals, faint with needless fear.
    Remember then:

With justice mold the present: all beside
Is borne as in the river's stream that now
In peaceful channel laves the Etruscan shore
    To reach the sea,

And now again carries away great rocks,
Tree trunks, and flocks and houses, while the woods
And mountains roar as now the torrential flood
    Transforms the stream.

He will live free and happy who can say
As each day passes: I have lived today,
Tomorrow, whether god send lowering clouds
    To hide the heavens

[169]

Or glorious sun, he cannot take away
That which I've had nor yet reshape the past
To render void what yesterhour has swept
    Into Time's stream.

Fortune, rejoicing in her cruel role,
Forever playing at her heartless sport,
Scatters her fickle gifts, now kind to me,
    Now to another.

Grateful the while she stays, if she spread wide
Her wings, I yield her gifts and wrap myself
In virtue's cloak of poverty, upright
    Though unendowed.

'Tis not my wont, if 'neath the Afric blast
The mast groans, to resort to wretched prayer
Or trade with heaven to save my Tyrian wares
    Or Cyprian

From adding to the greedy ocean's wealth.
Instead, within the little lifeboat safe,
The breeze and Castor's twin shall bring me through
    The Aegean storm.   (III. 29)

Horace's ode to Tyndaris (I.17) is less an invitation than
an adaptation by the lyric poet of a bucolic idyll by Theocritus
or Vergil. Tyndaris is not invited to some special occasion
but only to Horace's countryside where he imagines himself
as a (highly sophisticated) goatherd playing on his pipes.
Tyndaris will sing with him and, safe from the autumnal heat,
will escape the boisterous roughness of Horace's assumed
rival.

Swift in flight, to lovely Lucretilis,
Faunus ofttimes deserts the Arcadian mount

To guard my kids from summer's fiery heat
And threatening wind clouds pregnant with the rain.

So safely through enchanted groves they go,
Those wandering mates of my old smelly goat,
Seeking the arbute berries where they lurk,
Hunting the fragrant thyme, nor fear the snakes

Or hostile wolves along Haedilia's slope
Whenever, Tyndaris, my tuneful pipe
Sounds through the valleys or beside the cliffs
That friendly guard low-lying Ustica.

The gods protect me. Dear to the gods my faith
And dear my sylvan muse. 'Tis here for you
Shall flow abundance from the horn of plenty,
The generous store of simple country wealth.

Here in my sheltered valley you may shun
The Dog Star's torrid heat. On Teian lyre
Here you may sing how, rivals once, the twain,
Penelope and Circe, plied their charms.

Here in the grateful shade you'll quaff the cups
Of innocent Lesbian, and the Thyonian god,
Offspring of Semele, shall never rouse
Disgraceful brawls with Mars, nor shall you fear

That boisterous Cyrus, lest, incontinent,
He raise a hand against your helplessness
To tear the chaplet from your fragrant curls
Or roughly rend your undeserving frock.

Finally, Lyde is invited in III.28 to celebrate Neptune's feast day with Horace. Unlike other invitees, Lyde seems to be more or less in residence, and the ode is certainly less invitational than purely lyrical (see pp. 150–51).

In all of these poems of invitation there are common elements, a limited number of offered attractions, and these are significant. Wine is the one item always present. With it are sometimes flowers and perfume, usually a suggestion of song, and almost always a promise of release from cares. The particular cares vary with each invitation. They may be political worries or business concerns or the philosopher's search for truth: they may come from concentration on literary effort or from the unsatisfactory progress of a love affair. Sometimes they seem to arise merely from the frustration of city life, never from the hardships of life in the country. Never, I would say, are they truly tragic.

These are all invitations to share for a brief period the peace which another has found in life outside the metropolis. At the same time, it is also clear that Horace was not inviting his city friends to come out and picnic in the woods. He does not even suggest their strolling about his farm to admire his vegetables or his woodsmanship. He is definitely inviting them one and all to a party, but each to a party suited to his or her personality and social position. A bottle or cask of his wine—vin ordinaire or chateau vintage or sweet sauterne according to the guest—is the mainstay of every party, whether it be an evening of reminiscent talk or a night of serious drinking. There are no invitations to his local friends, who would hardly appreciate the wreathes, the spikenard, and the songs. We are forced in spite of ourselves to admit that, while Horace was at bottom a real countryman, he had in him enough of the suburbanite to enjoy an occasional renewal of his more sophisticated urban parties in an almost conventional pattern.

And so perhaps the invitation to Vergil is a little more understandable. It is in a younger vein than the others. It is to an intimate friend with simple tastes, like those of Horace. It is to a poet of country life, a poet young enough to be still fascinated by the Alexandrian novelties of the new poets. It is written by a poet young enough to feel the inspiration of returning spring, an inspiration which has induced in poets of every race and age an urge not toward tragedy but toward sentimentality, with a touch, at best, of the pathetic, at worst of the ridiculous. And this same nostalgic note made the invitation from the poet of the earlier days appropriate to the spirit of Horace's last lyric publication.

THE EPISTLES · *Odes* I–III came out in 23 B.C. When Maecenas urged Horace to write more, he responded in 19 B.C. with a small volume of *Epistles*. His explanation to his patron is that he has served his time as a poet and been given honorable discharge. He is now engaged in the search for truth and the study of sound philosophy, following no one school but gleaning what he finds of good in the teachings of both Stoics and Epicureans. He will begin with the fundamental elements of philosophy: the first step is the elimination of vices; the first function of wisdom is to abandon folly. The attitude of the world is opposed to this but, in the end, the philosopher is king, rising serene above the ills of life—until he catches a cold. The irony of the satires is clear in this last line, and in fact the whole of the first epistle might well be classed with the satires. As the book proceeds, however, many of the pieces are real letters and all are addressed to individuals and adapted to the character of the recipient. The prose epistle had been made a literary vehicle for philosophy largely by the Epicureans.

The second epistle is a letter to a young man studying rhetoric in Rome and is apparently sent to him by Horace from Praeneste. In subject matter it is almost a continuation of the first. Homer, says Horace, is a sound philosopher presenting in action the many types of human character. This occupies the first half of the letter; the second speaks directly to Lollius, urging him to heed the lessons of philosophy while he is young. These two epistles, concerned primarily with practical philosophy, are followed by three of a definitely personal nature. To young Florus, Horace writes asking about the literary activities of the group which is attending Tiberius on a voyage to the East. Who is writing the epic of Augustus? Is Titius writing Pindaric odes or rhetorical tragedies? Has Celsus taken my advice to use his own genius rather than the resources of the library? And you, so gifted in every line, why not give philosophy a chance? To Tibullus, in retirement in the country, goes a short and puzzling note (Epistle 4). Are you, the frank critic of my satires, writing works to rival Cassius of Parma or just browsing in the woods gaining physical and spiritual strength? The gods have given you everything; remember then to live as though each day were your last. Meanwhile you may laugh at me, who, in spite of my high moral preaching, am becoming a fat pig from the Epicurean sty. It is tantalizing not to be able to say positively what Horace thinks of Tibullus. The younger poet was not one of the group patronized by Maecenas, and Horace did not like the erotic elegy, which was Tibullus' medium of expression. And yet here, as in Ode I.33, the feeling seems to be one of almost intimate warmth. The two poets were evidently friendly enough to be outspoken: Tibullus is the *candidus judex* of Horace, and Horace warns Tibullus against too much mourning over Glycera in *elegi miserabiles*. The reference to Cassius also can hardly be complimentary. Cassius, in Satire I.10, is said to have written so carelessly and rapidly that rumor had him cremated on a pyre made of his own writings. It seems as if Tibullus, with his independent means and his independent personality, had been, as a poet, something of a disappointment to Horace, who still hoped to goad him into fulfilling the promise of his less erotic and more vigorous Roman verse.

The fifth letter is an invitation to Torquatus to come out to dinner in the country. It is reminiscent of the invitation odes but lacks the lyric atmosphere with which most of those invested the simple country. Whether the difference derives from some change in Horace's mode of life or from the character of Torquatus is not easy to say, but the latter seems more likely. These first five epistles are samples of the contents of the book.

Of the remaining fifteen letters, two (13 and 20) deal directly with Horace's published works. The first consists of the poet's directions to the messenger who is taking a volume to Augustus. It is full of assumed nervousness, and it puns rather heavily on the name of the messenger. It was, however, clever enough to lead Martial to imitate it with improvements. The second applies directly to the book of *Epistles* and is the envoi to the volume with the signature of the poet.

> So, when some kindly sun has favored you
> With listeners, you shall speak to them of me,
> A freedman's son in modest poverty
> That from the nest ambitiously took wing
> And won the favor of the city's great
> In war and peace. So what you have denied
> My lineage you'll add to virtue's score.
> You'll say beside, he's short and too soon bald,
> One who loves sunshine, quick to anger, yet
> One easily appeased. Perchance they'll ask
> My age; I've lived through winters forty-four
> In Lepidus' and Lollius' consulship.   (I.20.19–28)

Horace seems to be writing the final word to wind up his whole literary output and this impression is strengthened by his use of the phrase *libertino patre natum,* which had been used so emphatically in the first book of the *Satires*.

Eight of these fifteen epistles are real letters, two of them notes of introduction for his personal friends. One is a longer letter to Maecenas declining to come to Rome and defining his understanding of the proper relation between client and patron. This subject is treated from a somewhat different point of view in three letters (8, 17, 18) to young men giving them advice in the matter. One letter (15) asks about possible resorts to which Horace might go for relaxation, and another (11) is advice to a friend against the spirit of restlessness which keeps him always on the move.

Country life as contrasted with city life is the subject of three letters (10, 14, 16) and straight philosophy that of another (6). The last before the epilogue (19) is on literary matters to Maecenas.

It is surprising that Horace does not comment on the new type which he is using, the verse epistle. It almost seems as though he considered these letters as just another book of satires. They are, to be sure, in hexameters and not fundamentally very different from satires, but the address in each to a definite person determines in each case the tone of the letter and to some extent governs the choice of subject matter. There are practically no lyric touches and little discussion of literary doctrine. The latter is confined to the nineteenth epistle to Maecenas and consists of some mild ridicule of imitators and the registration of his own claim to lyric originality in his epodes and odes.

> I was the first to plant my footsteps free
> On virgin earth nor trod in others' steps.
> Who trusts himself shall one day rule the swarm.
> I was the first to show to Latin folk
> The Parian mode iambic, following there
> The verse and meter of Archilochus,
> Never the theme nor yet the words that brought
> Death to Lycambus. Nor should you refuse
> An ample wreath because I feared to change
> The measure and the order of his song,
> Remembering how heroic Sappho merged
> Her Muse with measures of Archilochus,
> Alcaeus too, yet both maintained intact
> Their matter and their form, nor hunted out
> A kinsman to defile with vicious verse
> Nor wove a noose of slander for the bride.
> Alcaeus 'twas, unsung before, I brought
> To fame with my new Latin harmonies. (I.19.21–23)

Into the book of *Epistles* Horace introduced the symmetrical arrangement which was sketchily present in the *Odes*. Number twenty is Horace's signature and therefore outside the formal symmetry, but it is tied with the first letter insofar as that serves as the dedication of the volume to Maecenas. So, considering the contents of the book to be nineteen epistles, the first obvious mark of deliberate arrangement is the placing of the letters to Maecenas and Augustus (1, 7, 13, 19) at equal intervals. At the center of each of the three groups thus formed is a letter to one of Horace's own personal friends: Tibullus, Fuscus Aristius, and Quinctius Hirpinus, friends of long standing and all of them recipients of earlier odes. In each group, flanking the central epistle, are pairs, one to his younger friends filled with advice or admonition, the other to older friends for the most part unknown to us otherwise. The first young man addressed, in the second epistle, is addressed again in the second from the end. This is young Lollius, presumably the son of the Lollius whom Horace would later eulogize in his fourth book of odes.

LITERARY EPISTLES · Independent of the volumes of poems in the four categories we have been considering, satires, epodes, odes, and epistles, Horace left the "Saecular Hymn" and three epistles much longer than those of the published volume. These longer epistles, usually referred to as the literary epistles and one of them known as *Ars poetica,* give us only a rough idea of their dates: after 17 B.C. for the first one, addressed to Augustus; between 20 and 17 B.C. for the second, to Florus; after 17 for the *Ars poetica,* addressed to the Piso brothers. Proof is impossible for even so vague a dating, but it can safely be said that these long hexameter essays represent Horace's final position on the literary questions which they raise. Unfortunately for our present purpose, Horace has become particularly interested in dramatic poetry, not as author but as critic. There is comparatively little criticism of lyric poetry. The effect of this dramatic interest is obvious in his picture of the stages of man's life:

> The young boy, smart to answer, firm of step,
> Is eager for the games of youth, is quick
> To wrath, soon mollified, changing each hour.
> The beardless youth, released from tutor's grasp,
> Rides happily and hunts o'er sunny fields,
> Wax in the hands of evil, spurning advice,
> Loth to be practical, spendthrift of wealth,

[177]

High-spirited and eager, fickle at best.
With changing goal, the age of manhood seeks
To gather wealth, make friendships, gain renown,
Avoid commitment that shall breed regret.
Old age brings sore discomfort in its train:
Acquisitive but miserly, it fears
To spend, treats all with calculation cold,
Postponing, hoping, grudging every hour,
Yet slow to act, complaining, difficult,
Worshiper of the past when life was fresh,
Scourge of the young and critic of the new.
The years, oncoming, bring us many joys,
Receding, filch them from us one by one.

(Ars poetica 158–76)

The lines lack the real fire of genius which Horace might have put into them when he was writing his satires. This is partly owing to the fact that in this essay he is to some extent rehashing Aristotle but more to the fact that he is thinking of the stages of life not as they are in life itself but as they are depicted on the stage. The lines are not a picture but directions for making a picture.

One objective fact about the literary epistles must be noted. There is no mention of Maecenas, no reference to him. Augustus, Florus, a protégé of the emperor's son, and the Pisos, a family in official position and intimate with Augustus, these are the recipients of the long essays. When Maecenas fell out of favor with Augustus, it would seem that Horace turned to the emperor as his patron and closest friend. The minister who, up to and including the first book of *Epistles,* always came first and to whom they were all dedicated is not mentioned in the long essays and in the final book of odes receives only casual attention. And yet something of mystery remains. The casual attention in Ode IV.11 is less casual than at first appears. Between two slight and not too pleasing odes to his past loves, Ligurinus and Lyce, the one about to lose his appeal, the other already bereft of hers, come two of the most

charming odes of the book: an invitation to Phyllis to celebrate Maecenas' birthday and an invitation to Vergil to come
and relax in the country. Vergil was long since dead; the poem
is included in the book in memory of the poet's best friend.
Maecenas is still living but banished from the circle of the
court: Horace may not invite him, but he loyally remembers
him and celebrates his birthday as he would have done under
happier circumstances with Maecenas himself. And some
years later when Maecenas died, still out of favor with Augustus, he commended "my Horace" most affectionately to his
onetime leader. Those who would have us believe that the
relation between Horace and Maecenas was a mercenary one
have given too much attention to the separation and too little
to other evidence.

But Horace was indeed poet laureate at least from 18 B.C.,
and Augustus had every right to expect from him the loyal
support he received. The fourth book of *Odes* and the literary
Epistles are not actually official expressions like the "Saecular
Hymn," but they are expressions of literary authority by the
official poet.

With this background it is not surprising to find in the
literary criticism of the long essays less of the combative spirit
against the poets' guild and a more general basis of criticism
than there was in the *Satires*. Also, another element has
entered into the situation since the late thirties. Lines 108–17
of the epistle to Augustus are significant, especially 117:
scribimus indocti doctique poemata passim (trained or un-
trained we write poems indiscriminately). The widespread
passion for writing is new and it has produced false standards
of judgment. Poetry is written to appeal to the audience, to
make an immediate impression. It would seem that public
readings, which in the satires was merely a personal nuisance,
had now become an established practice. Pollio's unhappy
innovation of inviting friends to hear his readings had flowered
too successfully. The door had been opened to rhetoric.
Horace therefore expounds a new classicism. The appropriate
meter for each branch of poetry has been determined by the
Greeks and must be followed.

[179]

The deeds of kings and captains and the woes
Of war, their proper meter Homer showed.
Alternate lines, unequal, first appeared
In lamentations but ere long in prayers;
But who produced our worthless elegies
The pedant schoolmen still deliberate.
Rage armed Archilochus with iambic verse
Which poets of sock and buskin made their own,
To conversation apt, appropriate
To picture action and to quell the mob.
The Muses gave to lyric verse the task
Of honoring gods and heroes, winners too
With boxing glove and chariot, then, beside
The heart concerns of youth, their flowing wine.

If ignorance forbids me to conform
To such convention, why salute me poet?

(Ars poetica 78–87)

He still insists on the duty of each generation of poets to improve on its predecessors. He believes in the best of his own generation. But now he emphasizes beyond all else the need for respect toward the great writers of the past, the maintenance of sound tradition and unending care and hard work. He assails the careless workmanship of the average poet, his inconsistencies, his use of the spectacular even when inappropriate. He concentrates on dramatic poetry and only incidentally shows his dislike for Callimachus, the erotic elegy, and the schoolteachers.

Like most poets laureate, Horace lost much of his fire when he became a public oracle. The literary epistles produce a number of immortal phrases but on the whole they are dull, too pontifical, and, for the most part, platitudinous. *Non est qualis erat bonae / sub regno Cinarae.*

VII · TIBULLUS

he elegiac couplet served two chief purposes in Greek literature. It was the standard meter for short inscriptional verse, such as epitaphs and tributes inscribed on monuments. This usage quite naturally spread to embrace epigrams not inscribed on monuments and, presently, to a wide range of subject matter without any content of grief or eulogy but usually with poignantly expressed emotion or wit. The meter served also for narrative of less dignity and long-sustained interest than the traditional epic in hexameters. Its suitability in both cases comes from its couplet character. The second line, the pentameter, with a pause in the middle, serves to bring the couplet to a natural stop, almost forcing the writer to complete the sense also within the couplet. For the epigram this is ideal, giving sharp distinction to a single idea. For the longer poems the same effect repeated at too great length tends to become monotonous and, for consecutive narrative, it breaks the continuity with too great regularity. Even in the hands of the most facile poet it is inevitable that the couplet should, after a while, produce a tedious effect of regularly recurring metrical breaks.

We have seen Catullus' experiments with elegiac verse, highly successful in the epigram, far less so in his longer efforts. These latter elegiac poems he did not follow up with any really serious productions. They were experiments which did not prove wholly satisfactory. They all (except the "Conversation with the Door") dealt with Catullus' own love affair with Lesbia and in this characteristic differed from the Hellenistic elegies which treated other people's love adventures. But the Lesbia affair is no longer a passionate matter of concern to Catullus: he views it rather in retrospect. The "Conversation with the Door" was destined to play a considerable part in the work of later elegiac poets.

Four major poets of the Augustan Age, Gallus, Tibullus, Propertius, and Ovid, did adopt the elegiac meter as their own particular medium and used it for a particular type of poetry that definitely sets them apart as a group. There were others who wrote elegies but their work is lost, as indeed are the poems of Gallus, but it is quite reasonable to assume that we have the best product of the school, if such it may be called. These poets considered Callimachus and Philetas their masters and models, but Gallus was also a worshiper at the shrine of Euphorion. It seems clear that while they probably got their first suggestion from Catullus, they went back to Alexandria for more extensive inspiration. Horace might speak of one of them as "that ape who knows nothing but Calvus and Catullus," but Callimachus was the real source of their elegiac type. This would not endear them to Horace.

It is perhaps significant that Gallus was a close friend of Vergil in their younger days, when Vergil was following the lead of the new poets and successfully using the elegiac meter in his light and artificial pastorals. Gallus followed a different line and established a new type in Latin poetry with his elegies to Cytheris. None of these has survived, but we know something about Gallus' work from later writers. Quintilian, for instance, rates Tibullus best of the elegiac poets (terse and elegant) though, as he says, some prefer Propertius, while Gallus was more stern (*durior*, perhaps more serious) and Ovid the gayest and most wanton (*lascivior*).

Cornelius Gallus, the first of the Augustan poets to publish, the man who probably introduced Vergil to Octavian, was a direct successor of the new poets of the days of Valerius Cato and Catullus. An enthusiastic translator and follower of Euphorion, he represents the group which Cicero in scorn called the singers of Euphorion. He adopted the elegiac meter of Catullus' experiments and extended its use beyond the Alexandrian practice by writing in it a new type of love poem. This was no passionate outburst of emotion direct from the heart, such as Catullus had presented to the world of Roman poetry. It was far more Alexandrian in both tone and technique. It expressed a self-conscious, nervously excited type of erotic experience, the temporary, superficial affairs of a self-pitying, purely sentimental, and highly sophisticated lover to whom each affair was a deliberately cultivated game carried on with conventional rules and portrayed with every device of Alexandrian contrivance. His four books of elegies to Cytheris established the Roman erotic elegy. In the next century he was considered rather stiff and perhaps crude, but, to his contemporaries, he must have appeared as wanton as Ovid did to a later generation.

It is with Gallus that we can begin to understand more clearly Horace's attitude toward the new poets and at the same time his position between the older poets of Rome and the moderns. Both are based on his partial view of both "new poets" and "moderns." Horace, no less than the new poets, believed in the obvious truth that Roman poetry was derivative from the Greek. Unlike the new poets, however, he knew and understood the difference between the classic poets of Greece and their successors at Alexandria, represented by Callimachus and Euphorion. While Catullus had enough passion as well as poetic genius to escape the worst artificiality of the Alexandrians, he was sufficiently attracted by their charm to experiment with some of their favorite literary types and to be influenced by their metrical novelties. Gallus adopted them all with enthusiasm and, combining the Alexandrian elegiacs dealing with love stories and the lighter love adventures of comedy, he started on its way the short-lived career of the erotic elegy of Augustan literature.

Horace had taken advantage of the revolt of the new poets that had given him the freedom to write personal poetry, but he had resisted the enervating influences of their Alexandrian fancies. He had gone back to the sounder models of earlier days: Archilochus, Sappho, Alcaeus, Pindar, Bacchylides. His quarrel with the new poets and the grammarians was not caused by their following Greek models but by their following what he considered the wrong Greek models. Presumably Gallus felt the same pride as Horace in naturalizing at Rome another product of the Greek genius, giving it a Roman variation in the process, and so rivaling his contemporaries, Vergil and Horace.

So when we come to the successors of Gallus whose work has survived, we find them producing poems of a type which seems to be fairly well established. But we should not make the mistake of condemning them (as perhaps Horace did) to a convention narrower than theirs actually was. Tibullus and Propertius were first writing in approximately 27 B.C., just after the appearance of Horace's second book of *Satires* and before he had published his first book of *Odes*. The elegy therefore was at first the rival not of lyric poetry but of satire. As is generally recognized, it had features in common with satire. It is a form of talk or conversation. It is addressed to an assumed listener: to the loved one, to a friend or patron, to an enemy, or merely to a listener among the general reading public. On the other hand, its overall field of interest and tone is sharply in contrast with that of satire. The one type is intellectually critical, morally concerned, serious in spite of its use of wit and humor. The other is emotional, concerned with illicit love, frankly amoral, and yet, by convention, prevailingly serious in spite of its subject matter. The urge which drove Catullus and the new poets away from highly serious, nationally significant poetry to personal expression was strong in the elegiac poets; hence, from one angle, Horace's antagonism toward them. And, because Tibullus displayed something of serious purpose and national interest, he seemed to Horace worth the attempt to save him from his "miserable elegies." But fundamentally the elegiac poets were perfecting one area of Latin poetry derived from Alexandria, suggested by Catullus but given distinctly Roman character by Gallus, Tibullus, and Propertius.

Tibullus must have published between 23 and 19, as evidenced by the references in Book I to the campaign of Messalla in 23 and Tibullus' death in 19. Horace twice addresses

Tibullus, in Ode I.33 and Epistle I.4. Book I of the *Odes* was published in 23, Book I of the *Epistles* in 19. It is generally assumed that the epistles of the first book were written not long before publication, probably after the appearance of the first three books of *Odes,* but there is no reason why the letter to Tibullus may not have been *written* before 23. In the ode, Horace speaks of Tibullus as grieving over unkind Glycera and writing "miserable elegies." In the epistle, Tibullus is in retirement on his farm. The ode would imply either that Tibullus wrote elegies earlier than those which have survived or that his individual elegies were circulated among the friends of Horace and Maecenas. That the Glycera named by Horace is in fact the Nemesis of the extant elegies is hard to believe. Nemesis appears only in the later work of Tibullus: the natural assumption is that Glycera was the subject of lost elegies. The sixteen poems which we have from the hand of Tibullus seem too few to sustain the reputation he won so soon and so surely. On the other hand, he cannot have been much over thirty when he died.

Tibullus opened his first published work with an elegy which, in the fifty introductory lines, might well (apart from the meter) have been an Horatian satire. The contrast between unhappy wealth and joyous "poverty" is summed up in the Horatian phrase, *contentus vivere parvo.*

> Let him who will heap up the tawny gold
> And till his mighty acres of rich soil,
> His labor wrought in terror of the foe,
> His slumbers banished by the trumpet's blast.
> For me, my frugal fortune shall support
> A quiet life beside a welcoming hearth.
> And so may I, content with little, live
> Free from the curse of constant journeying,
> Basking instead, when burns the Dog Star's heat,
> Beneath the cooling shade of my own tree
> Beside the waters of a running stream.
> I shall not blush at times to wield the hoe

Or prod the dragging oxen with the goad
Or in my arms bring home the wandering lamb
Or kid deserted by its careless dam.
In season I will plant the tender vines,
A proper farmer, and new apple trees.   (I.1.1–16)

He hopes for good crops and ample wine, for he pays his
due worship to Ceres and Priapus. The lares too shall have
their offerings. He pours libation from simple earthenware,
he cares not for riches: a small farm is enough. But when it
comes to the conclusion of this introductory section, the climax line, Tibullus gives a sharp turn to the argument, an
elegiac and not an Horatian turn:

Yea, perish all earth's gold, all emerald wealth
Ere for my absence any maiden weep.   (I.1.51–52)

The rest of the introductory poem is in a new key. We learn
for the first time at line 53 that it is addressed in part at least
to Messalla:

For thee, Messalla, wars by land and sea
To hang its trophies on thy palace front;
For me my bondage to a lovely maid,
Lying as watchman at her fast-barred door.
                                             (I.1.53–56)

Messalla, however, is addressed only by way of formal dedication. The real recipient of the poet's devotion is Delia:

I crave not glory, Delia mine: if I am thine
The world may brand me sloth and sluggard too.
Let me but look on thee as I face death
And dying clasp thee with my failing hand.   (I.1.57–60)

He urges her not to spoil her beauty in her distress. Meanwhile he will be the good soldier of love and enjoy its quarrels
and its delights. Real war he will not have.

But now while Fate permits we'll join in love:
Death will come soon with hooded head and dark

And sooner still old age that knows not love
Nor lovers' speeches, with its hoary head.
Now let me gaily live while 'tis no shame
To break down bolted doors or boldly brawl.
There is the field where I'm a soldier brave:
Begone ye standards and ye trumpet calls,
Bequeath your wounds to men of eager greed;
Give them your wealth: safe in my frugal home
I'll scorn alike both wealth and poverty. (I.1.69–78)

Here is a somewhat forced return to the theme of the opening lines after the manner of satire.

As if to show that he deliberately chooses the role of elegist rather than satirist, Tibullus places next in his book a
poem extreme in its elegiac tone and content, an elegy to Delia,
a confusion of almost all the motives associated with Roman
elegy. Here we meet the excluded lover, the conversational
door, the miraculous immunity of the faithful lover, the appeal to the loved one, the magic rites, the husband absent at
the wars, the futility of wealth, the integrity of the speaker,
the dastardly rival, and the appeal to Venus. About the only
thing missing is the learned mythological parallel.

Pour wine unmixed. With wine dissolve
These unaccustomed woes that sleep at last
May close my weary eyes. Let no one then
Awake me from that Bacchus-given rest
That suffers my unhappy love to sleep.
A cruel guard is stationed o'er my dear
And with harsh bolts her sturdy door is closed.
May the storms beat on thee, thou cursed door
Of stubborn master, may the lightning bolts
Hurtle upon thee by the will of Jove.
But yield betimes to my laments alone
Nor creak aloud as turns the stealthy hinge,
And if distraught I sometimes spake thee ill
Forgive me: let those curses fall on me.
Remember only now my suppliant prayers

Brought with the flowers I hung upon thy posts.
And thou too, Delia, give thy craftiest aid
Boldly to fool thy jailer: now's the time
For daring. Venus ever helps the brave.
She helps the youth who first assails the door
Of some new love, she helps the maid that lifts
The latch and frees the door. 'Tis she that shows
The skill to creep unheeded from the bed,
To move with silent footsteps o'er the floor,
How in her husband's presence she may speak
By nods that render the sweet words of love.
Yet not to all she speaks, only to those
Whom neither sloth retards nor fear prevents
From rising in the silence of the night.
Mark how I wander anxious through the town
All wrapped in darkness. Venus suffers none
In swift attack to harm me with his sword
Or strip me of my garments and escape.
Who is possessed of love may safely go
Secure from ambush wheresoe'er he will.
The rigors of the winter's icy night
Can never harm me nor the pelting rain;
My lover's toil shall leave no trace of hurt
If only Delia open to me the door
And give me silent summons to her side.

.   .   .

May I but hold you, Delia, in my arms,
I'll woo sweet slumber on the rugged earth.
What profit, if there be not love withal,
To lie on Tyrian couches while the night
In loneliness brings nought but wakeful tears?
Then neither downy feathers can bring sleep,
Embroidered coverlets nor purling streams.
Have I done violence to Venus then
That I must expiate my sinning word?
Have I, unpurified, approached her shrine

Or torn the garlands from her sacred hearth?
If so I'll gladly, at her temple's door,
Prostrate myself to kiss that threshold chaste,
A suppliant, crawl the earth on bended knee.

(I.2.1–32, 73–85)

The third poem pictures the poet, struck down by illness,
left behind on a foreign shore while Messalla and his retinue
move on. He mourns over his own hard lot: death threatens
with no mother at hand to bury him, no Delia to weep for
him, Delia who consulted the omens at the time of his departure and promised a safe return.

And wilt thou so, Messalla, o'er the sea?
Forget not then, I pray, this heart-sick friend
Whom, sick and lonely in a foreign land,
Phaeacia holds. Death, stay thy greedy hand!
Black Death, avaunt. No mother have I here
To gather to her bosom my burned bones,
No sister here to offer frankincense
Or, with disheveled locks, weep at my tomb.
Delia is far away who, when I sailed,
Besought the gods, they say, at every shrine.

(I.3.1–10)

There is no help in Delia's Isis, yet he prays to her to spare
him to return home.

Now, Isis, help me. Many a votive gift
Left in thy temple proves thy healing touch.
Help me that so my Delia make her prayer
Each night, all swathed in white, before thy door
And twice each day amid the Pharian choir
May, with dishevelled locks, intone thy praise.
So may I live to hail my household gods,
Give to my lares incense of gratitude.   (I.3.27–34)

The mere thought inspires him to draw a picture of the happy,
primitive days before Jupiter brought death and destruction

to earth. He proceeds to write his own epitaph, sure that because of his fidelity in love he will go direct to the Elysian Fields.

> But if I have fulfilled my allotted years
> Raise me a stone; inscribe thereon these words:
> Here lies Tibullus, snatched by unkindly Death,
> Following Messalla over land and sea.
> Then for my faithful service to her son
> Venus shall lead me to the Elysian Fields
> Where never fails the dancing and the song.
>
> (I.3.53–58)

In spite of his own destination he could not miss the chance to describe in passing the seats of the wicked. Then he pleads with Delia to remain faithful and closes with a fine, if inconsistent, picture of his sudden and joyous return.

Between these two poems and two others to Delia (5 and 6) comes one which turns out in the last few lines to be addressed to Marathus, the poet's favorite boy. But the poem is in form a Priapus poem. Tibullus asks the country god what cleverness he has which wins all the pretty boys, and the god answers at length. Tibullus preens himself as having become an authority but ends with another groan over Marathus. There is one mythological reference, to Nisus, the father of Scylla, already familiar to the literary elite through Vergil's Ciris.

The seventh poem divides the book into two unequal parts. It is in celebration of Messalla's triumph over Aquitania. It is a tribute to the poet's patron but not, strictly speaking, an elegy. It recounts other victories of Messalla in the "Tarbellian Pyrenees," in Gaul, Asia, and Egypt. Egypt furnishes the excuse for a long digression on Osiris. The poem ends with good wishes for Messalla and an appeal to his Genius.

After two more poems to Marathus, the book ends with a tirade against war and a eulogy of peace. As with the first poem in the book, this might well be a satire in elegiac verse until the poet comes to the last and, to him, most important attribute of peace: it makes possible the joys and quarrels of love and on this ground is earnestly urged to come.

The first book then, apart from the consistently elegiac meter, is a miscellany of satire, elegy, and Priapus poem. The poet would seem to incline toward the elegy. Its conventional situations are accepted, the self-pity and the self-analysis, the prevailing melancholy air. But the poems lack the abandon which we look for; the diction is restrained. Subtle and learned allusion is eschewed. Greek characteristics are not prominent. There seems to be justification for Horace who first, in the ode, recalled Tibullus rather flippantly from his despair over Glycera and later, in the epistle, tried more seriously to win him away from elegy. There was enough evidence in the first book to indicate the possibility that Tibullus might write either Roman satire or Roman epic and in a style which would have Horace's hearty approval. He might not yet be committed to the softer elegy with (in Horace's mind at least) its degeneracy and its degenerating influence.

The second book is not very different from the first. It opens with a poem on the country celebration of the Ambervalia, followed by one to Cornutus on his birthday. Poems 3, 4, and 6 are to a new love, Nemesis, a coarser type than Delia, apparently a skillful and practiced gold-digger. Into this series to Nemesis is inserted poem 5, a somewhat confused eulogy of Messalinus and Messalla. It is in the form of a prayer to Apollo featuring the sibyls and ancient Rome, Aeneas and the sibyls, war and peace, and the glories of country life.

Gilbert Highet would have us believe that Tibullus was a psychotic weakling (*Poets in a Landscape,* New York, 1957). Others consider him a romantic. Much sentimentality has been expended on his early death after what is pictured as a life of high tension and low vitality, overshadowed by unhappy love. There is no evidence to tell us whether his early death was due to lingering disease or sudden accident. It is well always to remember what Ovid insists on in his own defense, that a man and his book are two separate characters. Martial, whose real friends were among the best and most conservative

[191]

citizens of the day, could write for Sabine mothers or the saturnalia. Pliny indulged in indecent verse—or as indecent as he could make it. The subject matter of a man's poetry is not the proper basis for biographical material. With Tibullus, even if we were justified in abstracting his character from the conventional situations in his pages, we should still be at a loss. His poems would reflect too many variant faces.

What do we really know of Tibullus? He performed his military service without discredit and evidently with some distinction. He possessed the friendship of Horace and also of Messalla. He was an *eques* of some means with a country place outside Rome. He died young in 19 B.C. This is the sum total of our knowledge apart from his sixteen poems.

These sixteen poems give the impression of a young man trying out a new line of poetic production. Variety indicates experimentation. The poetic taste is there, the command of his vehicle. There are reminiscences of his reading: Catullus, Lucretius, Horace, Vergil (the juvenalia). He shows discrimination: Quintilian calls his style *elegans*. He is appreciative of the qualities of earlier Roman simplicity. In other words, he shows immense promise. He never, however, developed control of larger construction that required greater force of purpose to achieve unity. He is a Catullan experimenter without the passion of Catullus. He has the urge to write the kind of love poetry that Horace disliked but is inhibited by the finer restraint that Horace approved.

Our manuscripts of Tibullus contain, in addition to his two books, six elegies by one Lygdamus and six short poems, also called elegies, by Sulpicia, a lady of standing and connected in some way with Messalla. The first group opens with an introductory poem somewhat reminiscent of Catullus, whose "Peleus and Thetis" the poet actually cites in his concluding poem. The second poem is a complaint, in which Lygdamus confesses his despair at losing Neaera, avows his will to die, and gives directions for his funeral with a dictated epitaph. Elegy 3 is on the old theme, the worthlessness of wealth without love: better poverty with Neaera than wealth without.

Number 4 recounts at length the poet's dream of a visit from Apollo, who discloses the faithlessness of Neaera, an exhibition piece framed between two appeals to the gods to avert the evil omen. In the fifth poem Lygdamus complains to his friends of his probably fatal illness, how little his youth and innocence deserve such a fate, and begs them to sacrifice for his recovery. The sixth and last poem is a toast to Liber, with a picture of the poet's empty pretence of joy at a banquet when his heart is sick. This collection is a slight product of little distinction marked by some variety but permeated by an atmosphere of self-pity and melancholy love. This self-centered, rather tepid emotion must by now have been considered the proper theme of the elegy, for Lygdamus shows no signs of originality.

The poems of Sulpicia are also in elegiac meter, but they show more originality and more moving passion. They are short poems, not fifty lines in all. They express the authoress' passion for Corinthus, her first thrill at this love, her desire to be in Rome, where love flourishes, rather than in the country, the appearance of a rival, and a sick-bed effusion. They are really short lyrics or incidental trifles in elegiac verse. They have the ring of sincerity rather than elegiac convention and at times they present a moving passion. Some critics have gone as far as to discover a Roman Sappho in Sulpicia, with little harm to Sappho and little credit to the critics.

VIII · PROPERTIUS

ibullus was the favorite of the experts. Horace wanted to think well of his work and Ovid put him at the summit of elegiac composition. Quintilian later approved this estimate. His pure diction and Roman spirit and his human dignity weighed heavily in this verdict, but these are not the qualities which we have been led to look for in a writer of artificial, subjective love poetry. In the first line of his first published poem, Propertius opens a new vista: *Cynthia prima suis miserum me cepit ocellis.* This could be a new Catullus or it might even be another Horace. What immediately follows shows that it is neither, that we have here a pioneer launching boldly into the field which Tibullus tentatively explored in his rather prim and very tidy manner.

> 'Twas Cynthia first snared with her glorious eyes
> My innocence, by passion yet untouched.
> Then Cupid shamed my prim and proper glance
> And firmly set his foot upon my head,
> Till he had made me hate all maidens chaste
> And, mischief-maker, taught me how to live
> A life unfettered. So, the whole year round,
> This madness rules me, spite of unkind gods.
>
> (I.1.1–8)

This is a new field of love experience. At line nine the poet plunges into an artificial parallel drawn between himself and Milanion. It is deliberately made more learned and obscure by referring to Atalanta as Iasis. After the illustrative myth, Propertius calls on the wielders of magic to win for him his sweetheart, then on her friends to cure him of his love. The last theme merges into a final warning to these friends to avoid his melancholy fate. This would not be an impossible poem for Catullus to have written, but there is an overtone of insincerity which is foreign to the lyric poet. The writer almost accepts the situation as a recognized and chosen game.

Propertius was an Umbrian from the neighborhood of Assisi and was born about 55 B.C. His father was a well-to-do *eques* and the son was highly educated for public service, which he abandoned for poetry. He lost at least part of his property during the seizures following the victory of Antony and Octavian. His whole life centered at Rome where he came to be associated to some extent with Maecenas and his group. His first book seems to have been published about 29 B.C. It was dedicated to one Tullus, of whom nothing is known, and indicates acquaintance and perhaps friendship with the poets Ponticus and Bassus and a friendly rivalry with one Gallus. A second book of elegies appeared about 25 B.C., a third some years later, and the fourth and last after 16. The date of his death is unknown.

It is his first two books which really represent for us the subjective erotic elegy. Both are concerned chiefly with the love of Propertius for one whom he calls Cynthia. It is of little importance whether she was a real person named Hostia, as the ancient critics believed, or an unknown freedwoman of easy virtue or even a creation of the poet's imagination. As we have seen, he plunges directly into his chosen subject with the first line of his first poem, and in a general way the elegies of Book I follow very roughly the course of his love affair. From love at first sight it passes through a period of happy mutual devotion to one of suspicion and jealousy, to vituperation, reconciliation, infidelity, and final rupture. The earliest poems are perhaps the best. They have a vivid directness which appears not only in the opening lines already quoted but every now and again in the other elegies which immediately follow. But, almost naively, this sincerity is constantly interrupted by passages of learned obscurity or of sentimental reflection on the sorrow inherent in love. It should not be overlooked that even in his first exuberant outburst over the effect of Cynthia's eyes he speaks of himself as *miserum,* and the poem ends with his warning of *dolorem* for his friends if they do not avoid his fate. Melancholy was part of the convention.

The second elegy is rather conventional, urging Cynthia to give up her fashionable and expensive adornment, since natural beauty is the best and she need have no distrust of either her beauty or her wit. The flowers and the birds, the babbling brooks and the pebbles on the shore are not perhaps the most natural parallels for the man-about-town to be using but they are comfortably conventional and apt. The mythological illustrations are more sophisticated and less apposite.

Poem 3 opens with a show of learning, but the myths cited are familiar ones and, after the sixth line, the whole elegy is direct, realistic, and poetically charming.

> As on the deserted shore exhausted lay
> The Cretan princess while her lover's ship
> Sailed far away, or as Andromeda,
> Freed from the cruel cliff, first sank in sleep,
> Or as the Bacchant from the Edonian dance
> Stretched wearied by Apidanus' grassy bank,
> So seemed to me my Cynthia as she lay
> Soft breathing, resting her head on hands relaxed
> When I came dragging footsteps Bacchus bound
> With torches slave-borne in the festive night.
> So, with what sense was left me, I essayed
> To approach her as she lay there on the bed.
> And though with passion doubly fortified
> By Cupid and by Liber bidding me
> With arm beneath to lift her where she lay
> And pilfer kisses, yet I dared not so
> Disturb the quiet of my mistress' sleep,
> Fearing her cruel jibes I knew so well,
> But stood transfixed with eyes as vigilant
> As Argus' gaping on Io's newfound horns.
> Then, tearing the banquet garlands from my brow,

I placed them on your forehead, Cynthia,
And joyed to rearrange your tumbled locks;
Stealthily placed an apple in your hand,
Lavishing gifts on unresponsive Sleep.
Gifts that kept slipping from your careless breast.
And even as you stirred and sweetly sighed
I stood astounded at the portent vain,
Lest someone seeing her there should frighten her
Or seek by force to seize an unwilling prize,
Till through the lattice of her windowpane
The moon went slipping by with busy beams
Whose curious searching rays opened her eyes,
And resting on her elbow so she spake:
"At long last you would come to insult my couch
When closed doors of another shut you out.
Where have you spent the watches of my night
To come a'wearied with the setting stars?
Would, wretch, that you might spend such endless nights
As, by your cruel order, fall to me.
For now I baffled sleep weaving my wool
And now by weary singing to the lyre;
At times bewailed to my deserted self
The long delays of separated love.
Till Sleep o'erwhelmed me with his soothing wings.
That was the final ransom of my tears."   (I.3.1–46)

In the fourth poem, Propertius reiterates his devotion to
Cynthia alone, and the fifth is a warning to Gallus not to poach
on his preserves. Cynthia is still all golden in poem 6 as
Propertius refuses to go abroad with Tullus because he is the
thrall of love. The seventh is addressed to Ponticus, who is
writing epic to rival Homer. Propertius defends his own love
poetry: it too will live, for wretched lovers will read it and
know his plight and will recognize his power to express their
passion—if only at his tomb. One line of Mimnermus is worth
the whole of Homer. Number 8 is practically an elegiac propempticon to Cynthia, who is off on some voyage. He points

out the dangers but prays for her safety. His love will endure. Then there is a sudden break with poetic tradition: my plea has persuaded her, she will not sail, she is true to me. After two poems to friends, about love to be sure but not directly about Cynthia, the poet again addresses his mistress: what are you doing at Baiae? A strong suggestion of suspicion is evident and it develops in twelve that Cynthia has ceased to love him. Her stay in Baiae has made her forget. *He* can never forget: she was his first love and will be his last. He is still lonely and dejected as he addresses Gallus in 13. The fourteenth poem is a denunciation of wealth as compared with love, a trifle ambiguous but suggesting perhaps a wealthy rival and a hope for the return of Cynthia. In the next, however, he upbraids her for her perfidy, and 16 is the complaint of a chamber door framing the long lamentation of an *exclusus amator*. Cynthia is not mentioned. In the next poem it is Propertius who is abroad and very sorry for himself. He should not have left Rome. He may die in a foreign land and then Cynthia cannot give him burial. Finally, in 19, he tells Cynthia that it is not death he fears but only death away from her. Let us love while we can, no love is long enough. The remaining three elegies of Book I are not to Cynthia or about her. One is a miniature epyllion, the story of Hylas, framed between warnings to Gallus. The next is an epigrammatic appeal from Gallus' unburied ghost, and the last is a short signature poem telling Tullus about the poet's birthplace.

This is the first publication of a young poet, an inspired poet, one would think, who has chosen a particular field for his efforts, shows originality in developing it, and is slightly diffident perhaps but on the whole confident of success. That this confidence was not without foundation is evidenced by the fact that his second book (some five years later) opens with a poem addressed to Maecenas. And not only that: Maecenas has evidently made to Propertius his familiar suggestion that he turn from lighter verse and pay tribute to the regime of Augustus. Propertius' answer is a reiteration of his devotion to erotic elegy.

You ask me why so oft I sing my love.
How wins my wanton book to all men's lips?
'Tis not Calliope who frames my song
Nor yet Apollo: Cynthia inspires all.
For if I see her radiant in Coan silks
Then Coan silks shall be my constant theme.
Or if her ivory fingers pluck the lyre
I marvel at this most consummate art.
If her coy glance again invites to sleep,
A thousand motifs rush to my poet's pen.
If, mantle torn away, she strives with me,
Then do I straight produce long Iliads.
Whate'er she does, whatever she may say,
A mighty tale is born of nothingness.
But had the Fates, Maecenas, given me
To sing of heroes summoned to the fray
It would not be of Titans that I'd sing
Or Ossa piled upon Olympus' peak
To forge a way to heaven, nay, nor yet
Old Thebes nor Homer's famous Pergamum;
Not Xerxes joining into one two seas.
I should not sing of Remus or the might
Of Carthage, Cimbrian threats, or Marius,
But rather of the deeds your Caesar wrought
And, after Caesar, you would be my theme.

.   .   .

The sailor tells of storms, farmers of fields,
The soldier counts his wounds, the hind his sheep;
I sing the lesser song of bedroom strife.
Let each devote his day to his own art.

(II.1.1–26, 43–46)

This is only half of the poem. The poet makes his way through
a heavy undergrowth of mythological allusion to a conclusion
rich in self-conscious pathos.

So when the Fates have summoned back my life
And I become a name inscribed on stone

Then pray, Maecenas, hope of our Roman youth
And very glory of my life and death,
If chance should bring you riding by my tomb
Check there your chariot with its inlaid yoke
And with a tear pay tribute to my dust:
"This wretch was ruined by a cruel maid."

(II.1.71–78)

True to his assertion, Propertius makes his second book as much a "Cynthia" as the first. Only the tenth elegy, addressed to the exploits of Augustus, has no Cynthia content. In it he makes a firm but soon forgotten assertion that he will write more serious poetry, and the reader can hardly fail to note that more of the poem is concerned with the poet than with Augustus. His insistence that in mighty efforts the will to do is sufficent is a dubious if convenient conceit. In the final lines the poet confesses that his forte is not the grand style.

Now up and tread the slopes of Helicon
With other measures. Now's the time to give
Free rein for coursing to the Haemonian steed.
My pleasure now to tell of mighty hosts
Loosed for the battle and to sing the deeds
Of glorious Roman wars waged by my prince.
But if my powers avail not, still I'll win
The praise of boldness, for in mighty deeds
The will to do suffices. Youth should sing
The lure of love; let age sing war's emprise.
Wars will I sing for I have sung my love.
Now would I turn, more gravely countenanced,
To strike a nobler lyre for my Muse.
Up, up, my soul, leave thy too humble verse,
Pierian maids, a mightier call is there.
Euphrates now disowns the Parthian shaft
And mourns the long disgrace of Crassus' hosts.
India bends its neck beneath the yoke

Of your triumphant march, Augustus. Even
The unconquered Arab trembles at your thrust.
If there be any hidden lands beyond
The bounds of earth, let them now feel your might.
Yours be the camp I follow. I shall be
A mighty minstrel if I sing your wars.
May fate reserve for me that glorious day.
As when we cannot reach the statue's head,
We lay our wreathes more humbly at its feet,
So, impotent to soar in eulogy,
I here present my humble offering.

Cynthia is still his real subject. There is no attempt to present a sequence in the poems to his mistress: each represents
a situation or a mood and most of them are complaints or denunciation.

Let others laud thee or none sing of thee:
Let him give praise who sows in barren ground.
For all thy gifts, believe me, one black day
Shall sweep away upon thy funeral bier
And passing travelers shall scorn thy bones
Nor say, "A learned maid lies buried here."

The concluding elegy, like the first, asserts the poet's devotion to the poetry of love, but it is a perplexing poem. Editors
have practiced on it their endless game of subdivision, making
of the one poem either two or three. It seems wiser to take it
as tradition has presented it to us and accept a difficulty in
transition and a lack of unity that are faults not altogether
foreign to Propertius' practice.

Why ever trust one's love to Cupid's care?
'Twas so I well-nigh lost my sweetheart dear.
I speak who know: there is no faith in love.
Rare is the man that beauty will not bribe.
This god it is defiles the love of kin,
Wrecks friendship, plunges into bitter strife
Hearts firmly knit. Guests at his very hearth

Proved Menelaus' fate adulterous;
The Colchian followed a bold stranger's love.
Thus, treacherous Lynceus, could you violate
My darling? Did your hands not falter then?
What if she had not proved her constancy?
Could you have lived thereafter with that shame?
Slay me with sword or poison if you will
But 'gainst my mistress raise no wanton hand.
You shall be friend and all things else to me:
Only my couch of love I will not share,
Nay, not with Jove himself in rivalry.
When I'm alone apart from her I swear
I'm jealous of my shadow, shake with fear
Where no fear is. One plea alone there is
For you: your words wandered from too much wine.
Never again shall your stern, virtuous look
Deceive me. All the world may know at last
How powerful is love, for Lynceus too
Though late, so late in life, is mad with love.
For this then I rejoice: you hail our gods.
What boots it now to prate of Socrates?
What profit in the Aeschylean lyre?
Your ancient bard is nought against such love.
Come, learn the songs Coan Philetas sang,
The dreams less stately of Callimachus.
Now, though you tell again how, overwhelmed
By love, Aetolian Achelous flowed
Or how deceitfully Meander set
A wandering course along the Phrygian plain,
Betraying its own path, or how again
Adrastus' mount, Arion, found a voice
To speak his sorrow for Archemorus,
No help to you shall be the chariot
Of Amphiaraus or the overthrow
Of Capaneus that cheered the heart of Jove.
Give up the buskin of old Aeschylus,
Relax your limbs to suit the softer dance.

Begin to turn your verse on humbler lathe
And, poet grim, sing your own fiery love.
You'll be no safer than Antimachus
Or Homer's self: a lovely girl may flout
Even the gods. And yet the angry bull
Submits not to the yoke until his horns
Have first been captured by the stubborn noose.
Nor will you willingly accept hard love
Till your proud spirit's bridled by my verse.
No girl desires to know how Nature's law
Orders the universe nor how the moon
Toils with his brother's steeds, nor if there be
In truth a judge beyond the Stygian wave
Or reason in the crashing thunderbolt.
Nay, look on me. Paltry the wealth that came
To me by birth, no ancestors of mine
Triumphed of old for battles dear to Mars.
Yet witness how I reign amongst the maids
What time the banquet's spread, all by the wit
For which you now make solemn sport of me.
My joy it is to languish midst the wreaths
Of yesterday because the god of love
With certain aim has smitten me to the bone.
Vergil delights in power to tell the tale
Of Actium's shore under Apollo's guard,
Of Caesar's mighty ships; now calls to arms
Trojan Aeneas, pictures those new walls
Reared on Lavinian shores. Yield now to him
Ye poets of Rome, and yield, ye Grecian bards:
There comes to birth a greater Iliad.
Thou singest too beneath Galaesus' shade
Of Thyrsis and of Daphnis with his pipes,
The appeal of rustic gifts, fruit or a kid
Torn from its mother, to corrupt a maid.
Thrice happy who so cheaply buys his love
With apples. Even Tityrus may sing
To such a love, reluctant though she be.

[203]

And happy too your Corydon who seeks
To win Alexis, joy of his master's heart,
And so is praised even in his silent hours
By Hamadryads in their wanton play.
Thou singest too the precepts taught of old
By Ascra's bard: when best to plant the corn,
Where best the vine. Such music's yours
As once the Cynthian sang to his learned lyre,
The while his tapering fingers touched the strings.
None who may read but shall delight therein
Whether long skilled in love or innocent,
Nor shall the tuneful swan ever yield place
To the untutored cackling of the goose.
Such songs sang Varro too, his Jason done,
Varro the pride of his Leucadia;
And such songs, too, wanton Catullus wrote
Whose Lesbia lessened Trojan Helen's fame.
Such songs adorned the learned Calvus' page
Who sang Quintilia's unhappy death,
And Gallus sang the same, so recently
Washing in Hades' stream Lycoris' wounds.
My songs know naught of Ascra's fountainhead:
Love has but laved them in Parnassus' stream.
But Cynthia too shall live in Propertius' verse
If Fame but grant me rightful place with these.

This is certainly a loosely constructed poem. The chief
difficulty lies in the abrupt transition at line 25 from protest
to and forgiveness of Lynceus to a poem which, starting from
Lynceus, proceeds to a discussion of elegiac poetry. But Lynceus is directly addressed in both parts, and the first, which
depicts the downfall of the stern writer of epic, is not an un-
reasonable introduction for Propertius' appeal to him to turn
to poetry more suitable to his changed attitude. The difficulty arises from the fact that Propertius is even less specific
than usual in his handling of the transition. The whole forms
a plausible conclusion to the poet's two books of subjective
erotic elegy.

[204]

It is obvious that the urge toward creative poetry and the production of something new in Roman literature had a strikingly different effect on a disillusioned member of the non-political, sophisticated society of Rome from that which it exercised on such men as Horace and Vergil, who had accepted the policies of Augustus and joined his more intimate circle of friends. These elegies of Propertius breathe a wholly different atmosphere from that of the *Odes,* the *Georgics* or the *Aeneid.* In the first place, the poet admits and seems to glory in his surrender to carnal love. There is no feeling of depth or dignity aroused by his poetry. In the second place, there is no real expression of strong passion, either love or hate. The tone tends to be clinical, the poet studying his own emotions, often to the point of seeming to be an outsider. Again, the poet's experiences are not convincing as realities: the whole thing tends to appear as a complicated and artistic game, its narrative adorned with every available literary device, even obscurity now and again, deliberately created for a supposedly charming effect. The meter, already considered less dignified than the hexameter, more formal than the hendecasyllable or the iambic, becomes part of the artificial nicety of the elegy. Finally, the persistent self-consciousness, leading often to morbid self-pity, and an almost psychopathic pathos would seem to justify Horace's phrase, *miserabiles elegiae.*

All of this may be, and to me is, true without meaning that the elegies of Propertius are not a successful literary creation. They command the reader's interest whether or not they hold it consistently. At times they are moving. Always they are the product of great craftmanship, often exquisite in expression. The verse is wedded to the matter. The elegiac poets added a new type to the corpus of Latin poetry. When Propertius had published his first book, the volume to Cynthia, and it had been well received by those for whose delectation it had been intended, he spoke with more confidence in the introduction to his second volume. Addressed, as we have seen, to Maecenas, who must have found in the first the promise, at least, of genius, this introductory elegy expresses definitely the poet's refusal to change his medium. He is by no means ashamed of his field and, in the final poem of Book II, he reasserts his loyalty to the school of Callimachus and Philetas. With Book III there appears a marked change in the product of Propertius' pen. It was not published until after the appearance of Horace's *Odes* I–III and the introductory poem indicates at once the attention which Propertius had given to the *Odes*. While the opening lines are a manifesto maintaining the poet's adherence to the school of Callimachus and Philetas, there is evident a new pride in his pioneer achievement. Horace had boldly proclaimed himself the first to present the Grecian lyric in Roman verse and, in the Roman odes, had spoken as priest of the Muses. Propertius opens Book III:

> Spirits of Callimachus and the Coan poet,
> Let me, I pray, enter your holy grove.
> I am the first, priest from unsullied spring,
> To lead in Roman rites the choirs of Greece.
>
> (III.1.1–4)

No longer does Cynthia figure most prominently: it is the poetic achievement and the enduring fame of the poet which concern Propertius now. "Time renders all things greater after death." Otherwise no one would know today all the great tales of Troy, for even Homer's fame grew great with time. (In Horace's manner, Propertius introduces a thundering phrase which might well recall Homer: *Deiphobumque Helenumque et Polydamanta.* So generations of Romans to come shall render me the praise begrudged today.

The second poem continues the theme. "No ivory ceilings with rich gilded beams / bedeck my home." (Horace again?) But the Muses are his friends and Calliope never wearies of his music.

> Happy the girl my song shall celebrate:
> My verse shall be her beauty's monument.
>
> (III.2.15–16)

The pyramids shall perish by fire or storm or by the *ictus annorum* but not the fame my genius shall have won. It is not merely the Horatian touches so evident here that mark a change but the very real concern for literary achievement and recognition. Poem 3 carries on the theme with further Horatian reminiscences. Propertius pictures himself reclining in the shade of Helicon, on the point of following the lead of Ennius and writing Roman historical epic when he is brought up sharply by Apollo, who rebukes him for dallying with epic. Not thence thy fame. And he shows the poet "where leads a new path o'er the mossy floor." This path led to the cave of the Muses, whence Calliope drew him by the hand with firm instructions for his guidance.

> For thou shalt sing of lovers garlanded
> Before another's door and all the round
> Of drunken revelry by night. Thy song
> Shall teach the lover how to win his love
> By cunning from her jealous husband's keep.
> (III.3.49–50)

Almost perversely after these literary declarations, the fourth poem is a tribute to Caesar, with prayers for his success in Parthia. Propertius, like Horace, will cheer his triumphal return, one of the adoring crowd on the Via Sacra. But in the fifth poem he returns to his literary theme, expressing scorn for the lure of wealth—"the world goes emptyhanded to the grave"—and rejoicing that love, wine, and song have been his youthful pursuits. In old age he will turn to serious philosophy. In the ninth poem, he defends the elegy. It opens with a somewhat awkward echo of Horace: *Maecenas, eques Etrusco de sanguine regum* (Maecenas, knight of royal Etruscan blood), and defends his choice of elegy by appealing to Maecenas' own refusal of honors and office in favor of the life he loved. For the rest, the book contains poems to Paetus (7), to Postumus (12), on the death of Marcellus (18), to Tullus (23), and a denunciation of luxury (13). There are eight elegies to or about Cynthia, the last two being short poems denouncing her and wishing her a miserable old age when her beauty is gone. The change is even more obvious in Book IV. It opens with a dull and difficult poem, which Propertius begins with a survey of early Rome and a declaration that his poems will now be devoted (with glory to his native Umbria) to Rome's early tradition. His raptures over this program are cut short by a Babylonian astrologer named Horus, who spends many lines giving his own background and qualifications and warns Propertius against carrying out his plan. Nevertheless, four more of the eleven elegies deal with Roman cults and one with Actium. Another is a letter from a Roman matron to her husband, abroad with the army, and the final poem is a remarkable *apologia pro vita sua* spoken by the ghost of another Roman matron, Cornelia, the wife of one of Augustus' close associates. Of the other three poems, one is a compilation of curses on the head of a procuress named Acanthis, whose chief offense was to have given sinful and ribald advice to the poet's mistress. The other two are Cynthia poems and form a curiously contrasted pair. In the first, Cynthia's ghost berates Propertius for infidelity and neglect. The poem directly following presents a scene of gay celebration at which the poet is entertaining two ladies of light character when the living Cynthia bursts in and, like an outraged fishwife, breaks up the party with crockery and billingsgate.

All of the poems of Book IV are longer than the general run of poems in the other books and, except for the grace and ease of the verse and the learned cleverness and obscurity, they have little resemblance in kind. The book was certainly published after 16 B.C. Maecenas had fallen from favor. Augustus, after many disappointments, official and private, had been showing a tendency to tighten his grip on legislation and to stress his campaign for old-fashioned morality. All this may have had its effect on Propertius. He may also have been maturing. Whatever the secondary incentives, it seems to me clear that, starting with an urge like that of every poet since Catullus to create something new, Propertius chose the elegy, developed first the subjective erotic type, and then, still a restless pioneer, proceeded to embrace a wider range.

In the Hylas poem of Book I he had played with the miniature epyllion in elegiac couplets. Under the exciting influence of Horace's *Odes* he made some effort to apply the meter to the less lyric type of ode and at the same time to the epistle. Finally, in part at least to assure his patriotic reliability, he turned to the Roman religious tradition and created a new type of short epyllion.

It seems possible that in his elegy on Actium, Propertius was offering a challenge to both Horace and Vergil. It might have been expected that the latter, pioneering as he did with the elegiac meter, would have inspired more imitation in the elegiac poet. But Vergil's pastorals, with their rustic settings and their artificial simplicity, were foreign to Propertius' taste: he found much more to emulate in the love lyrics and literary ambition of Horace. Neither in any sense furnished him a model. Both he and Tibullus would seem to have derived from Gallus (and perhaps his lost contemporaries) and it was, as far as we can tell, Propertius who perpetuated and gave to the erotic elegy one characteristic dear to the earlier poet, that of erudite allusion to the tales of mythology.

Tibullus did not hesitate to use illustrative myth but he chose familiar stories which really illustrated his point. Propertius prefers the obscure myth which does not so much illuminate as decorate his poem. This is more conspicuous in the second book than in the first. In the monobiblos there is no massive accumulation of parallels. The second elegy has some not too familiar mythological characters, Phoebe, Hilaira, Marpessa, and Hippodamia, but only four. The third has three, all familiar to every reader. The ninth has a somewhat recondite allusion, referring to Thebes as *Amphioniae moenia lyrae* (walls raised to the music of Amphion's lyre). Fifteen has four reasonably well-known mythical ladies: Calypso, Hypsipyle, Evadne, and Alphesiboea.

Poem 20 is of particular interest in this respect. It is a miniature epyllion, telling the story of Hylas within a framework not of another tale but of advice to the poet's friend Gallus.

This, Gallus, is my warning word to you
In token of long friendship; heed it well.
The unwary lover oft encounters Fate.
Ascanius, cruel to the Minyans,
Can tell of this.   (I.20.1–4)

As an opening gambit, these lines set a high standard of obscure allusion. Ascanius was a river in the Propontic region. The Argonauts were, most of them, sons of the daughters of Minyas. But the obscurity may be excused, since the poet is leading up to the story of Hylas and the Argonautic voyage, to which the transition is clear.

Yours is a love as beauteous to behold
Nor less in fame than Hylas', he who claimed
Theiodamas as father. So, if now you sail
Along the wooded stream or bathe perchance
In Anio, or more likely stroll the shore
Gigantean, whatsoever flowing streams
Be your companions, guard your treasure well
Against the nymphs: Ausonian dryads too
Know love. Else art thou doomed to roam
The rugged mountains, icy cliffs, and lakes
Untraversed yet. So wandering Hercules
On unknown shores bowed to Ascanius.
                                          (I.20.5–16)

In the story of Hylas that follows there is no lack of learned obscurity, more permissible there than in the passionate expression of a lover's emotion. Zetes and Calais are referred to not only as *Aquilonia proles* (sons of Boreas) but in terms of their mother and great-grandfather: *Pandioniae Orithyiae*. The last two lines of the poem return to Gallus and the contemporary scene.

Whatever the reason may be, the second book is far less restrained than the first in respect to the show of learning. The first poem has 22 proper names in 13 lines and 62 in the full 78 lines. The high point is perhaps *Hic Ixioniden, ille*

Menoitiaden, indicating simply Pirithous and Patroclus. No other elegy is as conspicuous as this, but not more than half a dozen out of the total thirty-four are without some mythological reference. One reason for emphasizing this characteristic is to indicate the real interest of the poet. To Catullus the Hellenistic indulgence in learned allusion made slight appeal, for his emotions were too directly involved in his poetry. Horace and Vergil developed an active dislike for such display. But here in Propertius, who surely stemmed from the same current of individualism, learned allusion is a prime element of delight and seems to outweigh the sincere emotional element as a basic motive. It confirms a suspicion that the love affairs of the elegiac poets, even that of Cynthia and Propertius, are largely poetic creations, based no doubt on experience but on experience which has been fondly cherished, expanded, and adorned by trained imagination. In other words, the elegy is almost as artificial an appeal to a sophisticated audience as the pastoral, differing primarily in the assumed point of view. By its artificial perfection at the hands of Propertius, it justified his claim to have developed a new field of Roman poetry.

IX · OVID

vid is by tradition the fourth and final Roman elegist. Such a characterization is wholly proper provided we do not forget that it is but a partial characterization. For he also completes the roster of the new poets stemming from Calvus and Catullus. The urge which forced these earlier writers to break with tradition and venture into the realm of self-expression reached fulfillment in the output of the last of the Augustan poets, whose extreme individualism caused his exile from Rome. Calvus and Catullus had opened the way with their personal lyrics and their short epics of frustrated love. A serious poet, Lucretius, had created a philosophic didactic poem to exorcise the fear of superstition and death. Equally serious but less solemn, Horace had developed the satire, the iambic, and the Ionian lyric, Vergil the pastoral, the agricultural didactic, and the romantic epic. Following a different line, more akin to that of the first revolutionaries, Gallus and Tibullus and Propertius had produced the erotic elegy, largely artificial, wholly amoral and out of line with the official nationalism of their day. Ovid gave a new turn and the final touch to this erotic elegy. When he had proven his supreme art in this direction, he did many other things, but the perfecting of the artificial elegy was his first significant achievement.

Quintilian, the literary oracle of the later Romans, has left the verdict that fixed the position of Ovid in the category of the elegiac poets (*Inst. Orat.* X.1.93): *mihi tersus atque elegans maxime videtur Tibullus; sunt qui Propertium malint; Ovidius utroque lascivior, sicut durior Gallus* (Tibullus seems to me to be concise and polished; there are those who prefer Propertius; Ovid is more wanton than either of these and Gallus more austere). *Lascivus* is the adjective which Martial chiefly applied to Catullus, whose epigrams were Martial's avowed models. But it applied to only a part of Catullus' product; it is almost universally applicable to the work of Ovid. It suggests a frivolous gaiety undisturbed by any concern for morals or politics, a merry playfulness inherent in the character of Ovid but only occasional with Catullus. Horace and Vergil had demonstrated what the new freedom could create when controlled by a moral code and patriotic devotion. Ovid showed what it could produce with no such controls, in the hands of a sophisticated and flippant artist.

Ovid, never one to forget himself in his art, gives us the best account of his early life and ambitions.

> That you may know the man you read, the poet
> Of tender lovers, hearken, posterity.
> Sulmo's my city, rich in cooling springs,
> Distant by ninety miles from mighty Rome.
> That was my birthplace and, to know the date,
> 'Twas in the year two consuls met their fate.
> For what it's worth, my rank's inherited:
> A knight I am and not by Fortune's freak.
> I'm not firstborn, my brother came before
> To be my honored senior by twelve months.
> The same moon 'twas attended both our births
> And one day poured libations for us both.
> Well trained, when young we went, obedient to
> A father's will, to Rome to study at the feet
> Of learned men. My brother from his youth
> Followed the law and learned the mighty feats
> Of wordy battle in the courts; for me,
> While still a boy, I loved the sacred rites
> And stealthily the Muse captured my heart.
> Often my father said: "A useless trade:
> Even Maeonides bequeathed no wealth."
> I hearkened to his words, left Helicon
> And tried full hard to write in simple prose.
> But of its own accord the verse emerged

And forth in numbers came whate'er I wrote.

    .   .   .

I paid my court to all the reigning poets
And, whosoe'er they were, I thought them gods.
Often I heard old Macer read his birds,
What serpents sting, what herbs give benefit;
Often to me Propertius read his poems
By virtue of the friendship that was ours;
Ponticus in heroic verse and Bassus too
With his iambics were my comrades dear.
Inspired Horace held our attentive ears
Timing his polished verse to Ausonian lyre.
Vergil I only saw, and bitter fate
Robbed me of friendship with Tibullus too.
He followed Gallus' steps, Propertius his
And I, in that succession, followed fourth.
                             (*Tristia* IV.10.1–26, 41–54)

His success was immediate and impressive. His own estimate of his natural ability was entirely accurate: he was the
most facile of all Roman poets, his verse seems effortless. This
by no means indicates carelessness or crudity. His poetry is
polished, urbane, a work of extreme artistry. He himself tells
us that he destroyed much of what he wrote because it did not
measure up to his own standard of art. And still we have over
35 thousand lines which have survived, more than twice the
product of any other Roman poet and for the most part metri-
cally flawless.

It is important to remember the date of Ovid's birth, 43
B.C. This puts him definitely in a younger generation than
that of Horace and Vergil. He was only twelve in the year of
Actium and twenty when Horace published his odes, twenty-
four when the *Aeneid* was published. He himself did not publish before 13 B.C. By that time the burst of enthusiasm which
followed Augustus' disclosure of his program of peace and
reconciliation in the early twenties was spent. The era of ex-

altation and benevolence was over. The princeps, always serious and determined, had grown more so under the pressure of events and without the relaxing companionship of Maecenas. For Maecenas had been banished from his immediate circle of friends. After the bright noonday, the afternoon of Augustus' career was deteriorating into a chill grayness. His dream of a restored *Roma antiqua* and his plans for the royal succession failed simultaneously. He had not the saving sense of humor to meet with any resiliency the affronts of fate. As misfortune robbed him of Marcellus, Lucius, and Gaius, and at the same time of Vergil and Maecenas, he struck back unwisely at Julia and her lovers, at Agrippa Postumus and also at Ovid. Had he not lost the advice of Maecenas or if he had retained the happier tolerance of his best days, Ovid might have been won over to become the mediator who interpreted the ways of god to man, the beauty and value of Roman virtue to a pleasure-loving audience. As it was, there was first a lack of communication, then definite hostility, and finally banishment for the poet.

What Tibullus and Propertius took seriously, thus very understandably incurring the disgust of Horace, Ovid took lightly and gaily, making of illicit love a merry work of art as harmless in elegy as it had been in comedy. For Ovid never identified himself thoroughly with the unhappy lover as did Propertius: he was the expert and the amused spectator. What he might have been had he been won over by the matchless diplomacy of Maecenas, who must have understood him well, can never be known. Certainly to Augustus, in his chagrin at the failure of his moral legislation, Ovid was almost the incarnation of what he was striving to eradicate and he must have welcomed whatever misstep it was that gave him an opportunity to strike. In A.D. 9 Ovid was banished from Rome to spend the last years of his life in distant Tomi on the fringe of barbarism.

Augustus was fighting against the trend of the times. The audience to which the poems of Horace and Vergil were addressed was by no means the society of the earlier republic, and the transformation was continuing at an accelerated pace. The make-up of the governing class was different. The old republican families figured less and less in public affairs and the senatorial group were now mostly new men who had won their position by virtue of wealth or service to the state: origin counted for much less than in the old days. Provincials, transplanted to Rome, and freedmen or their sons, largely from Greece and the East, were beginning to figure in considerable numbers. Oriental cults and astrology were getting to be fashionable. The society of the court and the world of fashion which radiated from it took its character not from the preachments and edicts of Augustus but from the traditions and habits of its more sophisticated and less inhibited background. Horace had protested against the villas of the rich pushed out into the bay at Baiae, but the villas of the rich had multiplied not only around the Neapolitan resort but around and within the walls of Rome. This society of the newly rich was not at ease with itself or with the rest of the world. Ambitious, insecure, jealous, it was permeated with rivalries both social and political and only selfishly concerned with the rest of the populace of Rome and Italy. Such a society was surely conditioned to listen (if it ever stopped to listen) not to the philosophy of Horace or the dreams of Vergil but rather to the extreme individualism and selfish indulgence of the elegists, whose private concern found its last expression in the first publications of Ovid.

To Propertius, his vehicle is largely taken for granted, at least in the first two books. What determines his poetic line is the content: *me dolor et lacrimae merito fecere peritum* (as for me, grief and tears have properly made me an expert) (I.9.7). Tibullus would seem to have something of the same outlook. To Ovid the metrical concern comes first. He speaks as a poet first and always; vehicle and tone (including the matter which controls the tone) are inseparably one. In his first poem he renounces the hexameter, admitting its superior standing, and accepts the softer elegiac couplet. In the second he makes the same renunciation but in terms of subject matter,

ending however with a return to the metrical argument. It may
be well to quote both poems at length.

> Of arms and cruel wars I sought to sing
> In numbers dignified, appropriate,
> With equal lines. They say that Cupid laughed,
> And from my lines pilfered a single foot.
> "Who gave you power, my boy, over my verse?
> Priest of the Muses I, not of your camp.
> Should Venus don the maid Minerva's arms,
> Minerva wave the flaming torch of love?
> Who could brook Ceres ranging o'er the hills
> The while the huntress goddess tilled the fields?
> Who would arm fair-haired Phoebus wth a spear
> Or suffer Mars to strike the Aonian lyre?
> Wide is thy range, my boy, too great thy power:
> Why seek, ambitious, new adventurings?
> Or is all earth thy realm, fair Tempe too
> And Helicon: shall Phoebus lose his lyre?
> When my new page has risen with opening line
> That second verse relaxes all its force.
> My subjects are not tuned to lighter verse,
> To boys and girls, combing their lovely locks."
> Such was my plaint. He from his quiver drew
> An arrow fraught with my catastrophe.
> Against his knee he bent the willowy bow,
> Saying "My poet, accept what you shall sing."
> Ah, woe is me. His arrows won their mark.
> I'm all on fire. Love rules in my vain heart.
> Six feet my verse shall soar, shall sink in five:
> Farewell, ye wars, farewell the modes of war.
> Come, Muse, with myrtle wreathe my tawny locks,
> Muse that must e'er be wooed with eleven feet.
> *(Amores I.1.5–34)*

> Lo, I confess: your latest victim I.
> Cupid, in full surrender, I submit.
> No need for weapons: here I sue for peace:

Unarmed, I'll rob your weapons of all praise.
Wreathe brow with myrtle, yoke your mother's doves:
Apollo's self shall give you chariot,
And in the car, to triumph-shouting crowds,
You'll stand and drive your deftly harnessed birds.
The captive youths shall follow, captive girls,
And so your glorious triumph shall proceed.
I too, your latest prey, will show fresh wounds,
Bearing, in captive mind, unwonted chains.
Sound Mind shall follow too with hands fast bound
And Shame and all that's foreign to your power.
And while in fear of you they stretch their arms,
"Io Triumphe," loud the mob shall shout.
Soft Words attend you, Error and Fury too,
A rout that eagerly supports your cause.
With them you conquer gods and men alike,
Your soldiers without whom your power is nought.
From high Olympus shall your mother fling
In joy her roses on your triumphing.
Golden yourself, in golden chariot ride,
Gems on your wings and gems on every lock.
Then too full many victims you'll inflame—
I know you well—you'll wound as on you pass
Whate'er you will, your arrows shall not rest
Nor cease to wield their fiery potency.
So once wrought Bacchus in far Ganges' land
When tigers drew his car as doves draw yours.
So since I'm doomed to be your triumph's crown
Wreak not on me, great victor, your attack.
Look on your kinsman Caesar's happy power:
The hand that conquered spares the conquered foe.

                                    (*Amores* I.2.19–52)

Here speaks no melancholy poet inspired by woe and tears.
He yields to Cupid and undertakes to write elegiac couplets
rather than heroic hexameters, but that is the extent of his
yielding. He will be master in the lesser fields, not Cupid's

victim so much as his deputy. He will speak less as a harassed lover than as a tolerant, half-amused spectator. Only by a poetic fiction is Ovid's erotic elegy subjective; he is an elegant flaneur treating love as an absorbing game or as a contest in the lists of gallantry. He states himself that the frank immorality of his elegiacs is purely literary and that his own life was wholly respectable. There is every reason to believe that this is true. It cannot be overemphasized that Ovid is as much interested in the artistic development of his medium as Horace was in his. Two more examples of this attitude must suffice. Of these, the first is something of an expansion of the claim which he had already put forward, but with more specific illustrative detail.

> Brave deeds of war demand the Maeonian foot:
> What place is here for tender dalliance?
> The tragic poet breathes dignity and wears
> The buskin, comedy the common sock.
> The coarse iambic rails against its foe
> Or swift or slow its culminating foot.
> Bland elegy shall sing of quivered loves
> And, merry mistress, sport to her own tune.
> Achilles spurns your rhymes, Callimachus,
> Cydippe's alien, Homer, to your verse.
> Who could bear Thais playing your tragic role,
> Andromache, or you in Thais' part?
> Thais just suits my art—unlicensed love:
> Away with fillets: Thais just suits my art.
>
> *Remedia amoris* 375–88

Finally, in a defense against the jealous criticism which he either rightly perceives or conventionally assumes, Ovid writes a self-defense and a strong plea for serious literary recognition. It is reminiscent of Horace's similar claims and ends with a familiar note: *Vivam, parsque mei multa superstes erit.*

Why, Jealousy, berate my "wasted years"

And call my song the work of idle mind?
I have not sought, the while my strength was young,
As did our sires, the dusty prize of war,
Nor did I learn the wordy law, to sell
My voice to make the ungrateful forum ring.
The fame you call for is a mortal thing:
I seek eternal fame, forever sung.
Homer will live while Tenedos shall stand
And Ida, or while Simois shall roll;
The poet of Ascra too while grapes shall swell
Or Ceres fall before the curving blade.
The world will ever sing Battiades,
However weak in genius, strong in art.
Sophocles' buskin shall forever strut,
Aratus live as long as moon and sun,
And, long as tricky slave or father harsh,
Pander and whore survive, Menander's safe.
Ennius with no art, grand Accius
Have names no future time shall e'er erase.
What age to come shall lose the memory
Of Varro's ship that sought the golden fleece?
The song sublime Lucretius sang shall fail
Only when that last day destroys the earth.
Tityrus and earth's crops, Aeneas' arms
Mankind shall read while Rome still rules the world,
And while young Cupid's bow has fire to wield
Thy numbers, skilled Tibullus, shall be learned;
Gallus shall have his fame from East to West
And with that fame Lycoris shall be one.
So, though the solid rocks, the plowshare tough
Perish with time, poetry shall never die.
Let kings and triumphs yield to poetry
And all the fabled wealth of Tagus' stream.
The mob may worship trivia: for my taste
Apollo shall proffer the Castalian spring.
My brows shall wear the myrtle from warm climes
And I shall be the sage of lovers lorn.

[220]

Envy is for the living: after death
Each shall reap honor as his merit rules.
Therefore, even when my last day's fire is spent,
I shall live on, much of me shall survive.

(*Amores* I.15.1–42)

With such a passionate devotion to poetry, Ovid could not
be content to harp on the one string of melancholy despair.
Nor did he confine his raptures to one mistress. Corinna is indeed generally assumed to be the object of his devotion, but
her name does not appear until the fifth poem of the *Amores*.
He has already presented one poem in which he appeals to his
love to overlook his lack of noble lineage and great wealth and
to listen rather to his verses. He has given long and specific
directions to his sweetheart for flirtation at a dinner party. In
I.5 Corinna comes to him at the siesta and he rejoices in her
beauty and her love. But, in spite of poems on the bolted door
and its cruel janitor, on remorse for his rough treatment of his
lady love, on an old hag's advice to his mistress, to which he
listens from behind the arras, and on love as a battlefield, it
is not until the eleventh poem that Corinna is again named.
In this poem Ovid dilates on the use of writing tablets by lovers and sends a note to Corinna. The following poem relates
the unhappy outcome of the venture. The three remaining
poems of Book I are, first, a diatribe against Aurora, who always comes too early and quite unwelcome to farmers and
especially to lovers; second, an appeal to his love not to try
to beautify her hair with every cosmetic device; and finally,
the exposition of his own claim to fame already quoted.

In Book II Corinna's name appears more frequently but
also (in the fourth poem) Ovid confesses that every girl, every
type has a strong appeal for him: he is really in love with love.
He goes so far (in II.10) as to argue that he is equally in love
with two girls at the same time. In all, Corinna's name appears
in eleven of the thirty-four poems of these two books and she
may safely be assumed to be the subject in two others, each
of which forms a pair with a poem in which she is mentioned

by name. In other words, Ovid avoids the monotony which results from the constant appeals to the same mistress and is free to attain something of the variety which characterizes the love lyrics of Horace. He does make use of most of the conventional themes of the erotic elegy but there is little if any repetition and there is constant variety in subject matter and expression. Other topics than love are also introduced: poems on the festivals of Ceres and Juno, an epicedion for Tibullus and discussions of his own poetic vehicle.

Perhaps the contrast with the more melancholy elegists may best be illustrated by two poems from Book II which appear there in succession (7 and 8). In the first Ovid protests vigorously to his mistress (who appears from the sequel to be Corinna) against her charge that he has been tampering with her maid Cypassis.

> And lo, another charge: your clever maid,
> Cypassis, has betrayed her mistress' couch.
> Ye gods forbid—if lust were mine to sin
> How could a sordid slave invite my lust?
> By Venus and the arrows of her son
> I swear I am not guilty of the charge.
>
> (*Amores* II.7.23–28)

And yet this is immediately followed, without embarrassment, by a poem to Cypassis.

> Cypassis, skilled to deck your mistress' hair,
> Yet worthy so to serve a goddess too,
> Known well to me by tricks sophisticate,
> Apt to your mistress' call, more apt to mine,
> What was the sign that gave our love away?
> Whence did Corinna know we two had loved?
> I did not blush. I did not slip the word
> That gave the signal of our furtive tryst.
> What though in time past I have said perchance,
> Love of a serving maid shows menial mind:
> The lord of Thessaly burned for Briseis' love

[222]

While the maid Phoebas won Mycene's king.
I am not better, then, than Tantalus
Or great Achilles: kings excuse my shame.
But when she fixed on you her angry eyes
I saw a rosy blush cover your cheeks.
Yet I—remember how much less confused—
Confirmed our innocence by Venus' oath.
The goddess bids the pure heart's perjuries
Be borne by Notos o'er the Carpathian Sea.
So now, Cypassis, for such ready wit
Give me the sweet reward, your sweetest self.
Why do you start away, pretend new fear?
One clearance from your mistress is enough.
But if so stupid as to say me nay
I shall confess, betray my own misdeed,
When and how often I have lain with you,
Cypassis; I shall tell your mistress all.

(Amores II.8.1–28)

Such frivolous treatment of the serious game of love would
have been quite out of character for Propertius. In the same
way Ovid seems almost deliberately to treat airily other subjects too serious to be played with by a true elegist. Propertius would have his love spurn cosmetics, proud in her
unadorned beauty. Ovid at one time uses the same theme but
at others finds unadorned beauty a trifle rustic and was presently to write an *Art of Cosmetics*. Just so his avowal of love
for all the ladies is almost a challenge to Propertius' renunciation of all girls for Cynthia. The same tone of half-mocking
superiority pervades all of the more traditional of the *Amores*.
In III.11 he says farewell to Cynthia and, presumably, to the
strictly elegiac type of poetry.

Much have I borne, my patience dies.
Yield, shameless love, yield to my wearied heart,
I've claimed my freedom and escaped my chains.
I blush to have borne what shamed me not to bear.
I've won and trample on my vanquished love:

Late though it be, bold strength at last is mine.
Perfer et obdura—some day this grief
Like bitter medicine may salve your soul.
So then I did endure, turned from thy door
And stretched my freeborn self on the hard ground:
Like slave for him you held in fond embrace,
I watched on guard before your chamber door.
I saw him when he came worn out with love
Forth from your arms relaxed, lover discharged.
(Yet, worse than all, what must I seem to him?
Such shame I pray befall my enemies.)
When have I not gladly escorted you
Myself your guardian, very husband, friend?
My verses, sung for you, have brought you fame,
Our love it was taught others how to love.
And yet the lies you told I may not tell,
The gods forsworn to my eternal hurt,
The signs you gave to lovers at the feast,
The words ambiguous by a code prepared.
They told me you were ill: I madly rushed,
Arrived to find you, for my rival, well.
All this I bore and more that shall be hid.
Find you another now to suffer so.
My ship is crowned with votive wreaths of thanks
And hears the sound of softly lapping waves.
Waste not your charms, your words so potent once:
For I am not the fool of yesterday.

(Amores III.11.1–32)

When it comes to the poems which wander from the type, they are again the product of a fertile fancy unimpeded by any overpowering passion. He teaches his lady the lovers' secret code for conversing at a banquet and again the rules for a flirtation at the circus. He rallies a frustrated eunuch and appeals to Isis and Ilithyia (a sufficiently bizarre combination) to bless for once in Corinna's favor an operation for abortion. The poem to Aurora departs even further from the type but is well within the range of conventional love poetry, with an Ovidian turn.

Now comes across the sea on frosted wheels
The fair-haired herald of another day.
Whither so fast, Aurora? Stop. To Memnon's shades
Thus speeds with sacrifice the bird of time.
Now is the hour for love in tender arms
Of sweetheart, now most true she clings to me.
Now sweetly clear the slender bird-notes sound.
Whither so fast, offense to men and maids?
With rosy hand draw in the dewy reins.
E'er thou dost rise the sailor views the stars
More clear nor wanders ignorant at sea;
The traveler at thy coming must arise
However weary; grim soldiers don their arms.
Thou first dost see the farmer at the plow,
Thou first dost call the oxen to the yoke;
Thou cheatest boys of sleep as off to school
They go to suffer from the master's rod;
Thou sendest fools off to the money mart
To court disasters with one plighted word;
The plaintiff and the lawyer love thee not
When each must rise to meet new threats at law:
Thou, when the tasks of women well might cease,
Recallest to their toil the spinning hands.
I would bear all: but maids rising at dawn!
Who could bear that—save he who has no maid?
How often have I prayed Night should not yield
Nor wheeling stars retreat before thy face;
How often have I prayed the wind might wreck
Thy car or in thick cloud thy steeds might fall.
Unkind, whither so fast? Thy son so black
Argues the color of his mother's heart.
Would I might tell Tithonus what thou art:
No woman then so shamed in heaven's vault.
The while thou fleest him for his old age

Thou risest to what he, the old man, hates.
But didst thou hold thy Cephalus embraced
Thou wouldst cry out: slower, thou steeds of night.
Behold the sleep that Luna gave to his
Beloved boy whose beauty vied with thine.
The sire of gods himself, to see thee less,
Joined by behest two nighttimes into one.
My grumblings ended. She had heard: she blushed.
But no more slowly entered in the day.

(*Amores* I.13.1–48)

To make sure that he had covered in his own manner the
field of his predecessors, Ovid included not only the wholly
serious tribute to Tibullus but also poems on two Roman festivals, to Ceres and to Juno. And when he had finished his
three books of *Amores* he definitely closed the door on a task
completed. This he accomplished with a final poem, a most
tantalizing envoi to the volume. There is just enough similarity
to Horace's *Exegi monumentum* to give pause, and a slight
reminiscence of Catullus' *Cui dono,* but Ovid, with exquisite
taste, borrows no word or phrase, no particular idea from
either. He does point with pride to his accomplishment; he
looks for its survival; and he adds one characteristic item: he
is going on to greater achievement.

Find a new poet, thou mother of the Loves.
I've turned the last goal of my elegies.
These are my poems nor do they give me shame
Who am the child of Paeligina's countryside,
The heir by ancient right of ancestry
To knighthood, not by war's vicissitude.
Mantua boasts her Vergil and Verona's joy
Is her Catullus: I shall be acclaimed
Paelignia's crown, whose sturdy liberty
Forced her to arms when Rome faced civil war.
And so some stranger, viewing Sulmo's walls
Enclosing scanty acres, shall exclaim:
"You that produced a poet so eloquent,

However small you be I call you great."
Exquisite Cupid, Cupid's mother too,
Remove my golden standards from the field:
Lyaeus with his potent thyrsus calls.
With mightier steeds I'll steer an ampler course.
Soft Elegy, farewell, farewell, sweet Muse,
But spare my verse to live beyond my end.
(*Amores* III.15.1–20)

Before he mounted his mightier chariot Ovid made two
other essays into the field of erotic elegy, using the medium of
his first experiments to produce epistles in elegiac meter and
also didactic poems in the same. Characteristically the letters,
which we know as the *Heroides,* are appeals to their lost or
unavailable lovers by deserted heroines of mythology, Ariadne
to Theseus, Medea to Jason, Dido to Aeneas and so on. The
last six are in pairs, the man writing the first letter. These
pairs present rather different situations from those of the single
letters. The pairs are Paris and Helen, Leander and Hero,
Acontius and Cydippe. Nevertheless each poem in the *Heroides* presents an emotional crisis in an affair of true love. The
conventional, passing episodes of the *Amores* have no place
here. The tone is prevailingly that of tragedy, and the appeals
are often reminiscent of rhetorical argument in the schools of
Rome. The writer is still the sophisticated poet of the metropolis. Two examples will illustrate this fixation of a point
of view.

Vergil, a sympathizer with Catullus in his forward movement, and Horace, the skeptic, had both borrowed freely from
Catullus' account of the abandonment of Ariadne by Theseus.
Ovid, in the *Heroides,* presents Ariadne left behind on Dia,
but with no reminiscences of the earlier poet. The elegy has
taken on a character of its own, sophisticated, somewhat rhetorical, sentimental rather than dramatic. It is possible to find
slight resemblances, but they are not convincing: the mountain
view of the ocean, the fear of wild beasts, the inhumanity of
Theseus, all of these are really inherent in the myth. Ovid

presents Ariadne, not rescued by Dionysus, but collectedly sitting down to write a fairly composed letter to her faithless lover, urging him to come back and rescue her. The unreality of the elegy must be accepted: where did she find the writing materials? Also we must accept the conventional setting of the scene presented too artistically for a maiden in distress.

> 'Twas at that hour when first the morning earth
> Is sprinkled with the sparkling frost, the birds
> Begin to twitter 'neath the leafy boughs.
>
> (*Heroides* X.7–8)

But then she describes herself, half awake, reaching out for Theseus, slowly feeling for him across the bed. Here of course is the sophisticated elegy of the city poet, not the realistic lyric of passion. Whence the bed on an uninhabited island? Ours not to reason why, for the elegy had won its conventions as surely as did the pastoral of a never-never Arcadia. Ariadne is not a tragic heroine but the jealous mistress abandoned by her lover. She has not lost all reason under the pressure of fear and hate. She does not invoke curses on Theseus. She argues shrewdly for his return. One word is used unusually, *perfida*. In Catullus' poem Ariadne hurls the epithet at Theseus, justly and effectively. In Ovid, Ariadne addresses it in good elegiac manner to the hypothetical bed.

> Two of us laid us down—return thou two.
> Both came—why are not both arising now?
> False couch, where is that better part of us?
>
> (*Her.* X.57–58)

And finally in the last two lines comes the inevitable, from the point of view of the elegist.

> Turn, Theseus, turn thy sails, come back:
> If I am dead, thou'lt have at least my bones.
>
> (*Her.* X.149–50)

In the seventh letter of the *Heroides,* from Dido to Aeneas, there is the same lack of realism. The man addressed is on the high seas heading for unknown shores: how is a letter supposed to reach him? Only the easy convention of elegy makes this irrelevant. More interesting is the relation between Ovid's Dido and Vergil's. There can be no doubt that in the main Ovid takes his material from the fourth book of the *Aeneid*. The evidence is furnished by the speeches of Dido, two directly addressed to Aeneas, the rest either monologues or spoken to Anna. The parallels and the sequence of ideas are convincing. But equally interesting are the differences. With Ovid, Dido must make a reasonable and somewhat rhetorical opening.

> Not that you can be moved by prayers of mine
> Do I address you: fate denies my prayers.
> But since in vain I've lost fair deeds and fame,
> Honor in act and thought, waste words are naught.
> (Her. VII.3–6)

With clear reason rather than with vituperation, she makes her points. They are not the outpourings of a distracted soul but the arguments of a disillusioned realist. Nor does she invoke curses on Aeneas. One detail is definitely changed from Vergil's account. There *may* be a child born of the cave "marriage." She is bringing pressure on Aeneas, not taunting him with what might have been. Even more than in the Ariadne epistle the devices of Roman rhetoric are used persistently and effectively by the queen of primitive Carthage. And finally her threat of suicide (without the trappings of the *Aeneid*) adds the proposed epitaph:

> Aeneas furnished cause and means of death
> But Dido fell by none but her own hand.
> (Her. VII.193–94)

The *Heroides* are a more dignified product than the *Amores* and without offense to the official standards of morality. The same cannot be said of Ovid's version of the didactic poem. In his *Ars amatoria* the connoisseur of love gives a complete guide for men (two books) and girls (one book) as to how to win the object of their (passing) passion. It is typical of the poet's whimsicality that these were followed by a *Remedia amoris* in a single book. In the conventional game of love it was as important to know the tactics of retreat as of attack. And while concerned with the art of gallantry Ovid added an elegiac manual, *De medicamine faciei femineae,* of which all but one hundred lines is lost. In this he boldly repudiates the official ideal of the good old Sabine housewife in favor of the up-to-date charmer of Rome.

> It may be that in good King Tatius' time
> The ancient Sabine women chose to till
> The family fields while the old apple-cheeked
> Matron sat spinning with persistent thumb,
> Seated apart upon her thronelike chair.
> She too it was housed for the night the sheep
> Fed by her daughter, she that spread the hearth
> With kindling first, then piled high the logs.
> Not so today your mothers: they produced
> Delicate daughters. You will clothe yourselves
> In gilded garments, dress your perfumed locks
> In varied fashion, deck your hands with rings.
> About your necks, gems from the Orient
> With pendants hanging heavy from your ears.
> How right you are: do all you can to please,
> For this our age has men of culture too.   (11–24)

The borderline between serious and frivolous may not always be too clear, but Ovid never lets his verse become serious to the point of solemnity or his irony reach the point of bitterness. The lightness of his touch never fails. Any failure to please in these didactic elegies can be ascribed to the taste of the reader rather than to that of the poet. To the idle society to whom they were addressed they were most congenial. To the princeps and his immediate group of counselors their gay abandon and complete irresponsibility were all too sure to inspire resentment, and the opening of the *Ars amatoria* made no conciliatory advances to officialdom.

> Whoe'er in Rome knows not the art of love
> Let him but read these lines and love with art.
> By art swift ships are moved with sail and oar,

By art swift chariots: love too must move by art.
Automedon was master of the course
And Tiphys of the swift Haemonian ship.
Venus made me master of tender love
(Automedon and Tiphys I of love).
Cupid's a cruel boy, oft battling me
But he's a boy, fit for the potter's hand.
Phillypides molded Achilles' youth,
Softened by soothing art his spirit fierce
And he who ever frightened friend and foe
Trembled before an old man's reprimand.
The hands that soon would mangle Hector's corpse
Were stretched obedient to the master's rod.
As Chiron to Achilles, I to Love,
Both spirited boys and both of goddess born.
But as the ox is broken to the plow
And noble steeds learn to accept the bit
So Love shall yield to me, but with his bow
And hustling torch he'll often wound my breast.
The more he wounds, the more he scorches me,
So much the abler I to avenge the wound.
I make no claim to be the inspired poet
Of Phoebus: no birds ever taught my lyre:
I never saw the Muses tending sheep
In Ascra's vale: experience taught me all.
Yield to a poet who knows: I sing the truth.
Thou, mother of Cupid, bless my venturing.
No fillets here, mark of propriety
Nor modest garments reaching to the feet.
Free Venus I shall sing, permitted love,
No proper charge shall lurk behind my verse.
You who would be the soldier in my ranks,
First task for you: choose well whom you will love;
Next, how to win the lady of your choice;
Last but not least, how best to hold her love.

(I.1–38)

This is all very well, frivolous but harmless, and, as the

poet says, there is no intent to assail the morals of the Roman matron. But Ovid's cleverness was insidious and when he proceeded to picture vividly the splendid opportunities offered the adventurous lover in the temples and theaters of Augustus' rebuilt Rome, he was not likely to endear himself to the reforming princeps. Brilliantly he turned the familiar rape of the Sabine women into the origin of the use of the theater as a *locus amandi*. And presently he went further. The triumphs of Augustus he pictured with verve and color, but for him their chief interest was as a setting for amatory conquests, their significance not in their origin but in the frivolous crowd of Roman spectators. All of this in effortless and faultless verse. When he was through he had no doubt, as a citizen, become an object of some suspicion but, as a poet, he had added one more prize to his bag, the didactic elegy.

It was evidently about 2 B.C. that Ovid launched out into what he fittingly called his *area maior*. For the time being he abandoned his elegiac meter in favor of the hexameter, which he had always declared to be the nobler verse and more suitable for sustained narrative. The *Metamorphoses*, which occupied him for the next six years, were not, however, epic narrative, which he had renounced as, for him, out of character. They are a long poem consisting of a multitude of short tales held together by a framework which gave continuity rather than cohesion or internal unity. There are fifteen books which tell some two hundred and fifty myths, nearly all of which involve some miraculous change of form and also (for Ovid is the author) the all-pervading power of love. Insofar as there was any existing model for such a product, it may well have been the *Aitia,* in which Callimachus had, in somewhat similar fashion, strung together a series of myths. But the hallmark of Ovid's grace and fancy as well as the facility and lightness of his hexameter verse makes the *Metamorphoses* not only original but unique.

> To tell of change from old forms into new
> My purpose: look ye kindly on my work,

Ye gods. Surely the miracles were yours.
So from earth's first beginning to our day
Conduct my unbroken song. (I.1–4)

It is a striking detail that the first line begins: *In nova fert
animus* (My heart spurs me to new things). The emphasis on
nova delicately suggests that the poet is not only telling of new
forms produced by metamorphosis but is creating a new form
of poetry out of old ingredients. The opening is modest (as
was Catullus' *cui dono lepidum novum libellum:* to whom shall
I give this dainty new book) and the task is Herculean. At
the end of the fifteenth book Ovid is satisfied that he has
achieved his goal. With something very much like Horace's
claim, he asserts his right to immortality.

And now the tale is told, which neither Jove
In wrath, nor fire, nor sword, nor wasting time
Can e'er destroy. Come when it will, that day
Which rules my body only, let it end
My little span of life. The greater part
Of my real self shall rise above the stars
Immortal and my name inviolate.
Where Roman might rules over conquered lands
I shall be read and, famous through the years,
If poets speak the truth, I too shall live.
(*Met.* XV.871–79)

Probably no one will question the poet's right to the claim
of immortality or blame him for honest pride in a great achievement. To have made the old myths sparkle again in itself took
genius, but to have woven them into a sequence without betraying the unsubstantial quality of that sequence was the
magic of purest art. The individual tales have the freshness of
new inventions. They are presented with much of the technique of the epyllion sufficiently concealed by Ovid's light
touch.

The palace of the sun rose high aloft
On soaring columns, bright with sparkling gold

And flamelike bronze. Ivory sheathed its roof
And its great doors flung back a silvery flash.
More wondrous still the workmanship, for there
Mulciber had engraved the encircling sea
Around earth's orb, the heavens over all.
Caerulean gods peopled the sea and there
Triton with sounding horn and many-formed
Proteus; Aegaeon too, his muscles strained
To foil the monsters of the sounding deep.
Doris was there, her lovely daughters too,
Some swimming, others on a nearby cliff,
Combing their long green locks while other some
Were riding dolphins. All so much alike
Yet each herself, for all were sisters born.
The earth showed men and cities, woods and beasts,
Rivers and nymphs and all the country gods.
Above, the pattern of the shining sky
With all the constellations.   (*Met.* II.1–18)

So begins the tale of Phaethon, one of the longer stories.
This setting of the prologue in the palace of the sun, with the
account of the decorations by a master hand, cannot fail to
recall the house of Peleus with its tapestry in Catullus' epyllion. But there is no imitation. The interior decoration does
not present a story within a story. The elaborate form of an
independent epyllion would be out of place in this collection
of shorter epyllia. But the rich and vivid description is there
while, for brevity's sake, the familiar "messenger speech"
technique of the drama is employed to launch the tale. With
the setting complete, the hero of the story enters and the narrative is rapid and dramatic. With Phaethon's disastrous
plunge toward earth, Ovid at the same time extends the period
of suspense and horror and also embraces the opportunity to
exhibit his own virtuosity with a massive display of proper
names. In ten lines he introduces some twenty-four mountains, headlands, and ranges famous in myth and history.

So Athos burned, Cilician Taurus too,

Tmolus and Oeta, Ida, rich in springs
Now parched and virgin Helicon, Haemus, too
Not yet Oeagrian; far across the deep
The fires of Aetna blazed with double flame;
Two-peaked Parnassus, Eryx and Cynthus grim,
Othrys and Rhodope, bereft of snow,
Dindymus, Mycale, Cithaeron, reared
To serve the rites of gods. The Scythian cold
Saved not her mountains: Caucasus burst forth
In flames, Ossa and Pyndus, mightier still
Olympus and the heaven-reaching Alps,
The cloud-capped Apennines.   (*Met.* II.212–22)

This would seem a sufficient tour de force, but Ovid is not one
either to repeat a given performance or to waste an opportunity. So, having gotten off to a good start, he turns to the
springs and rivers of the world, dried up by the scorching sun,
and manages to produce forty-one names in twenty-three lines
while the disaster runs madly on, delaying only for the majestic
Nile, to glance at its lost sources and its sevenfold mouth. All
this might suggest that Ovid is parodying the learned elegists
who preceded him, but, if there is a touch of satire, it is self-
inclusive and merry rather than caustic. In the same vein is
the sketch of the golden age in the tale of Aurora in the first
book (lines 89 ff.) and many another bit of decoration. Such,
too, is the Homeric touch, *At pater omnipotens* (II.401), used
to resume a narrative, and such, I suspect, is the description
of the dogs' attack on Actaeon as they assume the character
of Homeric heroes in battle.

So, hesitant, the dogs caught sight of him,
Melampus first and wise Ichnobates
Gave barks of warning (Gnosian Ichnobates
But Spartan stock Melampus.) Up then rush
The other heroes swift as swirling breeze.
Pamphagus, Dorceus, and Oribasus,
Arcadians they, mighty Nebrophonus,
Theron the truculent with Laelape,

Pterelas, swift of foot, and Agre, keen
To follow scent, Hylaeus fierce but now
Wounded by the wild boar, Nape, conceived
Of wolf, Harpyia, squired by her twin sons.

(*Met.* III.206–25)

And so on through the catalogue of thirty-five canine heroes, concluding quite properly: *Quosque referre mora est* (and others to mention whom is mere delay) and proceeding to a rousing Homeric battle scene.

But to return to the tale of Phaethon. It rushes to its fatal close, and the hero, received by the river god Eridanus, is mourned by the Heliads. They in turn are metamorphosed into trees by the river bank. Jupiter must now make an inspection of the damaged world in the course of which he quite naturally lingers in his beloved Arcadia. Before we know it we are launched on the Arcadian story of Callisto.

In general the myths appear in a roughly chronological order. After chaos, creation, and the golden age come the giants and, presently, Deucalion and Pyrrha. After the flood and the recreation of mankind, nature puts forth spontaneously the various animals, the last of which is the great Python. What follows will illustrate further the neat but rather casual methods of transition from myth to myth.

This Python then the archer god who ne'er
Had used his weapon save for timid deer
Slew with a thousand shafts, his quiver's tale,
The poison oozing through the darkling wounds.
And lest old time destroy the victor's fame,
He founded then the Pythian games to keep
The monster's memory forever green.
And whatsoever youth gained victory
With hand or foot or wheel, each one received
As crown of victory a leafy wreath.
There was no laurel then, but Phoebus crowned
Their flowing locks with various foliage.
Phoebus' first love, Peneian Daphne, fell

[236]

By no blind chance to him: 'twas Cupid's wrath.
The Delian, proud of heart for Python slain,
Had seen the boy bending his little bow.
"And what, my sportive child," he said "have you
To do with powerful arms? Weapons like those
Become my shoulders who give deadly wounds
To beast or enemy, who only now
Laid low with countless arrows Python's self
With swollen belly stretching o'er miles of field.
Be thou content to pester with your torch
What loves you will nor emulate my fame."
To whom the child of Venus: "Phoebus, all things
Your arrows pierce: my arrow shall pierce you.
And by as much as beasts are less than gods
By so much is thy glory less than mine."

(Met. I.461–86)

And so begins the myth of Daphne who is eventually changed into a laurel tree, sacred to the god of prophecy. The transformation occurs on the bank of the river Peneus which issues from the Vale of Tempe. Peneus is the father of Daphne and to him, to comfort or congratulate, troop all the rivers except Inachus who is mourning for his daughter Io. And so the myth of Io.

Another type of transition occurs, mainly at the division between books. At the end of Book VI, for example, Ovid has been telling the tale of the nymph Orithyia which involves Boreas (Aquilo) and his sons Calais and Zetes. The book closes:

So when in course of time they reached the verge
Of manhood, with the Minyae they sailed
In the first ship to fetch the golden fleece.

(Met. VI.669–71)

Book VII, containing the story of the Argonauts, makes a fresh start.

And now the Minyae were coursing o'er
The sea in Pagasaean ship and came to where
Phineus was dragging out hapless old age
Within perpetual night until the sons
Of Aquilo drove into headlong flight
The Harpies who beset old Phineus' eyes,
Thus, suffering many ills at Juno's hand,
They came at last to Phocis' anchorage.

(*Met.* VII.1–6)

And so follows the story of Medea.

For fifteen books the *Metamorphoses* continue without slackening pace. The light touch, the genius for variety never fail. Toward the end the myths merge with the Roman tradition of Aeneas and his race, culminating in Julius Caesar and Augustus, with a prayer for the latter's continued stay on earth. The successful creation of a new category in Roman poetry justifies the author's concluding claim to a place among the immortal poets of Rome.

There can be no doubt, I think, that the *Metamorphoses* show Ovid to be a serious poet making a sustained effort to win recognition and fame. While occupied chiefly with this, his masterpiece, he was also working in a somewhat less congenial field. Once more he had conceived a project in his favorite elegiac meter, which should be new in Roman poetry. Tibullus and Propertius had written isolated poems on particular Roman festivals. The *Fasti* were to be a poetic calendar of all the Roman feast days as they came along through the year with some account of the origin of each. Like the *Metamorphoses*, the *Fasti* looked back in a general way to the *Aitia* of Callimachus but with no close imitation of the Alexandrian poet. Futhermore the *Fasti* were as near as Ovid, with his temperament, could come to a patriotic contribution. He may very well have sensed the hostility which his erotic poetry had aroused in Augustus and sought to mollify the prince. If so he was too late. The *Metamorphoses* were finished but not published, only circulated among his friends,

and the *Fasti* were only half done when Ovid was banished
by the emperor to spend the rest of his life in Tomi on the
farthest shore of the Black Sea. Some incident unknown to
us and which, with all his self-revelation, Ovid never speci-
fied, gave the harassed Augustus the excuse to get rid of the
poet whom he looked upon as a menace to his own cherished
reforms. Far removed from his reference books and bereft
of the will to write, Ovid did not finish the *Fasti,* but he never
ceased to turn out verse. It was not verse that could bring
him much credit. During his ten years of exile he wrote metrical epistles back to Rome in a constant stream, bemoaning his
fate, defending himself, assailing his enemies, real or imaginary, and begging monotonously for pardon and restoration.
He imitated Callimachus by writing a Latin "Ibis," a vituperative assault on an unnamed enemy who is supposed to be
maligning Ovid's reputation in Rome and making life impossible for his loyal wife. His anger almost inspires him once
more to real poetry. Of infinitely less distinction is a didactic
poem on the fish of the Black Sea. Ovid's muse required the
gaiety and flair of Roman high society to call forth the brilliant fancies of his earlier days. The epistles from Pontus and
the Tristia add nothing to his reputation as a poet in spite of
the metrical facility which never failed him.

To a certain extent the collapse of Ovid's gay career and
with it of his effervescent poetry is consistent with the whole
trend of affairs at Rome. The regime of Augustus, following
on the century of civil struggle, had opened with a fine enthusiasm for the program of peace and tolerance. It had the
eager support of Vergil and Horace. The less involved elegists
were looked on with forbearance and added their bit to the
brilliance of the regime. Maecenas on the one hand and Messalla on the other maintained the essential connection between
the court and the literary world. But as the second decade of
the new government matured, the predominance of the new
aristocracy, without roots in the old traditions of Rome and
without the restraining influence of either religion or philosophy, became well nigh absolute. Vergil died in 19 B.C., Tibul-

lus probably in the same year. Maecenas had offended the emperor and departed from his position of influence. For a little, Horace, ever closer to Augustus, kept up his courage and his output. But he, too, died in 8 B.C. Ovid remained, a thorn in Augustus' side. And, as the great cultural circle disappeared, so too Augustus' political plans for the succession, one by one, collapsed. And, in the family circle, the tragedy of the two Julias and the lurking suspicion of disloyalty within combined to darken the later years of the great patron of literature and founder of the empire.

APPENDIX

CATULLUS, "PELEUS AND THETIS"

Once on a time the pines on Pelion's height
Took form, they say, and swam through Neptune's waves
To Phasis' strand and King Aeetes' realm
When chosen youth, the flower of Argive strength,
From Colchis set to bring the Golden Fleece,
Dared in swift ship to scorn the salty sea
Whipping the darkling waves with oars of fir.
For them the goddess crowned in citadels
Herself created that swift wind-borne ship
Bending the pine planks on the curving frame.
That was the first that Amphitrite knew,
And when it cut the sea with curious prow,
Turning the blue to white before the oars,
Up from the sparkling waters came the heads
Of Nereids marveling at the miracle.
Then only on that day did mortal eyes
Behold the naked sea nymphs from the depths
Rising breast-high above the whitening surge.
Then Thetis kindled Peleus' fiery love,
Then Thetis scorned not human marriage ties,
Then Zeus himself decreed the two should wed.
Oh happy heroes borne in such an age,
Hail to you, race of gods, of blessed birth
From blessed mothers, hail. Of you my song
Shall ever sing, of Peleus too, the tower
Of Thessaly with happiest wedlock crowned
To whom great Jupiter resigned his love.
Did beauteous Thetis hold thee in her arms?
Did Tethys yield her darling to thy couch
And ocean too that circles earth with sea?

So when the long-awaited day had dawned
All Thessaly came thronging joyously
To crowd the portals of the royal home.

Gifts they bear with them, joy in their faces shines.
Cieros lies deserted; Tempe's vale,
The homes of Crannon and Larissa's walls
They leave behind to fill the Pharsalian home.
None tills the field, the bullocks' necks grow soft,
The vine no more is trimmed, with downturned share
The steer no longer cuts the stubborn glebe
Nor pruning hook the shadowy foliage,
And squalid rust devours the idle plow.
But Peleus' palace with its vistaed halls
Shines wth a blaze of silver and of gold.
Bright gleam the ivory couch, the goblets rare;
The house laughs with its royal treasure trove.
And in the central hall, the wedding couch
Awaits the goddess, its white ivory
Bedizened with a crimson coverlet.

With subtle art this tapestry portrays
The glorious deeds of heroes long ago.
For from the sounding waves of Dia's shore
Swiftly the ship of Theseus sails away
And Ariadne, fury in her heart,
Straining her eyes, believes not what she sees
Nor that at last, aroused from treacherous sleep,
She stands deserted on that lonely strand.
Heedless the hero fleeing with bended oar
Flings to the windy blasts his empty vows
And Minos' daughter on the weed-washed shore
Like a Bacchante wrought in stone still stands
Gazing in vain while mighty waves of woe
Surge over her, forgetful of the plight
Of woven mitre that had held her locks
Or the soft veil over her snow-white breasts
Now fallen from her, washing at her feet
This way and that, the playthings of the waves.
No thought was hers for mitre or for veil.
With all her heart, with all her very soul

She clung to Theseus in each tortured thought.

Ah, wretched maiden with what surge of grief
Did Erycine in thy frenzied heart
Sow thorny sorrows on that tragic day
When Theseus sailing from Pinaeus' shores
Hailed Gortyn's palace and its faithless king.
For once they say, by cruel plague constrained,
Cecropia sent from year to year the flower
Of all her youths and maidens doomed to sate
The Minotaur to avenge Androgeus' death.
To save his city, straitened by this fate,
Theseus himself chose to engage his life
For Athens' sake rather than send to Crete
These specious mockeries of life in death.

So came he in swift ship with favoring breeze
To noble Minos and his palace proud.
And when she saw him with her eager glance
The royal princess whose young innocence
Knew but the sweetness of her maiden couch,
Her mothers' loving care, like myrtle flower
Along Eurotas' stream whose varied hues
The breath of spring creates, her startled glance
Was fixed on him nor wavered till a flame
Kindling in all her senses spread the fire
Of burning passion to her inmost soul.
Alas with what cruel wantonness does he,
That child of Venus, mingling for mankind
Sorrow and joy, inspire mad ecstasy:
And she that rules leafy Idalia,
With what great waves of passion Venus swept
The maid as she beheld, with heart on fire,
This stranger, golden haired, and deeply sighing
Turned pale with fear that clutched her fainting heart.
For Theseus, firm to meet the ravenous beast,
Was seeking instant death or glorious fame.
And still, with promises that reached their goal,

She kindled on her lips a silent prayer.
For as some oak with branches far outflung
On Taurus' peak or pine with pitchy bark,
The storm wind with indomitable blast
Tears from the ground—it crashes headlong down
Uprooted, spreading havoc far and wide—
So Theseus laid the mighty monster low
Tossing in vain to heaven its spreading horns,
Then safe with glory he retraced his way,
Guiding his footsteps by her slender thread
Lest in those labyrinthine wanderings
By treacherous error he might forfeit all.

But why stray from my song to tell the tale
How Ariadne turned from her father's face,
Her sister's last embrace, her mother's too
Who still rejoiced even in her daughter's loss,
And chose instead to follow Theseus' love,
Or how she sailed to Dia's foaming shore
Or how, her eyes still closed in peaceful sleep,
Her lover left her with forgetful heart.
Often they say, o'erwhelmed by maddened grief,
She poured shrill protest from her inmost heart,
Mounted the sheer cliff, thence to scan the sea,
Or rushed impetuous into the salty waves
That washed about her feet. So in despair
With deep drawn sobs that burst chill from wet lips
She poured forth to the winds her last lament.

"Was it for this you brought me from my home,
Oh faithless Theseus, here to abandon me
On this deserted shore? So will you bear
Thy perjuries unmindful home with you
Nor reck the avenging fury of the gods?
Could nothing curb your cruel heart's conceit?
Had you no kindness that could pity me?
Not such the promises you gave me then
In vain; not this the fate you bade me hope,

But happy wedlock and the marriage hymn:
Hopes that the winds of heaven scatter stillborn.
Now let no woman trust a man's firm oath
Nor listen to a man's protesting words.
For when their hearts conceive desire for aught
They fear no oath, no promises they spare:
But when they have gained the object of their lust,
Their words forgotten, oaths have no terror then.
Surely when you were in the grip of death
I snatched you from it, choosing to sacrifice
My brother rather than fail you in your need.
Wherefore in death unburied I shall be
Left to be torn by beasts and birds of prey.
What lioness whelped you by some lonely cliff?
What sea conceived and spewed you from its womb?
What Syrtis or what ravenous Scylla? What
Charybdis taught you to repay my gift?
If you could not endure to marry me,
Shrinking before my sire's inhuman laws,
You might even so have borne me to your home
To serve you with sweet labor as your slave
To wash your fair feet in the cooling bath
Or spread your couch with crimson coverlet.
But why distracted by my sufferings
Do I lament in vain to unfeeling winds
That cannot hear my plaints nor answer me
While Theseus rides the distant sea and here
No sign of life—only the empty strand.
So cruel Chance exulting to the last
Denies me even an ear to hear my cry.
Oh Jupiter omnipotent, I would
That never to our Cretan shores had come
That ship from Cecrop's land—I would to God
Its treacherous captain, hiding his cruel plots
Beneath so fair a form, had never come
To harbor as a guest within our home.
Where can I turn: What hope can I invoke?

Flee to the hills of Crete, when grim between
The ocean spreads its gulf of truculent waves?
Or seek my father whom I basely left
Following the hero stained with my brother's blood?
Or look for comfort in that husband's love
Who even now flees under bending oars?
Here on a lonely isle where no man lives
Is no escape with oceans everywhere—
No hope, no answer—everything is mute
A silent waste where all things point to death.
Yet never shall my eyes be closed in death
Nor life depart from my poor weary limbs
Till I have summoned in my last appeal
The wrath of heaven on his accursed head.
Wherefore ye Furies that deal punishment
To human crimes, your hissing serpent locks
Spelling the furious anger in your breasts,
Come to me here, come, hearken to my cry
That bursts unbidden from the inmost depths
Of my soul's helpless fire of furious hate.
So, as it speaks my heart's sincerity,
Let not my plaint vanish on empty air.
With that contempt which left me here alone
May Theseus doom himself and all his house."

When from her broken heart she poured these words
Demanding vengeance on his cruel acts
The father of the gods nodded assent—
That nod which makes to tremble earth and sea
And all the constellations of the sky.
But Theseus all forgetful as he sailed
Remembered not the injunction hitherto
Held in his mind inviolate, nor raised
The happy signal to his grieving sire
That safe at last he sought Erectheus' port.

For when, long since, forth from Athena's walls
Aegeus had sped his son with fond embrace

He gave him, so they say, this last behest.
"My son, far dearer to my heart than life,
Restored so late to comfort my old age,
Whom now I must commit to dubious fate
Since my grim fortune and your gallant faith
Snatch you from me ere yet my dimming eyes
Are satisfied, beholding your dear self,
I will not send you forth with heart of joy
Nor let you spread the emblems of fair fate,
But, pouring forth to heaven my full complaint
Fouling my white hairs with the dust of earth
I'll set black sails upon thy swaying mast
Witness to my dark thought, my burning grief,
A canvas dyed with Spain's most ominous hue.
But if the goddess of Itonus grant—
She the defender of Erectheus' race—
That your right hand shall shed the monster's blood,
Then let my words, held fast in memory,
Be sacred in your eyes, untouched by time;
And when you catch the first sight of our hills
Then from your masts lower the sails of death
And raise instead white canvas gleaming fair,
That so beholding I shall instantly
Know in my glad heart of your safe return."
Such the behests, safe cherished hitherto,
That now from Theseus' heart forgotten flew
Like clouds from snow-capped hills before the wind.
But from the headland's height his aged sire,
Waiting in anxious watch, his weeping eyes
Seeing afar the fatal black-hued sails,
Plunged headlong from the cliff, sure in his heart
That cruel fate had robbed him of his son.
So coming in triumph to a mourning home,
Proud Theseus felt the self-same tragic grief
As Minos' daughter by his treachery.

But she aghast, watching his fleeing ship,

Nursed in her wounded heart her endless woe
When sudden from the hills in joyous rout
Came flowering Bacchus with his retinue
Of riotous Satyrs and Silenuses
Hailing from Nysa's slope, yearning to find
Thee, Ariadne, maddened with love for thee.
Around him danced in madly whirling maze
Frenzied Bacchantes tossing disheveled hair
Shouting euhoe, brandishing aloft
The ivy-covered thyrsus or anon
Tossing the severed members of a bull.
Some wreathed themselves with tortuous serpent coils
And others with their caskets held aloft
Pursued their orgies that none else may know.
With tapering hands some beat the tambourine
Some blew resounding blasts on echoing horn
Or shrilled barbarian music on the pipes.

Such the adornment of the coverlet
That in the palace graced the wedding couch.
And when the Thessalian youth had sated well
Their eager gaze, homeward once more they turned
To yield their places to the blessed gods.
Lo, then as Zephyrus with morning breeze
Ruffles the placid surface of the sea
Into gay ripples as Aurora lifts
Above the threshold of the roving sun,
Slowly at first before the gentle breath
They steal along with laughing merriment,
Then faster, ever faster as the wind
Blows ever stronger and from far away
They send forth flushes of the crimson dawn,
So as they left the royal vestibule
Each to his home they passed with vagrant step.

And as they vanished, first from Pelion's height
Came Chiron with great store of silvan gifts.
For all that Thessaly on plain and hill

Produces for man's joy, and all the flowers
That on her river banks the pregnant breath
Of warm Favonius brings forth to life,
All gathered in great masses Chiron brought
Till all the house was joyous with their scent.
Straightway came Penios, leaving Tempe's vale,
Tempe deep-girdled with o'erhanging woods
And filled with music of her Naiad choirs,
Not emptyhanded: with their living roots
He brought high beeches, laurels tall, and straight
And nodding planes, willows that ever mourn
For Phaethon, and cypress, lord of all,
All these close-clustered he bestowed about
The vestibule to wreathe a welcome shade.
And after Penios came the provident
Prometheus bearing still his ancient scars
That he had won long since, bound to the cliff
To pay in chains the penalty of pride.
Next came the father of the gods himself
With wife and sons leaving alone in heaven
Thee, Phoebus, and thy sister, wont to range
The hills of Idrus, for she too, as thou,
Scorned still the home of Peleus nor would grace
The marriage rites of Thetis and the king.

So as they lay then on the couches white—
The tables piled high with banquet meats—
The Parcae, swaying feebly as they sang,
Began their hymn of faithful prophecy.
Around their tremulous bodies, robes of white
With crimson border covered their shriveled age
And crimson fillets held their snow-white locks.
Their hands pursued their everlasting task:
The left hand grasped the distaff with its wool
The while the right on upturned fingers found
The thread, twisting it on the downturned thumb,
Twirling the spindle with its polished weight,
And ever as they spin, with aged tooth

[251]

They smooth the thread which ever leaves behind
Its flecks of wool upon their arid lips
And at their feet the rustic baskets hold
The billowing mass of whitely gleaming wool.
So with clean wool, the while they spin the thread
They chant the song of destined fate divine,
Song that no future age shall e'er find false.

Thou who dost build by virtue honor's gift,
Guardian of all Emathia's wealth, made great
By greater son, hear what the sisters gray
Foretell in truth. And ye that follow truth,
    Run on, ye spindles, weaving the thread, run on.

To thee shall come with all that bridegrooms wish
Bright Hesperus, and with the star the bride
That shall with pulsing passion fill thy heart
Sharing with thee the languorous might of love
Her smooth arms twined about thy sturdy neck.
    Run on, ye spindles, weaving the thread, run on.

No home e'er now has ever known such love
No love e'er now has held such lovers true
As now to Thetis and to Peleus dawns.
    Run on, ye spindles, weaving the thread, run on.

To you shall come Achilles lord of war
Known ever to the foe by his brave front
Who, oft victorious on the field of sport,
Shall overtake the swift deer in its flight.
    Run on, ye spindles, weaving the thread, run on.

No hero in the strife shall be his match
When Phrygian plain shall run with Trojan blood
And he, beleaguering the walls of Troy
In long-drawn war, conquers as Pelops' heir.
    Run on, ye spindles, weaving the thread, run on.

His glorious deeds of matchless valiancy
Mothers in mourning shall confess the while,

Over their sons' graves, beating their aged breasts,
They sprinkle ashes on their disheveled hair.
    Run on, ye spindles, weaving the thread, run on.

For like the harvester that scythes the stalks
'Neath the hot sun, reaping the yellowing grain
He shall lay waste with steel the Trojan born.
    Run on, ye spindles, weaving the thread, run on.

Scamander shall be witness to his might
That in its course to join the Hellespont
Choked with the countless bodies of the slain
Shall falter and grow warm with hero's blood.
    Run on, ye spindles, weaving the thread, run on.

She shall be witness too by sacrifice
When from the mound of his high funeral pyre
Death shall receive a maiden's purity.
    Run on, ye spindles, weaving the thread, run on.

For when at last Fate grants the weary Greeks
To loose the Neptunian bonds of Dardan Troy
Polyxena's blood shall stain his sepulcher
When like a sacrificial victim slain
The two-edged sword shall sever her life's thread.
    Run on, ye spindles, weaving the thread, run on.

So come, ye lovers, join in wedded bliss,
Bridegroom in faithful pact thy goddess take.
Thou, goddess bride, now yield thee to thy lord.
    Run on, ye spindles, weaving the thread, run on.

When comes tomorrow's dawn, her faithful nurse
No more may clasp the bands of yesterday.
Nor shall her mother find her hope deceived
That longs for happy issue from this night.
    Run on, ye spindles, weaving the thread, run on.

[253]

Such song inspired of future happiness
Of old the Parcae sang in Peleus' halls,
For once the denizens of Heaven were wont
To visit mortal man, when homes were chaste
Nor mankind scorned the worship of the gods.
Often within his sanctuary bright
The Father of the gods on festive days
Saw fall the sacrificial hecatombs.
Often came Liber from Parnassus height
His Thyads madly tossing their wild locks
As forth in frantic rout from Delphi's shrine
They caught the God's wild fire within their hearts.
Often as dread war surged would Mars himself
Or Triton's mistress or the Rhamnusian maid
In very presence urge on the embattled hosts.
But since our world, embracing impious crime,
Has banished justice from its covetous heart,
Brother sheds brother's blood incontinent
And children mourn no more a parent's death.
The father prays to lose his elder son
To lie untroubled in his marriage bed.
Mothers, seducing sons with treacherous guile,
Fear not the anger of avenging gods.
Our madness that knows nought of right and wrong
Has turned the gods against our guilty race
Till they consort no more with human kind
Nor share their glory in the light of day.

INDEX

[255]